BARRON'S

CBEST®

CALIFORNIA BASIC EDUCATIONAL SKILLS TEST

BARRON'S

CBEST®

CALIFORNIA BASIC EDUCATIONAL SKILLS TEST

Kathryn Henkins, Ph.D.

Stephen A. Reiss, M.B.A.

BARRON'S

All inquiries should be addressed to:
Barron's Educational Series, Inc.
250 Wireless Boulevard
Hauppauge, New York 11788
http://www.barronseduc.com

ISBN-13: 978-0-7641-3589-7
ISBN-10: 0-7641-3589-9

Library of Congress Catalog Card No. 2008001085

Library of Congress Cataloging-in-Publication Data

Henkins, Kathryn.
    CBEST / Kathryn Henkins, Stephen A. Reiss.
        p. cm.
    Includes bibliographical references and index.
    ISBN-13: 978-0-7641-3589-7
    ISBN-10: 0-7641-3589-9
    1. California Basic Educational Skills Test--Study guides. I. Reiss, Stephen A. II. Barron's Educational Series, Inc. III. Title. IV. Title: California Basic Educational Skills Test.

    LB3060.33.C34H46 2008
    370.76--dc22

                                                    2008001085

Printed in the United States of America
9 8 7 6 5 4 3 2 1

Contents

CHAPTER 1

INTRODUCTION

Introduction

Barron's CBEST offers the test-taking strategies, explanations, and sample tests you need to sail through the California Basic Educational Skills Test (CBEST). Passing the CBEST demonstrates that the test-taker has important skills necessary to the educator professional and is required for many of the public school teaching credentials in California and other states. (See below for details.)

Let's start with a few basics, the answers to What? Who? Where? When? How? and a few other important questions.

What Is the CBEST?

Administered by National Evaluation Systems (NES), the three-part test is based on guidelines created by the California State Superintendent of Public Instruction, the California Commission on Teacher Credentialing (CCTC), and an advisory board made up mainly of California teachers. California Education Code Sections 44252 and 44252.6 state that educators must demonstrate their abilities in basic reading, math, and writing.

Who Takes This Test?

Anyone seeking a California:

Substitute teaching authorization

Secondary (middle and high school) teaching credential

Multiple Subjects (elementary school) Teaching Credential—unless the candidate has passed the CSET–Multiple Subjects Writing subtest

Credential for teaching adults

Credential for teaching special education students

Emergency teaching permit

Short-term staff permit

School counseling credential

Administrative services credential

Admission into a California Teacher Credential accredited teacher preparation program

Also, recent federal legislation has prompted some California school districts to require their para-educators (instructional aides) to pass the CBEST.

Anyone seeking an Oregon:

Basic or Initial Teaching License
Basic or Initial School Counselor or School Psychologist License
Substitute Teaching License
Admission to a professional preparation program
Basic or Initial Administrative License

From outside of California, candidates who have an Exchange Credential, Sojourn Credential or a teaching credential from another state must pass the CBEST during the first year of validity of their credential.

All test-takers must have completed at least a high school diploma, GED, or the equivalent. The only exception is high school students who are concurrently taking college credit courses that lead to careers in teaching.

What Is This Test?

As its name suggests, the CBEST assesses reading, mathematics, and writing skills which educators need to fulfill their professional responsibilities. As a straightforward test of communication and computation skills, then, the CBEST does not test subject knowledge or ability to teach.

There are three sections:

1. Reading	50 multiple-choice items	Critical analysis and evaluation; comprehension and research
2. Math	50 multiple-choice items	Estimation, measurement and statistical reasoning; computation and problem solving; numerical and graphic relationships
3. Writing	2 essays	One "expressive"; one "informational"

Chapters 2 through 7 of this book cover all you'll need to know about passing the three sections. And Chapter 8 will give you additional practice exams.

There is no requirement to complete all three sections during one test session. The CBEST is a four-hour test, comprised of three sections in one booklet, and test-takers can begin at any part. Therefore, many successful test-takers elect to work on only one or two sections on a particular test date. The administrators of the CBEST keep track of which sections you have passed, and when you have passed all three sections, you have successfully accomplished your goal and need never take the test again!

You should also know, initially, that this paper-and-pencil test is just what it says: you will not be able to use dictionaries, pens, calculators, or scratch paper (though there will be some white space in the booklet for your use).

Planning ahead, therefore, is critical: After using this book, you will know how to approach this test efficiently and strategically. Chapter 2 provides strategies and details about your options.

When Is the CBEST Given?

The CBEST is given on a Saturday in February, April, June, August, October, and December—six times each year. The exact test dates and the deadlines for registration are given at *http://www.cbest.nesinc.com*

How Do I Register for the Test?

You may register by mail, phone, or on-line at the NES website listed above.

The CBEST phone number for registration is: (916) 928-4001. You can call from 9:00 A.M.–5:00 P.M. Pacific time, Monday through Friday.

When you register, you will be asked to supply contact information and your Social Security number. If you register through the Internet, you will receive an "I-Ticket" admission information by e-mail and your official Admission Ticket by U.S. mail. If registering by phone or mail, you will receive an Admission Ticket by U.S. mail. The address of your test site will be on the Admission Ticket, along with the test date and time.

Important! Make a photocopy of your Admission Ticket—it contains the CBEST I.D. number necessary to obtain your unofficial scores on the Internet or to make any changes to your registration. Your I.D. number is confidential and cannot be given to you by calling or e-mailing the CBEST administration.

And you must bring the original Admission Ticket and photo I.D. to the test site.

Where Is the CBEST Given?

On the registration application, you request to take the test in a certain area, like the Oakland area, Santa Rosa area, or Orange County area. The specific site (usually at a public school) will be noted on your Admission Ticket.

What Is a Passing Score on the CBEST?

For each of the three sections you complete, you will receive a "scaled score" between 20 and 80. The reading and math scores are derived from an equation the CBEST administration uses, taking the number of correct answers, subtracting items that were included for experimental purposes, and multiplying by a difficulty factor. The CBEST administration says that a "scaled score" of 41 is passing for these two sections, but that is not to be confused with a score of 41 correct out of 50 multiple choice questions since there is a "difficulty factor." Since the "difficulty factor" is not quantified, it is somewhat difficult for test-takers to truly know how "passing" is defined for the CBEST. However, an excellent rule of thumb is that around 70% to 75% is the minimum passing score.

The two essays are scored holistically by two human essay readers. They assign a score between 1 and 4 for each essay, and these numbers are put into an equation to come up with the "scaled score" for the essay section. These readers do not use a tally or point system for each feature of the writing. Instead, they make an assessment of the whole composition based on criteria they are required to use. This will be fully explained in Chapter 7.

> **TIP**
>
> Candidates who obtain a passing "scaled score" (41 or higher) on any section of the test need not repeat that section. However, the complete test only requires a total score of 123, meaning that if your score on any section is higher than 41, you can actually score as low as a 37 on another section and still pass the complete CBEST. The requirements disallow any subtest score lower than 37 to be included in the sum of the 3 subtest' scores.

It may be a smart step, then, to repeat a section already passed. An increase can help you to reach the total score of 123 required to pass the CBEST, provided that the lower test scores are at least 37. You should remember that the highest score you obtain on each section, no matter when earned, will be used to compute your total CBEST score.

What Do I Do After the Test?

You can get unofficial scores for the reading and math portions of the test on the CBEST website about two weeks after your test date. The writing scores are posted on the Internet about 3 weeks after the test. After about 4 weeks, your official scores will be mailed to you and to the institutions you requested when registering.

Your mailed score will include test details for your evaluation and reflection, including an indication of how well you did on each subcategory of the multiple-choice part of the test.

The subcategories are

Reading: critical analysis and evaluation
Reading: comprehension and research
Math: estimation, measurement, and statistical reasoning
Math: computation and problem solving
Math: numerical and graphic relationships
Writing: two essays

If you do not pass the writing section, you will receive feedback about areas needing improvement.

What Do I Do With My Scores?

When you register for the CBEST, you indicate which, if any, institutions you wish to send your scores. When you pass the entire test, you receive in the mail a verification card and two transcript copies officially stating you have passed the test. These can be used to present to the school district in which you have been hired, as well as to the California Commission on Teacher Credentialing or Oregon Teacher Standards and Practices Commission when applying for a copy of your credential or permit.

What Happens If I Don't Pass?

The CBEST may be taken as often as necessary until a passing score is achieved. As mentioned above, test-takers who receive a passing "scaled score" (41 or higher) on any section of the test have passed that section. It may be to your advantage, however, to repeat a section already passed. An increase can add additional points to help you to reach the total of 123 (with 37 being the lowest acceptable score on any single sub-test) required to pass the CBEST. The highest score that you obtain on each section, no matter when earned, is automatically used to compute your total CBEST score. In addition, if you retake the Math or Reading Section after passing the Writing Section, you will receive a refund of $4, but you must register and pay the full fee first.

CHAPTER 2

HOW TO PREPARE
FOR THE CBEST

How to Prepare for the CBEST

Before the test, review all areas of this book which you deem to be important. In this chapter, we provide many ways to be prepared for the reading comprehension and math sections of the CBEST or any other kind of multiple choice test. Chapter 7 discusses successful strategies for passing the CBEST writing section or any other kind of essay writing test.

OVERALL TEST-TAKING STRATEGIES

It is always a smart move to become familiar with a particular type of test and learn the best advice for succeeding at that type of test. In later chapters, you will learn specific strategies for choosing the best answers in the Reading and Math Sections. However, our first consideration is the general setup of the CBEST. Critical to your passing this test is an understanding of the time management options and the key strategies to choosing correct answers on multiple-choice items.

Time Management

Since the 4-hour CBEST allows test-takers to manage their own time, there are different time schedules that are the most successful for different people. As yet, you may not know the wisest options for your particular abilities, but after reading and practicing with our book, you will!

There is no time limit for any section of the test; therefore, one could simply begin with the first page of the test—the Reading multiple-choice questions—and bubble in the 50 answers sequentially until coming to the Math Section, and proceed, item-by-item, through those 50 questions. Then, one would hope to have enough time remaining to write the two essays.

This isn't the smartest approach, though. The majority of successful CBEST test-takers know in advance that at one scheduled test date they will be spending the 4-hours on one of these options:

Option #1—the Math multiple-choice section only

Option #2—the Reading multiple-choice section only

Option #3—both multiple-choice sections (Reading and Math) only

Option #4—the Math and the Essay sections

Option #5—the Reading and the Essay sections

Option #6—the Essays only or

Option #7—all three sections (Reading, Math, Essays)

How do they know this in advance? They have strategically planned their approach to the test. After using this book, you will also know how to plan strategically. As you read the next chapters and take the sample tests, prepare to make an individualized plan for the option that is best for you, based on answers to these questions:

1. How long did it take me to correctly answer at least 35* questions on the Math Sample Test?
2. How long did it take me to correctly answer at least 35* questions on the Reading Sample Test?
3. How long did it take me to write two essays which I assessed at the 3–4 level?

For instance, if your answer to #1 and #2 are both between 90 to 120 minutes, you should consider taking the CBEST using Option #3, and then 2 months later take it again using Option #6. On the other hand, if your answers to #1, #2, and #3 are all between 60 and 75 minutes, you should consider using Option #7.

Chapters 2–7 will give you specific, time-proven strategies to maximize your correct answers on each particular section of the test. And after you complete several sample tests, you will have a good sense of your optimal time for successfully completing each of the three CBEST sections. Here we give you a few, important general test-taking strategies.

MULTIPLE CHOICE SHOULDN'T BE MULTIPLE GUESS

There are many smart methods of approaching multiple-choice tests, and you may already know many of them. Let's review all the angles related to this kind of test-taking.

First, there are five possible answers (A–E) to each question. Thus, five separate, possible best answers are always listed. "Best" answer is the term used by the test-makers, and it is important to remember. You may not find a single, entirely "right" answer, but there is always one that is the best of the five given. **Remember, too, there is no penalty for guessing.**

There won't be much need for guessing, though, when test-takers use all of these strategies:

1. *Read the directions* for any question or set of questions *at least twice*. Underline the key words which give the approach to take: "The author's *main point* is that" or "Put the fractions in order from *least to greatest*." Then rephrase the question in your own words to ensure that you understand it.
2. Complete the easy questions first. Make a check mark in the test booklet next to any question or set of questions that you left blank as you moved on to something easier. And, of course, be careful when skipping items to remain on the appropriate number on your answer sheet! When all of the easy questions are answered, you can return to the more difficult ones, knowing that you

---

As explained in Chapter 1, your score is not based on the simple total of correct answers. Test items are weighted by level of difficulty, and the number of correct answers out of a total of 50 becomes a "scaled score" between 20 and 80. Nevertheless, the rule of thumb is to be able to correctly answer at least 35 questions in each multiple-choice section.

have already acquired points for the correct answers to all that were easily within your grasp. Even if you do not have time to read and answer all the items, be sure to bubble in a random guess for all items. Wrong answers do not count against the right answers.

3. *Read the questions* at the end of a reading passage, chart, math problem, or geometrical diagram *before* reading the passage or looking at the chart or diagram. Knowing what kind of answers you must provide gives you a focus for the actual reading or necessary analysis. It may seem backwards, but it's truly strategic!

4. After you have read the question or the "stem" of the test item, anticipate the correct answer before reading among the answer choices. This will help you to spot the right answer when you do read it.

5. Read *all* the answers; don't select the "correct" answer before looking at all of them because you are expected to find the "best answer," and more than one may be accurate. If that is the case, you must choose the most accurate among the choices.

6. Use the process of elimination whenever possible to maximize your selection of the best answer. On many CBEST items, you will be able to spot at least one incorrect answer choice among the set. Since you can write anywhere on the test booklet, you should mark through any answer choice that you know is incorrect. That increases the odds of choosing the best answer, even when you're not certain. Also, do not be discouraged if you can not answer a ques-

---

Maximizer #1—Process of Elimination in the Math Section

- If you are not sure of the answer, you can at least select number answers that are in the middle of the range of answers. It is more likely that the correct answer will be in the midrange, while the extreme numbers are exactly that, "extreme."

- Use "E&E." Much of the math subtest relates to fractions and decimals. Frequently, these operations can be very time-consuming. For example, if time is short, using estimation and elimination (E&E) is useful. For example, consider adding $5\frac{1}{8}$ and $7\frac{7}{11}$. Just finding a common denominator squanders precious time. We can round $5\frac{1}{8}$ to 5 and $7\frac{7}{11}$ to 8. Since $5 + 8 = 13$, we can usually eliminate two or three answer choices.

- Use "P&C." Answers are usually arrayed in ascending or descending order. If time is short, a "plug-and-check strategy" is helpful. Always start at selection "C" and "plug" numbers into the equations; adjust upward or downward as necessary if C is not correct.

- Put yourself into word problems. There are process problems where the correct sequence of operations form the right answer. For example, if you know a runner was running at 7 mph and arrived at his or her destination at 2 P.M., what more do you need to calculate the distance covered? The test-taker should step back from the problem and consider what additional information is needed if he or she were the runner (in this case the starting time). What seems cryptic on the test becomes clear when the test-taker puts himself or herself into the problem.

tion. Leave it and go on. You may find the answer or clues to the answer in subsequent questions. Even if you do not find any help, be sure to go back to that item and bubble in a guess.

Maximizer #2—Process of Elimination in the Reading Section

• Choose the longer answers. If you are not sure of the answer, you can at least make a guess to your advantage by choosing the longer and more descriptive answer. These usually have more details; the details are necessary to make the answer correct. Shorter answers are sometimes created quickly by test-makers; they are the "throw aways."

• Never choose "never." Answer choices beginning with *always, never, except, none, most,* or *least* are very likely NOT correct. Absolute statements containing those words are too broad and far-ranging to be the specific, correct answer.

Write in your test booklet, wherever you wish, for instance, underlining the key words in the directions or summarizing key ideas in a few words in the margin next to the relevant sentences.

On the day before the test, prepare by setting aside your pencils, a watch, photo I.D., and your Admission Ticket. Know *exactly* how to get to the test site and plan to get there at least 30 minutes early. Feeling rushed may result in feeling stressed. Get a good night's sleep so you can focus on the task ahead. Wear comfortable clothes that can be added in layers if the room is too cold or removed if the room is too warm.

Answer Sheet

READING DIAGNOSTIC TEST

1 Ⓐ Ⓑ Ⓒ Ⓓ Ⓔ	14 Ⓐ Ⓑ Ⓒ Ⓓ Ⓔ	27 Ⓐ Ⓑ Ⓒ Ⓓ Ⓔ	39 Ⓐ Ⓑ Ⓒ Ⓓ Ⓔ
2 Ⓐ Ⓑ Ⓒ Ⓓ Ⓔ	15 Ⓐ Ⓑ Ⓒ Ⓓ Ⓔ	28 Ⓐ Ⓑ Ⓒ Ⓓ Ⓔ	40 Ⓐ Ⓑ Ⓒ Ⓓ Ⓔ
3 Ⓐ Ⓑ Ⓒ Ⓓ Ⓔ	16 Ⓐ Ⓑ Ⓒ Ⓓ Ⓔ	29 Ⓐ Ⓑ Ⓒ Ⓓ Ⓔ	41 Ⓐ Ⓑ Ⓒ Ⓓ Ⓔ
4 Ⓐ Ⓑ Ⓒ Ⓓ Ⓔ	17 Ⓐ Ⓑ Ⓒ Ⓓ Ⓔ	30 Ⓐ Ⓑ Ⓒ Ⓓ Ⓔ	42 Ⓐ Ⓑ Ⓒ Ⓓ Ⓔ
5 Ⓐ Ⓑ Ⓒ Ⓓ Ⓔ	18 Ⓐ Ⓑ Ⓒ Ⓓ Ⓔ	31 Ⓐ Ⓑ Ⓒ Ⓓ Ⓔ	43 Ⓐ Ⓑ Ⓒ Ⓓ Ⓔ
6 Ⓐ Ⓑ Ⓒ Ⓓ Ⓔ	19 Ⓐ Ⓑ Ⓒ Ⓓ Ⓔ	32 Ⓐ Ⓑ Ⓒ Ⓓ Ⓔ	44 Ⓐ Ⓑ Ⓒ Ⓓ Ⓔ
7 Ⓐ Ⓑ Ⓒ Ⓓ Ⓔ	20 Ⓐ Ⓑ Ⓒ Ⓓ Ⓔ	33 Ⓐ Ⓑ Ⓒ Ⓓ Ⓔ	45 Ⓐ Ⓑ Ⓒ Ⓓ Ⓔ
8 Ⓐ Ⓑ Ⓒ Ⓓ Ⓔ	21 Ⓐ Ⓑ Ⓒ Ⓓ Ⓔ	34 Ⓐ Ⓑ Ⓒ Ⓓ Ⓔ	46 Ⓐ Ⓑ Ⓒ Ⓓ Ⓔ
9 Ⓐ Ⓑ Ⓒ Ⓓ Ⓔ	22 Ⓐ Ⓑ Ⓒ Ⓓ Ⓔ	35 Ⓐ Ⓑ Ⓒ Ⓓ Ⓔ	47 Ⓐ Ⓑ Ⓒ Ⓓ Ⓔ
10 Ⓐ Ⓑ Ⓒ Ⓓ Ⓔ	23 Ⓐ Ⓑ Ⓒ Ⓓ Ⓔ	36 Ⓐ Ⓑ Ⓒ Ⓓ Ⓔ	48 Ⓐ Ⓑ Ⓒ Ⓓ Ⓔ
11 Ⓐ Ⓑ Ⓒ Ⓓ Ⓔ	24 Ⓐ Ⓑ Ⓒ Ⓓ Ⓔ	37 Ⓐ Ⓑ Ⓒ Ⓓ Ⓔ	49 Ⓐ Ⓑ Ⓒ Ⓓ Ⓔ
12 Ⓐ Ⓑ Ⓒ Ⓓ Ⓔ	25 Ⓐ Ⓑ Ⓒ Ⓓ Ⓔ	38 Ⓐ Ⓑ Ⓒ Ⓓ Ⓔ	50 Ⓐ Ⓑ Ⓒ Ⓓ Ⓔ
13 Ⓐ Ⓑ Ⓒ Ⓓ Ⓔ	26 Ⓐ Ⓑ Ⓒ Ⓓ Ⓔ		

CHAPTER 3

READING DIAGNOSTIC TEST AND ANSWERS

Reading Diagnostic Test and Answers

DIAGNOSTIC TEST

Here's your chance to practice taking the Reading test. Use the answer sheet preceding this sample test; then check your answers with the answer key.

> Read the passage below; then answer the five questions that follow.

For many decades in North America and Europe, children in public schools have received music training from preschool through high school. Music training seems to have added cognitive benefits; it is conducive to learning such basic skills as counting, cooperation, and concentration. In addition, it facilitates understanding of language and recalling information, as well as teaching children the fundamentals of playing simple musical instruments.

Children often learn about different Western music eras, learn to sing in small groups, play the bells or recorders while in elementary school. In secondary school, choirs, marching bands, jazz bands, and orchestras are <u>prevalent</u>, and students may elect to enroll in semiprivate music classes.

(1) When in college, students can receive credit for studying music; this is usually in the form of courses on the history of music or music appreciation. (2) Learning about different musical styles and how to listen to music generally forms the core content of music appreciation classes. (3) Students who plan to be elementary school teachers also are often required to learn how to use music in their classrooms.

(4) While colleges in North America are enhancing their curriculum to include music of non-Western cultures, such as the music of Bali or Africa, Western music courses are becoming more common in Asian countries, such as Japan, China, and South Korea. (5) This curriculum usually emphasizes the study of classical music.

1. Which of the following best describes the writer's pattern of organization in the passage?

   (A) Chronological order
   (B) Problem-solving format
   (C) Spatial order
   (D) Explaining with examples
   (E) Order of importance

2. Between the third and fourth paragraphs of the passage, the writer's approach shifts from

   (A) demonstration to analysis.
   (B) generalization to exemplification.
   (C) description to comparison.
   (D) analysis to persuasion.
   (E) cause to effect.

3. Which of the following is the best meaning of the word *prevalent* as it is used in the second paragraph of the passage?

   (A) private
   (B) common
   (C) uncommon
   (D) united
   (E) loud

4. Which of the following best organizes the main topics addressed in this passage?

   (A)   I. Music in Public Schools
        II. College Music Courses
       III. K–12 Music Opportunities
       IV. Western and Non-Western Music Curriculum Changes

   (B)   I. Why Children Like Music Classes
        II. K–12 Music Opportunities
       III. College Music Courses
       IV. Western and Non-Western Music Curriculum Changes

   (C)   I. Children's Music in North America and Europe
        II. Why Children Like Music Classes
       III. K–12 Music Classes
       IV. Western and Non-Western Music Curriculum Changes

   (D)   I. Children's Music in North America and Europe
        II. K–12 Music Opportunities
       III. College Music Courses
       IV. Western and Non-Western College Music Courses

   (E)   I. Music in Public Schools
        II. K–12 Music Opportunities
       III. College Music Courses
       IV. Western and Non-Western College Music Courses

5. Which of the following numbered sentences is *least* relevant to the main ideas of the last two paragraphs in the passage?

   (A) 1
   (B) 2
   (C) 3
   (D) 4
   (E) 5

> Read the passage below; then answer the three questions that follow.

When one looks at the human brain without the skull covering, one can easily see that it has two halves—a right side and a left side. Each side performs special functions. The left half, or lobe, of the brain dominates when analytical thinking is involved—mathematics, reasoning, and writing; _____ the right lobe of the brain is used, among other things, for thinking about a whole, rather than its separate parts. _____, when seeing a person coming towards us, the right side of our brains will look at the person's whole face for recognition, while the left side focuses on individual features, like the shape of the nose, eye color, or hair color.

6. Which words or phrases, if inserted in order into the blanks in the passage, would help the reader understand the sequence of the writer's ideas?

   (A) in fact, Therefore,
   (B) when, In contrast,
   (C) on the other hand, For example,
   (D) when, consequently,
   (E) in fact, For example,

7. An inference that can be drawn from this passage is that

   (A) a person with a damaged left half of the brain might not be very skilled in math.
   (B) playing the piano requires the work of the right half of the brain.
   (C) We can't distinguish a person's features without looking at them.
   (D) Writing an essay only requires the work of the right side of the brain.
   (E) We should look at a person's face by first concentrating on its left side, then the right.

8. Which of the following would be the most appropriate title for this passage?

   (A) The Human Brain
   (B) Right Brain Thinking
   (C) Left Brain Thinking
   (D) Reasons to Use Both Sides of the Brain
   (E) Two Sides of the Brain

Read the passage below; then answer the five questions that follow.

(1) Dances from European culture before the twentieth century are called "folk dances." (2) Dances from non-European cultures before the twentieth century are called "ethnic dances" or "traditional dances."

(3) European "folk dances" are ones which originated in that area of the world in times when a large divide existed between the common "folk" and aristocratic society. (4) (a)_____, more modern dances like hip hop are not deemed "folk dances" because they evolved in a different environment; they are part of the "street dance" or "vernacular dance" categories. (5) Certain ballroom dances originated from folk dances.

(6) Dances which highlight the dancers' culture are called "ethnic" or "traditional." _____ (7) They can also be ritual dances which convey important aspects of the ceremonial traditions of the culture. (8) Occasionally, the variations of the dance determine whether it is considered a "folk" or an "ethnic" dance. (9) For example, the polka might be considered a folk dance, (b)_____ since there are distinct ethnic varieties, such as the German Polka or the Czech Polka, they are actually categorized as "ethnic" dances.

9. Which sentence, if placed in the space in the second paragraph, would best suit the author's purpose and audience?

(A) These include sun dances, rain dances, and Whirling Dervish dances.
(B) Ethnic, traditional, and ritual dances are the same.
(C) Folk dances can be learned by plain ol' folks of all ages!
(D) Children enjoy all kinds of ethnic and traditional dances.
(E) Rituals are customs and ceremonial procedures.

10. Which of the following numbered sentences is *least* relevant to the main ideas in the reading selection?

(A) 1
(B) 3
(C) 5
(D) 7
(E) 8

11. One inference that can be drawn from this passage is that

(A) Many folk dances are, strictly speaking, ethnic dances.
(B) German Polka is more popular than Czech Polka.
(C) A divide still exists between the aristocratic and the common "folk."
(D) Hip hop is not a folk dance.
(E) None of these

12. Which of the following is the best meaning of the word *vernacular* as it is used in the first paragraph of the passage?

    (A) Green
    (B) Common
    (C) Variegated
    (D) Difficult
    (E) Predictable

13. Which words or phrases, if inserted in order into the blanks (a) and (b), would help the reader understand the sequence of the writer's ideas?

    (A) Therefore, in fact,
    (B) In contrast, when
    (C) Similarly, for example
    (D) However, but
    (E) Similarly, when

Read the passage below; then answer the four questions that follow.

The Periodic Table contains a symbol for each chemical element, including its atomic mass and atomic number. The elements are arranged by increasing atomic number. Simple abbreviations, of one and two letters, are used for each element. This table did not exist until the 1850s.

In the mid nineteenth century, the chemist J.A.R. Newlands first noticed that when arranged according to mass, each eighth element in a table of elements seemed to have the same properties. His ideas were ridiculed, however, until five years later when another scientist, Dimitri Mendeleev, published accurate predictions about three blank spaces in Newlands' "periodic table." Based on the hypothesis that any three adjacent elements contain a middle element with close to the average of properties of the elements just above and just below it, Mendeleev predicted the chemical and physical properties of the missing elements. When these elements were discovered, they were called scandium, gallium, and germanium.

14. The order of events which led to the acceptance of the Periodic Table are

    (A) (1) Mendeleev experimented with chemicals; (2) he discovered scandium, gallium, and germanium; (3) Newlands put the chemicals into his Periodic Table.
    (B) (1) Newlands ridiculed Mendeleev's idea about a Periodic Table; (2) Newlands discovered that there was a pattern in every eighth element in a table of chemical elements; (3) Newlands changed his mind and published his findings.
    (C) (1) Newlands invented every eighth element in a table of elements; (2) his inventions were ridiculed; (3) Mendeleev discovered he could use Newland's periodic table
    (D) (1) The Periodic Table was invented in the 1850s; (2) it was first used by Newlands; (3) later it was used by Mendeleev.
    (E) (1) Newlands discovered a pattern in every eighth element in a table of chemical elements; (2) his ideas were ridiculed; (3) Mendeleev was able to use this pattern to predict properties of three missing elements in the table.

15. One inference that can be drawn from this passage is that

    (A) Mendeleev accurately predicted the existence of scandium, gallium, and germanium.
    (B) Mendeleev didn't appreciate Newlands' ideas.
    (C) Newlands and Mendeleev were co-workers.
    (D) Newlands accurately predicted the existence of scandium, gallium, and germanium.
    (E) Newlands and Mendeleev were rival chemists.

16. What pattern of organization is used in the second paragraph of the passage above?

    (A) General to specific
    (B) Order of importance
    (C) Spatial order
    (D) Problem–solution order
    (E) Chronological order

17. Which of the following statements is true about the Periodic Table, based on the passage above?

    (A) A chemical element with a larger atomic number is found after an element with a smaller atomic number.
    (B) A chemical element with a larger atomic number is found before an element with a smaller atomic number.
    (C) A chemical element with a large atomic number will be abbreviated with two letters.
    (D) A chemical element with a small atomic number will be abbreviated with one letter.
    (E) None of these

Read the passage below; then answer the four questions that follow.

In the silent era of movies, the visual quality of the films, especially in those made in the 1920s, was often extremely high, but second- and third-generation copies from neglected stock have led to the misunderstanding that these films were low quality. On-screen intertitles were used in silent films to narrate the story and present dialogue. This required a skilled professional who wrote the titles, which often became graphic elements themselves, offering decoration and illustrations that commented on the film's action.

Silent movies were accompanied by musical scores, usually performed live at the theater. Small town theaters generally had a pianist, while large city theaters had an organist or even an entire orchestra. In fact, playing at the movie theaters was the largest source of employment for American instrumental musicians until the introduction of "talkies."

In other countries, a variety of methods was used to bring sound to silent movies. In Brazil, singers lip-synched behind the screen to filmed operettas, called *fitas cantatas*. In Japan, a live narrator, called a *benshi*, added commentary and character voices.

18. The best statement of the main point of this passage is

    (A) silent movies were professionally made.
    (B) musicians added to the silent movie experience.
    (C) unusual additions enhanced the silent movie experience.
    (D) other countries made silent movies more interesting than in the United States.
    (E) the silent movie era remains with us.

19. Several specific examples of 1920s silent movie supplements are provided in this passage. They include

    (A) the use of intertitles, live music, lip-synchers, and narrators.
    (B) the visual, graphic, and musical quality of films.
    (C) small theaters and large city theaters.
    (D) second- and third-generation copies of silent films.
    (E) silent movies vs. "talkies."

20. The best definition of *intertitles* as it is used in the first paragraph of the passage is

    (A) talking movie.
    (B) written comments placed between film segments.
    (C) tiles of celluloid.
    (D) titles of great interest.
    (E) the material placed between the movie's titles.

21. One inference that can be drawn from this passage is that

    (A) a benshi would be a more interesting on-stage performer than a Brazilian lip-syncher.
    (B) when "talkies" became popular, many American musicians found it hard to find employment.
    (C) the 1920s silent movies were of inferior quality.
    (D) full orchestras were used more than pianists at movie theaters during the 1920s.
    (E) the stock of silent movie films should not have been neglected.

Read the passage below; then answer the four questions that follow.

The term *perspective* refers to the representation on paper, or other flat surfaces, of a two- or three-dimensional image. To represent the way the eye perceives images in the real world, objects are drawn on paper smaller as their distance from the observer increases and forshortening is used. Foreshortening is based on the fact that when viewing at an angle, our eyes perceive a distorted image. Parallel lines, like those seen when viewing a railroad track, appear to the eye to be converging at a distance before they vanish completely. The artist can, therefore, render a "realistic" depiction of a railroad track on one-dimensional paper by drawing converging lines.

22. The best summary of the passage above is:

    (A) To draw a realistic railroad track, the artist must make the rails in the distance smaller and closer together.
    (B) The eye perceives the world in a distorted way, so an illustrator must also distort his drawing.
    (C) An artist's perspective can change the way the artist illustrates the three-dimensional world because he or she may not be accurately seeing things at a distance and may, therefore, distort the real world.
    (D) One-dimensional drawing can use perspective to illustrate the three-dimensional world by imitating the way the human eye sees things at a distance as smaller and distorted.
    (E) Using flat surfaces, an artist can represent the three-dimensional world by choosing the correct angles and shortening his or her perspective of the given object.

23. Which of the following best describes the writer's pattern of organization in the passage?

    (A) Chronological order
    (B) Problem-solving format
    (C) Explaining with examples
    (D) Spatial order
    (E) Order of importance

24. In this passage, the author's attitude toward the situation is one of

    (A) sharp criticism.
    (B) dismay.
    (C) exaggerated optimism.
    (D) dispassion.
    (E) cynicism.

25. The passage's author makes the point that

    (A) artists use perspective in a variety of ways.
    (B) the word *perspective* has a variety of meanings.
    (C) artists must understand the problems related to the human eye.
    (D) parallel lines are not truly parallel.
    (E) artists can represent two and three dimensions on a one-dimensional piece of paper.

Read the passage below; then answer the four questions that follow.

Dysgraphia, which is not the same as dyslexia, is a difficulty in coordinating fine motor tasks, like those used when tying shoes. Children with dysgraphia will also lack basic spelling skills and will write words they did not intend. It is a disorder of written expression and can be identified in a child whose writing skills are substantially below those expected, given the child's age and intelligence.

(1) Students with dysgraphia may have higher than average IQ, but the coordination dysfunction affects their ability to write appropriately sized and spaced letters and also influences them to write wrong or misspelled words even after thorough instruction. (2) Nevertheless, children with this disorder usually have no other academic or social problems, so they are not identified as behavior problems in the classroom. (3) Cases of dysgraphia beginning in adulthood generally occur after some physical damage to the brain.

(4) Other symptoms that may lead to a diagnosis of dysgraphia include mixing upper and lowercase letters, using unfinished letters, maintaining an odd writing grip, experiencing pain when writing, talking to self when writing, and demonstrating general illegibility. (5) Often children with dysgraphia will become extremely frustrated with the task of spelling and writing; younger children may cry or refuse to complete written assignments.

26. The intended audience of the passage above is

    (A) doctors.
    (B) students.
    (C) teachers.
    (D) speech therapists.
    (E) general audience.

27. The fact that dysgraphia is a coordination disorder is evident because

    (A) it is a disorder of written communication.
    (B) students with this disorder write with overly large or overly small letters and may experience pain when writing.
    (C) students with this disorder have other social problems.
    (D) students with this disorder often have a higher than average IQ.
    (E) dysgraphia is not the same as dyslexia.

28. Which of the following best organizes the main topics addressed in this passage?

    (A) I. How to recognize dysgraphia
        II. The effects of dysgraphia
        III. Symptoms of dysgraphia

    (B) I. Why children may exhibit dysgraphia
        II. What dysgraphia involves
        III. How to recognize dysgraphia

    (C) I. Characteristics of dysgraphia
        II. Parameters of coordination difficulties
        III. Symptoms of dysgraphia

    (D) I. How to recognize dysgraphia
        II. Social and emotional problems associated with dysgraphia
        III. Treatment of dysgraphia

    (E) I. How dysgraphia affects spelling
        II. How dysgraphia affects writing
        III. Treatment of dysgraphia

29. Which of the following numbered sentences is *least* relevant to the main ideas of the last two paragraphs in the passage?

    (A) 1
    (B) 2
    (C) 3
    (D) 4
    (E) 5

Read the passage below; then answer the four questions that follow.

    (1) The director of a play determines its "blocking," the movement and position of each actor on the stage. (2) This is an important stage of play production because the actors' positions can enhance the dramatic effect of a scene, _____ they must move in ways that don't block the sight lines of the audience.

(3) The stage manager is generally responsible for monitoring the blocking of each performance of a play because the director is not always present for each performance. (4) _____, the stage manager has taken notes during the blocking stage of play production, specifying actors' positions and their movement patterns on stage. (5) "Blocking" also refers to the arrangement of actors in the frame of a movie scene.

30. One inference that can be derived from the passage above is

    (A) the stage manager is more important than the director of a play.
    (B) the use of the term *blocking* in film-making is an extension of the word's use in theater.
    (C) actors' positions can enhance the dramatic effect of a scene.
    (D) blocking refers to actors' positions which block the sight lines of the audience.
    (E) the director of a play may sometimes become ill and not attend a performance.

31. What pattern of organization is used in the passage above?

    (A) General to specific
    (B) Comparison-contrast
    (C) Spatial order
    (D) Problem-solution order
    (E) Chronological order

32. Which words or phrases, if inserted in order into the blanks in the passage, would help the reader understand the sequence of the writer's ideas?

    (A) for example, For instance
    (B) yet, In fact
    (C) but, On the other hand
    (D) and, Thus
    (E) in contrast, Now

33. From the information in the passage, it is possible to project that

    (A) It is more difficult to block a play with a small cast than a play with a large cast.
    (B) Actors who monitor the blocking of other actors are more readily cast in plays.
    (C) A play that is blocked is quite traditional and unimaginative.
    (D) Stage managers are often fired because they fail to remember all the blocking notes.
    (E) It is more difficult to block a play with a large cast than a play with a small cast.

Read the passage below; then answer the four questions that follow.

Mainstreaming children with Down syndrome, placing Down syndrome children in class with their chronological peers, is controversial in the United States. Down syndrome is a developmental disability; individuals diagnosed with Down syndrome usually have a tendency toward naiveté and are not capable of abstract thinking. As children move into higher grades, the intellectual and emotional difference between children with and without Down syndrome is greater. On the other hand, separating children with Down syndrome into special classes can result in a misperception of their potential, setting lower standards for their learning than they are capable of. Mainstreaming students with Down syndrome is handled differently in other countries.

For instance, in the United Kingdom, it is common and expected. In Germany and Denmark, two teachers are in each classroom so that one teacher can take responsibility for the group of children with disabilities, including Down syndrome. Another system involves two schools. The mainstream school is the place where children with Down syndrome have recess, art instruction, eat their meals, and generally socialize in the larger population. The alternate school is the place where the children with Down syndrome have their academic lessons.

34. The best expression of the main idea of the passage above is:

(A) Other countries have less controversy surrounding the best learning environment for children with Down syndrome.
(B) Children with Down syndrome may have difficulty when they are placed in class with students their own age.
(C) Germany and Denmark usually mainstream children with developmental disabilities, whereas in the United States those children usually are not mainstreamed.
(D) Children with Down syndrome can be inappropriately identified as having lower academic potential than their peers of the same age.
(E) Down syndrome is a developmental disability occurring more frequently in the United States than in other countries.

35. The best definition of *mainstreaming* as it is used in the passage is

(A) placing students in alternate schools.
(B) placing students with developmental disabilities in two schools.
(C) placing students with developmental disabilities in classes with children their own age.
(D) providing recess, art, and other socializing activities for students with Down syndrome.
(E) abstract thinking at a lower level than students who do not have developmental disabilities.

36. Between the first and second paragraphs of the passage, the writer's approach shifts from

    (A) description to analysis.
    (B) comparison–contrast to example.
    (C) analysis to inquiry.
    (D) description to persuasion.
    (E) cause to effect.

37. One inference that can be derived from the passage above is:

    (A) Teachers should identify students who may have Down syndrome.
    (B) Children in Denmark and Germany have better schooling than children in the United States.
    (C) Individuals with Down syndrome are not capable of abstract thinking.
    (D) Children in the United States with Down syndrome are more easily mainstreamed in middle school than in primary grades.
    (E) Children in the United States with Down syndrome are more easily mainstreamed in the primary grades than in middle school.

Read the passage below; then answer the three questions that follow.

Energy is never depleted; this is the First Law of Thermodynamics. In chemistry, this law is seen in the fact that the amount of heat and work equal the total energy change in the system. The distribution of heat versus work can change, but they will always equal the same energy change because they are part of a closed system.

The First Law of Thermodynamics can be expressed as an equation [E (energy) = q (heat) + w (work)]. To think of this another way, if heat (q) were money in a checking account, the exact balance can be determined by subtracting the money spent (w) from the money deposited (E).

38. The best statement of the main point of this passage is:

    (A) According to thermodynamics, the proportion of heat and work is always the same.
    (B) An equation can explain the First Law of Thermodynamics.
    (C) Work and energy can be exchanged any time.
    (D) According to thermodynamics, energy is always conserved.
    (E) It is not wise to withdraw money from a checking account.

39. Based on the passage above, a *closed system* in thermodynamics can be understood as

    (A) a system of interlocking doors.
    (B) a system where heat and work are exchanged, but never depleted.
    (C) a process whereby heat is changed into energy.
    (D) a process whereby heat, energy, and work can be expressed as a mathematical equation.
    (E) a system that can be used to determine the optimum production during a work day.

40. An explanatory technique used by the author of the passage above is

    (A) analogy.
    (B) comparison–contrast.
    (C) exemplification.
    (D) description.
    (E) persuasion.

Use the table below to answer the next two questions.

**Ag University: Sales of Fruit by Semester—in hundreds
2007–2009**

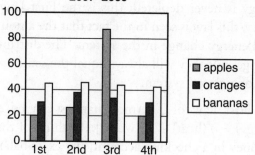

41. In which semester was Ag University's sale of oranges and bananas the highest?

    (A) First
    (B) Second
    (C) Third
    (D) Fourth
    (E) First and fourth are the same

42. In which semester was the university's sale of apples approximately twice that of bananas?

    (A) First
    (B) Second
    (C) Third
    (D) Fourth
    (E) The sale of bananas was always greater than the sale of apples.

Using the table of contents from a history of education textbook, answer questions 43, 44, 45, and 46.

Contents

43. The reader is looking for an explanation of the kind of lessons taught in earlier eras. The reader would probably find this information most quickly and easily by looking first in which part of the book?

    (A) Part One
    (B) Part Two
    (C) Part Three
    (D) Part Four
    (E) Glossary

44. The reader is looking for a technical definition of "hybrid class"; he or she would probably find this information most quickly and easily by looking first in which part of the book?

    (A) Part One
    (B) Part Two
    (C) Part Three
    (D) Part Four
    (E) Glossary

45. The reader looking for information about the Puritan education in America would probably find this information most quickly and easily by looking at the section beginning at which page of the book?

    (A) 5
    (B) 42
    (C) 157
    (D) 188
    (E) 233

46. The reader looking for information about on-line education would probably find this information most quickly and easily by looking at the section beginning at which page of the book?

    (A) 5
    (B) 42
    (C) 157
    (D) 188
    (E) 233

Read the passage below; then answer the two questions that follow.

In the early nineteenth century, Russian fur trappers moved south from Alaska as far as modern-day Sonoma county. The Russians sought sea otter pelts and continued to advance down the coastline. Russian trading posts dotted the landscape from Alaska to the Channel Islands. When a Russian Imperial nobleman fell in love with a young woman from a leading Californio family, they were set to create a new <u>dynasty</u>; however, the man died of disease while traveling to Siberia to get dispensation from the Russian Orthodox leaders to marry a Catholic.

47. An inference that can be drawn from this passage is that

    (A) the sea otter population has been made extinct due to Russian trapping.
    (B) Russian trade could have continued south to San Diego if the couple had been married.
    (C) Russians were looking for gold as well as furs.
    (D) disease can cause death.
    (E) Californio families disliked Russians.

48. Which of the following is the best meaning of the word *dynasty* as it is used in the passage?

    (A) Philosophy
    (B) Attack
    (C) Dessert
    (D) Opposition
    (E) Family

Based on the following graph; answer questions 49 and 50.

Number of New Games Created in 2007

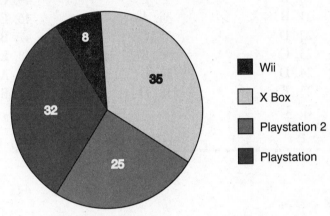

GameBook International

49. In 2007, creation of new video games was highest for what type?

    (A) Wii
    (B) X Box
    (C) Playstation 2
    (D) Playstation 1
    (E) X Box and Playstation 2 tied

50. Which two types of video games, if merged together, would have the greatest number of new games created in 2007?

    (A) Wii and X Box
    (B) Wii and Playstation 2
    (C) Wii and Playstation
    (D) X Box and Playstation 2
    (E) X Box and Playstation 1

Answer Key
READING DIAGNOSTIC TEST

1. **A**	14. **E**	27. **B**	39. **B**
2. **C**	15. **A**	28. **C**	40. **A**
3. **B**	16. **E**	29. **C**	41. **B**
4. **D**	17. **A**	30. **B**	42. **C**
5. **C**	18. **C**	31. **C**	43. **C**
6. **C**	19. **A**	32. **D**	44. **E**
7. **A**	20. **B**	33. **E**	45. **C**
8. **E**	21. **B**	34. **A**	46. **E**
9. **A**	22. **D**	35. **C**	47. **B**
10. **C**	23. **C**	36. **B**	48. **E**
11. **A**	24. **D**	37. **E**	49. **A**
12. **B**	25. **E**	38. **D**	50. **B**
13. **A**	26. **C**		

ANSWER EXPLANATIONS

1. **(A)** The information is in time order, in fact in two overlapping time sequences: (1) the passage of time from pre-school to college, and (2) the established tradition of teaching music in European and North American public schools to the more recent music training in Asian countries.

2. **(C)** Strategizing in a way similar to the method for answering organization questions, you can focus on the first of the two terms in each answer choice, eliminating answer (A) because the third paragraph is not a demonstration and (E) because it is not an explanation of reasons or causes. Taking, then, the second term in the remaining answer choices, one can eliminate (B) and (D) because the fourth paragraph is neither a demonstration nor a persuasive paragraph. The fourth paragraph compares North American music curriculum to Asian curriculum, so (C) is the best answer.

3. **(B)** Using the strategy of substitution, you can determine that . . . . *jazz bands and orchestras are* **common**, *and students may elect* . . . . is the statement that makes the most sense in the paragraph. Did you notice that the opposite, "uncommon" was also an answer choice? Did you recall what clue that gives you? (Chapter 3)

4. **(D)** The answer to No. 1—that the passage is arranged chronologically—can help you select the correct outline organization. You can eliminate answer (C) because Roman numbers II and III are not reflecting the time sequence of K–12, then college and you can eliminate (A) because the time order (college first) is inaccurate. Then focusing on only Roman number I statements in the remaining answers, you can eliminate (B) since the first paragraph does not concern children's preference for music classes. Finally, if you annotated the selection, you probably noted that the first paragraph is only about North American and European schools, so (D) is a better answer than (E).

5. **(C)** Since this long passage provides information about music training for all students in school, the idea that is least related to the main point is about specific training for future elementary school teachers (even though the point may be very related to your personal life!).

6. **(C)** Mentally placing the first term in each pair into the passage, answer (C) is the best choice since the two ideas are different (about the left lobe and the right lobe). It also checks out when mentally placing the second term because the details about visualizing a person are part of an example of the way the two lobes work differently.

7. **(A)** Given the information about the main functions of the left and right sides of the brain, you can deduce that playing the piano and writing an essay might require the left, the logical, side as much as the holistic side. Therefore, answers (B) and (D) are eliminated. Answer (C) is a statement of fact, not related to the

information in the passage and answer (E) is not suggested by the passage; thus, answer (A) is the best choice. The passage says that the left side of the brain operates during logical thinking in mathematics, among other things, so the conclusion drawn is a reasonable one.

8. **(E)** When you came up with your own title, it probably had something to do with both sides of the brain, so that eliminates answers (B) and (C). The passage doesn't emphasize "reasons" for using the different lobes, so answer (D) is also eliminated. The more accurate of the two titles remaining is (E) – answer (A) is more general than (E), and therefore not as appropriate for the title.

9. **(A)** Answer (A) is an appropriate list of examples to follow the generalization which begins the second paragraph. Answer (B) is not accurate, so it should not be included in the passage. In addition, answer (C) can be eliminated because its tone is not compatible with the educated, informative tone of the passage. And answer (D) would inappropriately include a statement about children when children have not previously been referenced in the passage. The last to eliminate, answer (E), is another generalization, defining rituals, a term which is already defined at the end of the next sentence, so it can be eliminated.

10. **(C)** Each of the other choices refers to sentences which are important to the overall understanding about folk and ethnic dances.

11. **(A)** Like the polka, which is explained in the passage, other folk dances probably have varieties developed in distinct areas or countries, so the statement in (A) is logically deduced from the passage. Answers (B), (C), and (D) contain statements which are inaccurate conclusions drawn from the reading.

12. **(B)** Substituting each term, the best resulting sentence is . . . . *they are part of the "street dance" or "common dance" categories.*

13. **(A)** Introducing the first term of each pair into the "a" location, you will find that answers (A), (C), and (E) are eliminated because they do not reasonably introduce the contrasting information in Sentence 4. Trying out the second term in answers (B) and (D) points to (D) as the best answer because *when since there are distinct ethnic varieties* shows that inserting "when" is not helpful in that sentence.

14. **(E)** Answers (A), (B), and (C) are easy to eliminate, especially if you have annotated the passage, because (A) begins with Mendeleev, while the part of the passage in question begins with Newlands. And (B) and (C) are inaccurate statements, based on the passage. Reading more closely, answer (D) also has an inaccurate statement when it says that Newlands <u>used</u> the periodic table, rather than he *created* the table. Thus (E) is the best answer.

15. **(A)** Clearly, answer (D) is inaccurate, so it cannot be a good inference. Answers (B), (C), and (E) have to do with the friendly/unfriendly relationship between the two scientists, but the passage doesn't provide anything about their relationship aside from the fact that Mendeleev used the table Newlands cre-

ated; thus Mendeleev probably didn't ridicule Newlands. More appropriate as a choice, therefore, is (A). The passage does not state directly that Mendeleev predicted those specific elements, but one puts "2 + 2 together"—in this case puts the last two sentences together—to form the conclusion.

16. **(E)** The second paragraph discusses what Newlands did first to create the table, then explains how Mendeleev later used the table to makes his predictions. This is chronological, or time, order.

17. **(A)** Based on the second sentence in the passage, answer (A) provides the only true statement about the Periodic Table.

18. **(C)** Annotations made alongside the passage would probably include words like *intertitles, pianist, orchestra, lip-synch,* and *live narrator.* From these, it is easy to select the statement about "unusual additions" as the best answer for the main point of the passage.

19. **(A)** Again, your annotations should make this choice fairly easy. Also, answers (B) through (E) are not "specific examples" of anything—they are generalizations.

20. **(B)** According to the passage, intertitles presented narrative and dialogue or decoratively "commented on the film's action." Therefore, they were not "talking movies," "tiles of celluloid," or "material placed between the movie's titles." They might be "of great interest," but they are definitely as described in answer (B): "decorative, written comments placed between film segments."

21. **(B)** The passage does not provide any details which could be collected to form the conclusions expressed in answers (A), (D), or (E). Answer (C) is inaccurate; the passage actually says the quality was superior, not inferior. It is logical, though, that if the "largest source of employment for American . . . musicians" before the 'talkies' " was the silent movies, then after "talkies" became popular, many musicians would have become unemployed.

22. **(D)** The passage centers on the creation of three-dimensional images through "perspective," which uses the techniques of size diminishment and foreshortening. Answer (D) expresses that idea. Answer (A) is not a statement which encompasses the whole passage, and answers (B), (C) and (E) do not correctly render the information from the passage into more general terms.

23. **(C)** The passage ends with the example of the railroad track; it begins with an explanation of the term "perspective." Thus it explains with examples.

24. **(D)** The information is presented in a matter-of-fact way with formal wording. No "tone of voice" is apparent, so the attitude is neutral or "dispassionate."

25. **(E)** Locating the portion of the passage that mirrors one of the statements, you can find the first sentence "perspective refers to the representation on paper . . . of a two- or three-dimensional image," which has virtually the same meaning as answer (E).

26. **(C)** Since the passage refers to identifying this learning problem "in the classroom," the passage is intended for teachers.

27. **(B)** Writing "overly large or overly small letters" and experiencing pain when writing are the result of physical coordination problems.

28. **(C)** Taking each item's Roman numeral I, we eliminate (B) and (E), for the passage does not begin with a paragraph about the causes of dysgraphia or the associated spelling problems. Looking, then, at Roman numeral II, we can eliminate answers (A) and (D) because that paragraph is about the characteristics of children with dysgraphia, not just the effects on the children, as well as about the cause of adult-onset dysgraphia. Children with dysgraphia have "no other academic or social problems" besides inappropriately sized letters and misspelled words, so (D) is not an accurate rendering of the second paragraph's main topic. That leaves (C), which does present accurate main topics as organized in the passage.

29. **(C)** As you may have noticed when you were annotating this passage or when you were working out the answer to No. 27, the one sentence about adults with dysgraphia is irrelevant to the rest of the passage.

30. **(B)** While the major part of the passage discusses staged plays, the last sentence discusses movie-makers' use of the term "blocking." It is a reasonable conclusion that the concern that stage actors "move in ways that don't block the sight lines of the audience" can be transferred to the concern about "sight lines" of the camera. Answer (C) is directly stated in the passage, so it cannot be an inference.

31. **(C)** The first paragraph presents the problem—sight lines of the audience must not be blocked by the actors. The second paragraph presents the solution—the stage manager monitors the position and movement of the actors to ensure that the problem does not present itself.

32. **(D)** Testing the first terms in each pair allows for the elimination of answers (A), (B), (C), and (E). Answer (D) is left, and its second term also makes sense in its position.

33. **(E)** You might have seen the clue in the presentation of opposite answers. Since the director and stage manager must determine and remember the positions on stage of every performer, a play with a large cast would be more difficult to block than one with a small cast.

34. **(A)** Since the first paragraph describes the United States' controversy over mainstreaming and the second paragraph discusses the mainstreaming situation in the United Kingdom, Germany, and Denmark, answer (A) is the best choice for an expression of the main idea of the passage.

35. **(C)** The term "mainstreaming" is re-stated in the first sentence of the passage: *Mainstreaming . . . placing Down syndrome children in class with their chronological peers . . . .* This sentence is very similar to the sentence in answer (C).

36. **(B)** The first paragraph compares the advantages and disadvantages of mainstreaming children with Down syndrome. The second paragraph provides examples of countries in which mainstreaming "is handled differently."

37. **(E)** Answers (A) and (B) are not reasonable conclusions based on any of the ideas in the passage. Answer (C) is not an inference, for it is stated in the middle of the first paragraph. That leaves (D) and (E) which are opposite statements. Since the passage says as children get older, the difference, intellectually and emotionally, between children with and without Down syndrome is greater, the logical inference is that children with Down syndrome are more easily mainstreamed at an earlier age, in this case "in the primary grades."

38. **(D)** The topic sentence states that *Energy is never depleted*; this is the same as saying "energy is always conserved."

39. **(B)** The third sentence says the energy change remains equal regardless of the "distribution of heat versus work," so a closed system must be one in which "heat and work are exchanged, but never depleted."

40. **(A)** The passage contains a description of a bank account as a method to "think of this (the equation in the passage) another way." Thus, the components of the bank account can be compared to the components of the equation for the First Law of Thermodynamics. This comparison is called an analogy.

41. **(B)** Since the sale of bananas is constant over all four semesters, the feature to concentrate on is the bars representing sale of oranges. The bar for the second quarter is the tallest, so (B) is the best answer.

42. **(C)** Since the apple bar must be twice as tall as the banana bar, it is easy to spot the third semester as the best answer.

43. **(C)** Part Three has sub-topics about medieval curriculum and training clerics under the broad heading of "history of curriculum," so it is the section most likely to explain "lessons taught in earlier eras."

44. **(E)** Definitions are found in a glossary.

45. **(C)** The Puritans were a religious denomination in Colonial America. You should have looked at the page number answers, first, rather than going through the whole index to find the best answer. In this passage, another possible answer would be the chapter beginning on page 80, but this isn't listed as one of the choices. So it is more time-efficient to read the answers first, before tracking through a Table of Contents or Index.

46. **(E)** On-line education, classes over the Internet, is an alternative system for delivering learning, so it would be discussed within Part Four.

47. **(B)** The only reasonable conclusion to draw from the facts is that if the Russian nobleman had lived and married the Californio woman, the Russian trade route might have extended to the southern part of that region.

48. **(E)** Substituting each term, we find that *they were set to create a new family* makes the most sense, given that the man fell in love with the woman.

49. **(A)** The pie chart shows 35% of the number of new games created in 2007 were for the Wii.

50. **(B)** The two largest percentages on the chart are 35% and 32%, so Wii (at 35%) and Playstation 2 (at 25%) would have the greatest number of new games created in 2007 (67%).

CHAPTER 4

READING SECTION REVIEW

Reading Section Review

In this chapter you will find:

the types of questions in the Reading Section,

- the approach you should take in the Reading Section,
- examples of Reading Test items with correct answers and explanations,
- **Maximizer** strategies to optimize your reading and answering time.

The Reading Section does not require test-takers to have any outside knowledge to answer the questions. The 50 multiple-choice questions are based on material provided in the excerpts or passages, and the answers variously require you to:

- Select the correct meaning of a designated word within the context of the passage
- Select supporting details from the passage
- Identify the main idea of the passage
- Identify accurate paraphrases or summaries of the passage
- Identify certain techniques used by the author of the passage (like the tone or organization principle)
- Make an inference (logical conclusion) from the passage

According to the CBEST preparers, approximately 40% of the multiple-choice questions in this section requires you to analyze and evaluate the reading, and the other approximately 60% requires you to select correct answers based on accurate comprehension of written passages, indexes, charts, and graphs. (Indexes, charts, and graphs are the means used to test your researching skills.)

As you can tell, you are tested on your ability to understand and manipulate information presented in written form. This kind of reading is very different from pleasure reading: you are reading for a *specific purpose*—answering specific questions.

Since you are reading for a specific purpose, you should read all the questions BEFORE reading the passage. *Previewing the questions* and circling or underlining the key words give you the ability to focus on the information you most need to identify in the reading passage.

Maximizer #3—Transitions

Pay attention to *connecting words* in the reading passages because they communicate important information or change of direction.

- Indications of a change of direction: *However, In contrast, Instead of, But, Still, Otherwise*

- Indications of a new, but similar, thought: *Likewise, Similarly, In addition*

- Indications of cause and effect: *As a result, Therefore, Thus, Hence*

As you carefully read the passage, you should also underline, circle, annotate, or number parts of the reading passage itself when you find possible answers or clues.

Example Annotation	Example Passage
Hans = horse. *Master thought horse could count.*	(1) Clever Hans was a horse which stamped his hoof the correct number of times when his master said a number. (2) Hans and his master went about the German countryside early in the twentieth century demonstrating Clever Hans' ability to count. (3) This was not <u>charlatanism</u> because Clever Hans' master believed Hans could indeed count. (4) Eventually, it was demonstrated that Hans could count only if his master performed with him and only if Hans could see his master.
When master tense → *horse stamped.* *When master relaxed →* *horse stopped.* *Horse was conditioned by master's actions, approval, and reward.*	(5) Hans was actually stamping his hoof as long as his master maintained a tense stance. (6) When Hans got to the correct number of stamps, his master unconsciously would relax a bit and take a breath. (7) Hans' clever behavior is the result of conditioning. (8) The positive reinforcement came from the affectionate approval, including lumps of sugar perhaps, given to Hans by his master when Hans was successful.

After annotating the passage in this way, read the answer choices again—all of them—before selecting one. It is just as likely for the last answer choice to be correct as the first.

As you are reading the choices, cross out ones you are certain are not correct. Sometimes you will find that two answer choices are opposites. When this occurs, it is likely that one of the two choices is the "best answer." In addition, you should look for hints about the correct answer in other questions for the same passage. The best answer may be part of another question on the test, as well.

The Reading Section tasks listed at the beginning of this chapter can be more simply categorized into three types:

- Questions based on the entire passage
- Questions based on sections of the passage
- Questions based on particular words or sentences

A question based on the entire passage above might be:

Which of the following would be the most appropriate title for this passage?

Before you read further, try to answer the question on your own. A title should encapsulate the overall point of the passage. You can also think of it as the *primary purpose* of the passage or the *author's main idea*. In fact, in all CBEST exams, there are questions about appropriate title and the author's main idea or primary purpose.

In main idea questions, answers that emphasize factual information can usually be eliminated. Generally, choices that are very narrow or very broad are also incorrect. Instead, those answer choices which contain key words and concepts from the passage are most likely to be correct.

Now, select the most appropriate title for the example passage above:

(A) Clever Hans
(B) Fooling the Audience
(C) Conditioning by Positive Reinforcement
(D) Charlatanism
(E) Training Horses

EXPLANATION The best answer is **C**. The story of the horse serves as an example of the overall idea of conditioning through positive reinforcement. Only choice **C** expresses that idea, and it is actually expressed at the end of the second paragraph, following the long narrative about Clever Hans and his owner's unconscious behavior. Choice A just names the horse; the horse itself is not the point, the conditioning of the horse to the master's body language is the actual point. Choice B expresses a minor detail in the passage. Choice D inaccurately refers to what the horse's master did as deliberate trickery. Choice E inaccurately summarizes the passage as a "how to" about training horses.

In addition, when the reading passage is more than one paragraph long, be sure to choose a title which expresses the overall point of <u>all</u> paragraphs in that passage.

Another question based on the entire passage above might be:

What can you infer from the fact that Clever Hans' master didn't know what was truly happening?

(A) Clever Hans deliberately fooled his master.
(B) Clever Hans' master was unaware of his physical signals.
(C) The audience for the shows knew more than Clever Hans' master did.
(D) The master loved Clever Hans.
(E) Clever Hans' master could not count well.

EXPLANATION The best answer is **B**. Because the horse's master was not aware he was tense or breathing in a relaxed way (the passage says he did this *unconsciously*), he didn't sense he was giving signals to the horse. Choice A is an inaccurate understanding of the passage—the horse was conditioned to perform; it did not do anything of its own volition. Choice C may or may not be true, but first, the passage doesn't convey this idea, and second, what the audience knew is not relevant to what the horse's master didn't know. Choice D is probably an accurate reading of the passage (he rewards the horse with *affectionate approval)*, but again, it is not a conclusion drawn from the details about what the horse's master did or did not know. Choice E shows inaccurate comprehension of the passage since counting correctly was the basis of the demonstration.

Another question based on the entire passage above might ask about a writer's *attitude* or *tone*. Tone means something like the "tone of voice" which we interpret when we hear someone speak. Similarly, a writer's tone can be interpreted as cynical, depressed, sympathetic, cheerful, outraged, positive, angry, sarcastic, prayerful, ironic, solemn, vindictive, intense, excited, to name a few. In the Reading Section of the CBEST, determining the purpose of the passage is often a key indicator of the tone or attitude of the writer. For instance, when the purpose is to explain a serious issue, the writer's tone will usually be neutral, written in standard English. In contrast, if the purpose is to entertain or satirize, the writer may use slang, jargon or informal English to produce the desired effect. So given the fact that the author of the passage about Clever Hans is retelling an event about a man who was not trying to entertain, not trick, people with his "clever" horse, it is told without intense emotion. For instance, part of the passage says that Hans "went about the German countryside early in the twentieth century demonstrating Clever Hans' ability"—this is neutral, explanatory language.

So what is the best answer for the author's attitude?

In this passage, the author's attitude toward the situation is one of

(A) sharp criticism.
(B) dismay.
(C) exaggerated optimism.
(D) indifference.
(E) delight.

EXPLANATION The word choice in the passage is neutral; there are no words which describe the actions of any of the characters as positive or negative. The horse is, indeed, described in the 7th sentence as "clever," but that is simply reinforcing the horse's given name and the *appearance* (not the reality) that the horse could think and count. Therefore, the author is indifferent: **C**. The demonstration was "not an act of charlatanism"; therefore, the writer is not criticizing it—Choice A is therefore not correct. Neither does the author express worry or concern (dismay) about how the demonstrations fooled everyone—Choice B. Since this event happened in the past and since it is described without a lot of exclamatory or positive words or exclamation marks, we cannot accurately say that the author felt "exaggerated optimism"—Choice C—or "delight"—Choice E.

The second category of reading task is a question based on a section of the passage. These somewhat "factual" questions may seem to be the easiest ones, but they often take more time than first imagined since they require careful reading of each possible "best" answer.

An example based on the passage above is:

The author makes the point that

(A) To perform his counting trick, Clever Hans had to be in the line of sight of his master.
(B) The audience was often disappointed when Clever Hans made a mistake.
(C) Hans' master deliberately signaled to the horse.
(D) Hans' master always gave the horse lumps of sugar after a performance.
(E) The horse was treated cruelly by his master.

> **NOTE**
>
> These somewhat "factual" questions may seem to be the easiest ones, but they often take more time than first imagined since they require careful reading of each possible "best" answer.

EXPLANATION Sentence 4 in the passage states that the horse had to perform with his master and be able to see him; otherwise, the horse could not perform. Therefore, choice **A** is the best answer. The passage does not mention anything about the audience's reaction—choice B. (Be careful to avoid adding into the selection your own ideas or feelings.) Choice C expresses the opposite of the point made in the first half of the passage—Hans' master was not doing anything deliberately to affect the horse—only subconsciously. Choice D is not correct because that idea is expressed in the passage with "perhaps"—this is the author's conjecture, not a proven fact. And choice E is fairly obviously incorrect because the master gave *affectionate approval* to the horse.

Another question based on a section of the passage above might be:

What can you infer about the owner of Clever Hans?

(A) He made a lot of money from the performances.
(B) He could neither read nor write.
(C) He felt anxious when his horse was performing.
(D) He tried to make the performance entertaining.
(E) When his master found out what was really happening, he was very embarrassed.

> **TIP**
>
> Inferences are logical conclusions drawn from information, so the answer will not be explicitly found to a question asking what you can "infer" in the passage. Instead, you "put 2 + 2 together" to come to a conclusion or judgment not literally stated in the reading. So after reading about Clever Hans' owner, what do you know that is not directly stated?

EXPLANATION The best answer is choice **C**. The passage states that the owner was *tense* as the horse began stamping and *would relax* when the horse got to the right number of stamps. Thus, the owner didn't feel entirely confident or carefree until his horse got it right—he was anxious. Choice A is not correct because the passage doesn't mention payment at all; the passage also fails to mention whether the owner was literate, so choice B cannot be correct. Aside from having the horse stamp its foot, there are no other details about the performance, so we cannot accurately state that choice D is correct; and the passage doesn't take us into the time when the reality was revealed to the horse's owner, so we cannot say that choice E is correct, either.

A question based on particular words or sentences in the passage above might be:

Which of the following is the best meaning of the word <u>charlatanism</u> as it is used in the second paragraph of the passage?

(A) con artistry
(B) spiritualism
(C) tomfoolery
(D) indignation
(E) desperation

EXPLANATION The best answer is choice **A**. Let's go through all of the answers while considering the best approaches to these kinds of "fill in the blank" test items.

1. Clearly, the first step is to re-read the sentence that has the underlined word and to understand the general meaning of the sentence.

2. It is also helpful to decide which part of speech needs to be used at that point of the underlined word: noun, verb, adjective, adverb (these are the most common possibilities). For example, in the passage above, in the sentence *This was not an act of <u>charlatanism</u> because Hans' master believed Hans could indeed count,* the key word is a noun (person, place, thing, or idea). Therefore, the meaning of *charlatanism* must be expressed as a noun. Unfortunately, in our Clever Hans question, all 5 possible answers are nouns. Not much chance of elimination of wrong choices yet.

> **Maximizer #4—A Rich Vocabulary**
>
> You may have noticed that reading test questions such as this one assess the test-takers' vocabulary level. And therefore if a person doesn't know what *spiritualism* or *tomfoolery* means, he or she may have to resort to guessing. This situation suggests, of course, that a rich vocabulary will help a test-taker pass the CBEST.
>
> Anyone can build a larger vocabulary by reading fiction and non-fiction and recording and looking up unfamiliar words. There are many well-designed vocabulary building books to learn from, as well.

3. The context of the sentence or passage may also help us work out a rough meaning of the unfamiliar word. Clues from the context, or surroundings help us to reason out the meaning of a word or phase. They come in several categories:

Definition clue—Example: *<u>Etymology</u>, which is the historical tracing of a word's origins, is presented in square brackets in most dictionary entries.* Here, the sentence itself provides enough information to define an unfamiliar term. In our example sentence, however, *charlatanism* is not re-defined for us.

Restatement clue—Example: *The <u>dromedary</u>, commonly called a camel, stores fat in its hump.* So if we are unfamiliar with the word *dromedary*, its meaning is restated, camel. These kinds of clues are often enclosed by commas.

> **Maximizer #5—Restatement Clues**
>
> Restatement context clues are often surrounded by commas and are often introduced by words and phrases like: *Or, Such as, That is, In other words, Commonly called*

Unfortunately, in our Clever Hans sentence, *charlatanism* is not restated, either.

Antonym clue—Example: *Unlike his quiet and somber siblings, Julio is garrulous.* The two contrasting ideas, *quiet and somber vs. garrulous,* help us determine the meaning of the new word in the first sentence. *Garrulous* is the opposite of quiet and somber—so it means *talkative* or *lively.* Example: *I am very strict about children crying, but I am very <u>lenient</u> about children yelling.* Here, the word but is the clue that *lenient* is the opposite of *strict,* so it must mean *flexible* or *easygoing.*

There is no contrasting term, though, in our example sentence about Clever Hans.

> **Maximizer #6—Antonym Signals**
>
> Antonym context clues are often signaled by: *However, Yet, But, On the other hand*

General clues—Example: *The cat had such a <u>tenacious</u> grip on my shoe that when I lifted up the shoe, I also lifted the cat off the floor.* What kind of grip would allow the cat to be lifted with the shoe? Something very strong and unyielding, and that's what *tenacious* means. Sometimes we must use all the ideas in the sentence or context to reason out the meaning of the unfamiliar word.

<u>Example</u>: *Students who work over 20 hours a week face <u>adversities</u> such as lack of adequate time to study, sleep, or socialize.* Here, we are provided with illustrations or examples of *adversities*: no time to study, sleep, or socialize. These are negative things that are hard to cope with. So *adversities* must mean *hardship*s or *difficulties.*

Example: *People who suffer from asthma are advised to avoid things that can <u>precipitate</u> an attack, such as strong odors and sprays, changing weather conditions and chemical exposure on the job.* The various things listed at the end of the sentence "do something" to the asthma attack, and asthma sufferers are warned to avoid them. Thus, those things must bring on or create an asthma attack. And *to precipitate* does mean to *hasten* or *trigger.*

> **Maximizer #7—Example Clues**
>
> Example context clues are often signaled by: *For example, For instance, Such as, Including*

Now, back to the question about the best meaning for *charlatanism*. If its meaning is not already known to us, we use the general context clues. Clever Hans' master genuinely thought the horse could actually count, so, hmmm, he was not

- (A) a <u>con artist</u> (one who practices con artistry)
- (B) a <u>spiritualist</u> <u>(one who practices spiritualism)</u>
- (C) <u>a tomfool</u> <u>(one who practices tomfoolery)</u>
- (D) <u>indignant</u> <u>(one who feels indignance)</u>
- (E) <u>desperate</u> <u>(one who feels desperation)</u>

Based on the general context of the sentence, you can eliminate any obviously incorrect answers. For instance, the horse's master was proud of Clever Hans, so it's unlikely that Clever Hans' master was indignant or desperate, right? Then try substituting your remaining selections for the underlined word and re-read the sentence.

> *This was not an act of <u>con artistry</u> because Hans' master believed Hans could indeed count.*
>
> OR
>
> *This was not an act of <u>spiritualism</u> because Hans' master believed Hans could indeed count.*
>
> OR
>
> *This was not an act of <u>tomfoolery</u> because Hans' master believed Hans could indeed count.*

EXPLANATION The best answer is choice **A**. What may have seemed the case, but was not, was that Clever Hans' master was trying to swindle people, and a *charlatan* is a *swindler* or *pretender*. So is a *con artist*. Given the context of a performance where an animal supposedly can count like humans, the word *charlatanism* is related to swindling, not related to mysticism—choice B—*spiritualism,* or misbehavior—choice C—*tomfoolery.* And the demonstration itself wasn't negative or offensive, so it didn't cause—choice D—*indignation,* or worry—choice E—*desperation.*

To summarize, the multiple-choice reading section of the CBEST will assess your ability to answer questions based on (1) an entire passage, (2) a section of the passage, or (3) particular words or sentences in the passage.

Here are more examples of these types of reading questions. First, questions based on an entire reading passage. (If this were the actual test, you, of course, would read the questions *before* reading the passage, so here they are: *Which of the following is the best summary of this passage? Which of the following is the most reasonable inference from the passage?* And *Which of the following would be the most appropriate title for this passage?*)

ENTIRE PASSAGE

TIP

You may also use this to practice your annotating, circling, and underlining of the key material.

California is named for Queen Califia, a Black Amazon warrior queen who was purported to rule an island nation. Some European maps as late as 1700 depicted California as an island, which was near the earthly Paradise and "at the right hand of the Indies" as Garcia Ordonez Rodriguez de Montalvo's novel claimed. Since Queen Califia's nation used gold as its only metal, this legend helped encourage the Spanish to hunt for gold in North America. In fact, when Spanish explorer Hernando Cortez landed in Baja California, he told his crew they had arrived at Califia's domain. By 1770, the entire coastal area controlled by Spain was called California; the Spanish-speaking people who lived there were called Californios.

Which of the following is the best summary of this passage?

HINT

a summary rephrases the key ideas in a text.

(A) It took only 70 years for Spain to discover Baja California and conquer its native people. It was supposed to be on the "right hand" of the Indies, but the Spanish decided to explore in North America instead, and eventually they found California.

(B) Ruled by Queen Califia, an island which had a lot of gold was sought by explorers. When Hernando Cortez arrived in Baja California, he thought it was that legendary island. But he never found Queen Califia; later it was discovered that it wasn't an island, but the coast of the Pacific, so the Spanish called all of the Pacific coastal area they conquered California.

(C) The Californios began as subjects of Queen Califia. After their conquest by Hernando Cortez, they were made to speak Spanish because they were ruled by the Spanish.

(D) Queen Califia's domain was conquered by the Spanish; Hernando Cortez and his men sought for gold in her land. After her death, in her honor, the coastal area ruled by Spain was called California and the people living there were called Californios.

(E) Legendary Queen Califia's island domain, which had gold in abundance, was sought by explorers including Hernando Cortez. Eventually, the Pacific coastal area controlled by Spain was called California and its inhabitants, Californios.

EXPLANATION The best answer is choice **E**. All the other answers contain misreadings of the passage: Choice A mistakenly assumes that the 70 years between 1700 and 1770 were spent trying to find Baja California. Choice B mixes legend with fact and includes an idea not in the passage, that Cortez was seeking, but never found, Queen Califia.

Choice C mistakes the final point in the chronology with the first points, confusing the Californios with the Queen's subjects. Choice D adds an assumption which erroneously mixes fact with legend: Queen Califia actually died and then the name for the area was created in her honor. These mistaken assumptions and confusions can be avoided if you will read the passage attentively, annotating key ideas, circling important words, and so forth. Those emphasized areas will help you see the main parts of a passage which are subject to summary.

TIP

Summaries ONLY include the key ideas in the original.

Which of the following is the most reasonable inference drawn from the passage?

(A) The island of the Black Amazons is located near the Indies.

(B) The people living on Queen Califia's island were rich.

(C) Everyone who lived on the Pacific Coastal area conquered by the Spanish spoke Spanish.

(D) The name for the whole coastal area was later applied to the state of California after that territory became part of the United States.

(E) Cortez and his men became rich after they conquered Baja California.

EXPLANATION The most reasonable inference is choice **D**. Choice A infers that the island actually exists, which it does not. Choice B tries to reason that since the legendary islanders' only metal was gold, that gold made them "rich," but there is no supporting information which would prove that there was a lot of gold or that the gold—for those islanders—was precious and, therefore, something that made them wealthy. Choice C makes an erroneous over-generalization that since there were Spanish-speaking people in that area, all the people spoke Spanish. Choice E is not logically based on anything in the reading passage; nothing about the explorers' plunder is described.

Which of the following would be the most appropriate title for this passage?

(A) Amazon Queen

(B) The Spanish Conquerors

(C) How California Was Named

(D) Gold in California

(E) Cortez Seeks Califia

EXPLANATION Choice E sounds like the title for a personal ad, but it is not the best answer. Neither is choice A because it features the queen, only, while the passage was about the area on the Pacific Coast which was named for the queen, as well. Choices B and D are similarly limited, rather than encompassing the whole main idea of the passage. Choice B focuses on the Spanish, but the passage did not solely discuss the activities of the Spanish, and choice D focuses on the gold, which is only one detail in the text. Finally, choice **C** is the best answer; it encompasses the whole reason for the passage—to detail the process by which California got its name.

A SECTION OF THE PASSAGE

Moving now to the second category of reading questions, here are some samples based on a section of the same passage used before.

California is named for Queen Califia, a Black Amazon warrior queen who was purported to rule an island nation. Some European maps as late as 1700 depicted California as an island, which was near the earthly Paradise and "at the right hand of the Indies" as Garcia Ordonez Rodriguez de Montalvo's novel claimed. Since Queen Califia's nation used gold as its only metal, this legend helped encourage the Spanish to hunt for gold in North America. In fact, when Spanish explorer Hernando Cortez landed in Baja California, he told his crew they had arrived at Califia's domain. By 1770, the entire coastal area controlled by Spain was called California; the Spanish-speaking people who lived there were called Californios.

The author of the passage makes the point that

(A) Spain eventually controlled not only Baja California, but also other parts of the Pacific Coast.
(B) The Rodriguez de Montalvo novel gave Cortez clues to find Baja California.
(C) The crew and Cortez believed they had found Califia's domain.
(D) Califia's land was indeed an earthly paradise.
(E) The 18th century European maps showed gold in the land ruled by Queen Califia.

EXPLANATION Various sections of the passage are called into focus by answers A–E. Choice **A** is the best answer, based on the information provided in the last two sentences of the passage. Choice B refers to the novel in the passage, which only described the island (sentence 2) in ways that would *not* help Cortez, especially since Cortez sailed to North America, not the Indies. Furthermore, choice C is a misreading of sentence 4, which indicates what Cortez supposedly said, but not what Cortez or the other men believed. Choice D takes a phrase from sentence 2 and mistakenly applies it to Califia's island when it is actually referring to a place near Califia's island, while choice E also misreads that sentence, mistakenly adding references to gold to the European maps.

Which details from the passage support the idea that Queen Califia, real or legendary, was held in high esteem during the time period referred to in the text?

(A) That the famous Spanish explorer Hernando Cortez was searching for Queen Califia's island.
(B) That she was said to rule an island; that she was mentioned in a novel; that her name was applied to the Pacific coastal area ruled by the Spanish.
(C) That her island was on a map; that she lived near an "earthly paradise."
(D) That she was made into a legend.
(E) That Cortez's men, as well as Cortez himself, knew about her.

EXPLANATION The best answer is choice **B**. (Did you apply Maximizer #2—that the correct answer is often the longest answer?) Choice A is not the best answer because Cortez was not necessarily looking for an *island*. In choice C, the details about Califia's island's proximity to some kind of paradise and its presence on a map are not as clear proof of the queen's "esteem" as are choice B's details. Furthermore, choice D is not an accurate detail from the passage—so far as we know from the text, the Queen was always a legend. Choice E is not a detail from the passage; in fact, it may be a misinterpretation of the passage, so it can't be a good choice in answer to this prompt.

WORDS OR SENTENCES IN A PASSAGE

Since you know it so well by now, let's use the same passage to point out the reasoning behind correct answers to questions about particular words or sentences in a reading.

California is named for Queen Califia, a Black Amazon warrior queen who was purported to rule an island nation. Some European maps as late as 1700 depicted California as an island, which was near the earthly Paradise and "at the right hand of the Indies" as Garcia Ordonez Rodriguez de Montalvo's novel claimed. Since Queen Califia's nation used gold as its only metal, this legend helped encourage the Spanish to hunt for gold in North America. In fact, when Spanish explorer Hernando Cortez landed in Baja California, he told his crew they had arrived at Califia's domain. By 1770, the entire coastal area controlled by Spain was called California; the Spanish-speaking people who lived there were called Californios.

Which of the following is the best meaning of the word "purported" as it is used in the passage?

(A) proven
(B) destined
(C) presumed
(D) determined
(E) chosen

EXPLANATION First, we can determine that "presumed" is part of a verb, and all the answers are also parts of verbs. No answers to eliminate yet. Then we can substitute the selections for the underlined word and re-read the sentence.

California is named for Queen Califia, a Black Amazon warrior queen who was proven to rule an island nation.

OR

California is named for Queen Califia, a Black Amazon warrior queen who was destined to rule an island nation.

OR

California is named for Queen Califia, a Black Amazon warrior queen who was presumed to rule an island nation.

OR

California is named for Queen Califia, a Black Amazon warrior queen who was determined to rule an island nation.

OR

California is named for Queen Califia, a Black Amazon warrior queen who was chosen to rule an island nation.

As we substitute and look for the best answer, we must remember that the queen's nation was "claimed" by the novel to be at the "right hand of the Indies," and the idea that the island contained gold was a "legend." Therefore, choice **C** is the best meaning of "purported:" it isn't a fact, it was a *presumption*, at the most. (Did you notice that choices A and C are opposites and therefore it was likely that one of them is the best answer?) And since the passage begins with this statement, it is a given that the queen rules, and we are not questioning the accuracy of that idea; it does not need to be *proven*—choice A. Also, nothing about the queen's rule was indicated as her fate, so she wasn't *destined*—Choice B. Choice C is also not an accurate substitute for "purported," mainly based, again, on the general context of the word within the passage. There is no mention of the queen's attitude toward her reign, so she has nothing to be *determined*—answer D—about, and the idea that the queen was selected, or in some way *chosen*,—Choice E—also fails to correlate with the rest of the passage.

Which of the following is the best meaning of the word "domain" as it is used in the passage?

(A) home town
(B) abode
(C) realm
(D) valley
(E) world

EXPLANATION First, we note that "domain" is a noun, as are all the answers. So we are unable to eliminate any of them. (This will usually be the case on the CBEST, but it doesn't hurt to check quickly.) Substituting for the word in the passage, we have

. . . he told his crew they had arrived at Califia's <u>home town</u>.
OR
. . . he told his crew they had arrived at Califia's <u>abode</u>.
OR
. . . he told his crew they had arrived at Califia's <u>realm.</u>
OR
. . . he told his crew they had arrived at Califia's <u>valley</u>.
OR
. . . he told his crew they had arrived at Califia's <u>world</u>.

The word "domain" must indicate a place because the domain was previously referred to as an "island nation." All the answer choices refer to places, as well, though a nation is bigger and more important than a *home town*—choice A. And a nation is also a geographical and political entity, while *abode*—choice B—is merely a residence. Choice D, *valley*? No. And while we might informally call the territory which Queen Califia ruled her "world,"—choice E—it is much more appropriately called her "domain" or "realm"—choice C.

Now, we have a new reading passage with questions and answers separated by the types of tasks involved.

Why did the newly formed United States wage war against Great Britain only a few years after gaining independence through a bloody insurrection against the same country? We are told that the United States had grievances against Great Britain for sovereignty violations in several areas. First, forts promised to the United States in the 1783 Treaty of Paris were not surrendered by the British. Second, the British Royal Navy was boarding American ships, supposedly to search for deserters, but also to force Americans to serve on British ships. Finally, in an attempt to damage Napoleon's ability to continue his war against England, the British had seized hundreds of American merchant ships to stop supplies being shipped to France.

Speaker of the House Henry Clay agitated for a declaration of war, and in June of 1812, the United States declared war against Great Britain. This is now called the War of 1812. However, it must not be denied that besides the need to act on its grievances, the United States also hoped to gain Britain's colonies in what is now Canada.

Although the British were already at war with Napoleon, they declared war on the United States. After turning back an American invasion of Upper Canada in the summer of 1812, the British soon captured Detroit. Then the United States defeated combined British and Native American armies with victories at the Battle of the Thames, in October 1813, and the Battle of Horseshoe Bend, in March 1814. By this time, Britain had successfully concluded the Napoleonic wars and the British were finally able to divert more resources to North America.

The most significant event, in some ways, was the British invasion of Washington, D.C. When the British general sent in a flag of truce, defenders who remained in the evacuated area fired on the general and the flag-bearing party, killing the general's horse. This ignited a retaliation; lives were lost, although the British army followed orders in only setting fire to the government buildings, not homes. In addition to the burning of Washington, D.C. the British captured part of the District of Maine, but their counter-offensive was turned back at Lake Champlain, Baltimore, and New Orleans.

The United States ended the war without gaining any territory, its invasion of British North America having been defeated by British, Canadian, and Native American forces. Some will be glad to know, of course, that the British did revoke the restrictions on American commerce and cancelled all attacks on its sovereignty; in fact, the news of this arrived in the U.S. only days after war was declared!

ENTIRE PASSAGE

What is the main pattern of organization employed in the excerpt above?

(A) spatial order
(B) order of importance
(C) general to specific
(D) problem-solution order
(E) chronological order

EXPLANATION The entire passage is arranged in chronological, or time, order—choice **E**. Choice A—spatial order—refers to the arrangement of items in physical space (to the right of something, in back of something, etc.), and the information about the War of 1812 is not arranged by geographical locations. Choice B—order of importance—is not followed in the passage because the most important point, the burning of Washington, D.C., is not in the final paragraph. Choice C is not a correct answer because the text is arranged chronologically, not from a general overview of the war to a series of paragraphs that provide particulars about the war. Similarly, choice D does not define the arrangement of ideas in the excerpt since the passage does not first define the problem (the British crimes against the United States) and then follow up with the means by which the Americans addressed the problems.

In this passage, the author's attitude toward the situation is one of

(A) criticism.
(B) excitement.
(C) exaggerated optimism.
(D) indifference.
(E) delight.

EXPLANATION The attitude of the author, or the author's tone in the passage, is much like a speaker's tone of voice. When listening to someone speak, we take particular note of words or phrases that are louder, have a change of pitch, and so on. Similarly, when reading this passage, unusual phrases and words should spark questions in your mind, including "bloody insurrection" (why not "revolution"?)—"agitated for a declaration of war," (why not "advocated for . . ." or "demanded a declaration of war"?)— "it must not be denied that" (why the emphasis on this fact?). As you answer these questions, you come to the conclusion that the writer who included the words "bloody" and "agitated" is not excited—choice B—or optimistic—choice C—or delighted—choice E—with the events of the War of 1812. And clearly the writer is not indifferent, or without bias—choice D. The writer who ended the passage with the apparently ironic information that the British had ceased, at the very beginning of a two-year war, to do what had aggrieved the Americans at the outset was certainly criticizing—choice A—the justification for the war.

Which of the following best organizes the main topics addressed in this passage?

(A) I. American complaints against British
    II. Declaration of war
    III. Britain fights France and the United States
    IV. The British attack on Washington, D.C.
    V. Outcomes of the war
(B) I. Declaration of War
    II. American complaints against the British
    III. Britain fights France and the United States
    IV. The British attack on Washington, D.C.
    V. Outcomes of the war
(C) I. America's grievances lead to declaration of war against Britain
    II. Britain fights back
    III. Outcomes of the war
(D) I. British declaration of war against the United States
    II. American complaints against British
    III. Declaration of war
    IV. Britain fights France and the United States
    V. The British attack on Washington, D.C.
    VI. Outcomes of the war
(E) I. British declaration of war against the United States
    II. America's grievances lead to declaration of war against Britain
    III. Britain fights back
    IV. Outcomes of the war

EXPLANATION The Roman numerals used in a list as in the answers above is a typical way of outlining, or organizing, a reading passage. Each Roman numeral represents one main idea from the reading, and the main ideas should be listed in the same order as they appeared in the original text. So choice **A** is the best answer, as it accurately renders the main ideas from each of the five paragraphs in the passage. Choice B, instead, reverses the first two key points—and an organization pattern, or outline, must maintain the points in their original order. In choice C, the third point, "Britain fights back" is too general; it does not comprehensively reflect the information about England's war on two fronts and its subsequent ability, once the war with France was over, to address more strength to the war in North America. Choices D and E are both poor answers to the prompt because they inaccurately imply that the War of 1812 was begun by the British declaration of war. You should have been able to immediately cross them out as possible correct answers.

A SECTION OF THE PASSAGE

In the second category of reading questions, here are more samples based on a section of the same passage used before.

Why did the newly formed United States wage war against Great Britain only a few years after gaining independence through a bloody insurrection against the same country? We are told that the United States had grievances against Great Britain for sovereignty violations in several areas. First, forts promised to the United States in the 1783 Treaty of Paris were not surrendered by the British. Second, the British Royal Navy was boarding American ships, supposedly to search for deserters, but also to force Americans to serve on British ships. Finally, in an attempt to damage Napoleon's ability to continue his war against England, the British had seized hundreds of American merchant ships to stop supplies being shipped to France.

Speaker of the House Henry Clay agitated for a declaration of war, and in June of 1812, the United States declared war against Great Britain. This is now called the War of 1812. However, it must not be denied that besides the need to act on its grievances, the United States also hoped to gain Britain's colonies in what is now Canada.

Although the British were already at war with Napoleon, they declared war on the United States. After turning back an American invasion of Upper Canada in the summer of 1812, the British soon captured Detroit. Then the United States defeated combined British and Native American armies with victories at the Battle of the Thames, in October 1813, and the Battle of Horseshoe Bend, in March 1814. By this time, Britain had successfully concluded the Napoleonic wars and the British were finally able to divert more resources to North America.

The most significant event, in some ways, was the British invasion of Washington, D.C. When the British general sent in a flag of truce, defenders who remained in the evacuated area fired on the general and the flag-bearing party, killing the general's horse. This ignited a retaliation; lives were lost, although the British army followed orders in only setting fire to the government buildings, not homes. In addition to the burning of Washington, D.C. the British captured part of the District of Maine, but their counter-offensive was turned back at Lake Champlain, Baltimore, and New Orleans.

The United States ended the war without gaining any territory, its invasion of British North America having been defeated by British, Canadian, and Native American forces. Some will be glad to know, of course, that the British did revoke the restrictions on American commerce and cancelled all attacks on its sovereignty; in fact, the news of this arrived in the U.S. only days after war was declared!

What can you infer from the fact that the British general sent a flag of truce into Washington D.C. and authorized his troops to burn only American government buildings?

(A) The British felt the need to defend themselves against the Americans.
(B) The British wanted a ruthless retaliation.
(C) The British acted according to general rules of warfare.
(D) The British general was fearful of immediate attack by the Washington, D.C. defenders.
(E) The British wanted to end the war at Washington, D.C.

EXPLANATION Taking various details and drawing a conclusion, or as it is called, an inference, we can determine that the best answer choice is **C**: offering a truce and destroying only government buildings, as explained in the third paragraph, was conforming to rules of warfare at that time. Therefore, they were not "ruthless," as answer choice B suggests. And if they were "fearful" of being attacked by the Americans in Washington, D.C., they would not have come into the area with a flag of truce, so choice D is not appropriate. On the other hand, choice A refers to the British need to defend themselves, yet most of the discussion in the third paragraph shows English forces in offensive, rather than defensive, acts. The final choice, choice E, is not supported by any of the information in the third paragraph or anywhere else in the reading passage.

Which of the following is the best paraphrase of this sentence from the passage? "In addition to the burning of Washington, D.C. the British captured part of the District of Maine, but their counter-offensive was turned back at Lake Champlain, Baltimore, and New Orleans."

(A) The British succeeded in their objectives in Washington, D.C. and the District of Maine, but failed at Lake Champlain, Baltimore, and New Orleans.
(B) In addition to burning Washington, D.C., the British captured part of the District of Maine, Lake Champlain, Baltimore, and New Orleans.
(C) The British were turned back at Lake Champlain, Baltimore, New Orleans, and the District of Maine, while they successfully burned Washington, D.C.
(D) The British succeeded in their objectives in Washington, D.C., and also at Lake Champlain, Baltimore, and New Orleans.
(E) The British war strategies won in some areas and failed in others.

EXPLANATION You may have noticed that choices A and D have similar parts to them. As mentioned earlier, this is a clue that one or the other choice is the best one. Looking more carefully, choice A restates the activities of the British accurately, while choice D is not accurate when paraphrasing the activities in Lake Champlain, Baltimore, and New Orleans. In addition, choice B is not an accurate paraphrase because it erroneously indicates that the British were successful in Lake Champlain, Baltimore, and New Orleans, but the passage says they were "turned back." However, they were not turned back at the District of Maine, as choice C indicates, so that, also, is not an accurate paraphrase. And choice E is too general to be a true paraphrase because paraphrases retain all the information from a text, only rephrasing it. This is how a paraphrase is different from a summary.

WORDS OR SENTENCES IN A PASSAGE

Let's examine only the last paragraph in the passage used before as we consider the reasoning behind correct answers to questions about particular words or sentences in a reading.

> The United States ended the war without gaining any territory, its invasion of British North America having been defeated by British, Canadian, and Native American forces. Some will be glad to know, of course, that the British did revoke the restrictions on American commerce and cancelled all attacks on its sovereignty; in fact, the news of this arrived in the U.S. only days after war was declared!

Which of the following is the best meaning of the word *revoke* as it is used in the passage?

(A) realize
(B) purchase
(C) agree to
(D) withdraw
(E) enact

EXPLANATION To ensure that we know what "revoke" means, we can look at the word parts it is made from: "re" meaning "again or back" and "voc" meaning "call." So literally, this word means to "call again" or "call back." Putting the meaning into the context of the sentence, we get: The British did call back restrictions on American commerce. We can also find a clue in that sentence from the passage when we see that the second action describes that the British "cancelled" something. So "cancelled" may be a synonym of "revoke." Surely, then, choice **D**—withdraw—is the best answer, while the others might be quickly reviewed by substituting them into the sentence.

. . . the British did <u>realize</u> the restrictions on American commerce . . .

OR

. . . the British did <u>purchase</u> the restrictions on American commerce . . .

OR

. . . the British did <u>agree to</u> the restrictions on American commerce . . .

OR

. . . the British did <u>enact</u> the restrictions on American commerce . . .

None of these new sentences makes sense given all the information in the entire passage, and you probably also noticed that "enact" is the opposite of "withdraw," so again you were given a clue that one or the other of those two answers was the correct choice.

> Which of the following best answers the question—Why is there a special punctuation mark at the end of the last paragraph in the passage?
>
> (A) The punctuation mark registers the writer's intense sadness.
> (B) The punctuation mark registers the writer's posing a question.
> (C) The punctuation mark indicates the writer places emphasis on this sentence.
> (D) The punctuation mark indicates that there is a long pause at the end of this sentence.
> (E) The punctuation mark was placed at the end of the sentence to show that the readers are supposed to re-read that sentence.

EXPLANATION Most test-takers know that the exclamation mark (!) indicates emphasis, just as an exclamation is a loud or forceful crying out. So choice **C** is the best answer, while choice B describes a question mark—the last sentence is not a question, choice D describes a comma or dash, and a pause at the end of the last sentence in a four-paragraph passage is not practical. Also, there is no punctuation mark in English which indicates sadness or a command to re-read the sentence, so choices A and E are poor answers and should have been immediately eliminated from your consideration.

One last consideration. The CBEST will have one or two charts, graphs, or tables (generally Tables of Content or Indexes) to test your ability to interpret them as you would when doing research. A graphical representation of a series of numbers or other data points can impart a more comprehensible picture of the meaning of the data, as well as making it easier to see patterns or trends. Here is an example of this kind of task.

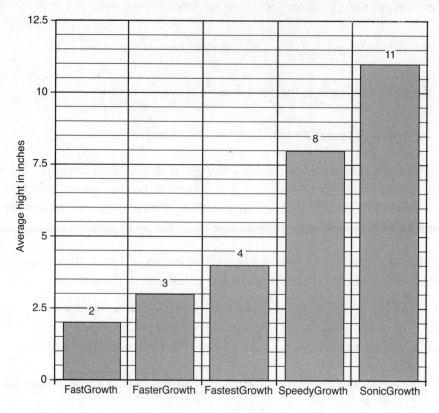

What is the relation between the radish growth achieved by FastestGrowth and SpeedyGrowth?

(A) They achieved the same amount of growth.
(B) The radishes grew twice as tall with FastestGrowth as compared with SpeedyGrowth.
(C) The radishes grew twice as tall with SpeedyGrowth as compared with FastestGrowth.
(D) The radishes grew three times as tall with SpeedyGrowth as compared with FastestGrowth.
(E) The radishes grew twice as tall with FastGrowth as compared with SpeedyGrowth.

EXPLANATION Bar charts like these are fairly easy to comprehend. The vertical axis, or side, shows the number of inches of growth, and the horizontal side shows separate growth measurements for each type of fertilizer. Each axis is always labeled for you. In addition, the charts and graphs in the CBEST are generally not more difficult than this sample. Here, it should be easy to calculate that since FastestGrowth enabled the radishes to grow 4 inches high and SpeedyGrowth grew radishes 8 inches high, choice **B** is the best answer.

SUMMARY

The examples, explanations, strategies, and Maximizers presented in these sample reading questions can make a big difference in your performance on any reading comprehension multiple choice test. As you work through the book's practice tests, you will become increasingly comfortable using these strategies.

Answer Sheet

MATH DIAGNOSTIC TEST

1 Ⓐ Ⓑ Ⓒ Ⓓ Ⓔ   5 Ⓐ Ⓑ Ⓒ Ⓓ Ⓔ   9 Ⓐ Ⓑ Ⓒ Ⓓ Ⓔ   13 Ⓐ Ⓑ Ⓒ Ⓓ Ⓔ

2 Ⓐ Ⓑ Ⓒ Ⓓ Ⓔ   6 Ⓐ Ⓑ Ⓒ Ⓓ Ⓔ   10 Ⓐ Ⓑ Ⓒ Ⓓ Ⓔ   14 Ⓐ Ⓑ Ⓒ Ⓓ Ⓔ

3 Ⓐ Ⓑ Ⓒ Ⓓ Ⓔ   7 Ⓐ Ⓑ Ⓒ Ⓓ Ⓔ   11 Ⓐ Ⓑ Ⓒ Ⓓ Ⓔ   15 Ⓐ Ⓑ Ⓒ Ⓓ Ⓔ

4 Ⓐ Ⓑ Ⓒ Ⓓ Ⓔ   8 Ⓐ Ⓑ Ⓒ Ⓓ Ⓔ   12 Ⓐ Ⓑ Ⓒ Ⓓ Ⓔ

CHAPTER 5

MATH DIAGNOSTIC TEST AND ANSWERS

Math Diagnostic Test and Answers

DIAGNOSTIC TEST

Here's your chance to practice an abbreviated math test. Use the answer sheet provided at the end of the chapter; then check your answers with the answer key. (Note: The actual test will have 50 questions).

1. $25.6 \div 0.16 = ?$

   (A) 1.6
   (B) 16
   (C) 160
   (D) 180
   (E) 194.2

2. $\frac{1}{3}n + \frac{1}{6}n = 27$

   $n = ?$

   (A) 9
   (B) 36
   (C) 48
   (D) 54
   (E) 243

3. Gary has 7 nickels, 3 pennies, and 5 dimes in a jar. If he draws a coin from the jar, what is the probability the coin will be a dime?

   A) $\frac{1}{3}$

   (B) $\frac{4}{15}$

   (C) $\frac{3}{5}$

   (D) $\frac{7}{10}$

   (E) $\frac{4}{5}$

4. A regular hexagon has a side length measuring 7 inches. What is the perimeter of the hexagon?

   (A) 7
   (B) 13
   (C) 42
   (D) 56
   (E) 70

5. Which of the following expressions can be used to calculate 29% of 271?

    (A) $271 \div 29$
    (B) $271 \div 0.29$
    (C) $271 \div \dfrac{29}{100}$
    (D) 271×29
    (E) 271×0.29

6. The sixth-grade class at Rohrbach Elementary School donated $3\frac{1}{5}$ tons of clothes to the Salvation Army. The fifth-grade class donated $2\frac{2}{3}$ tons of clothes as well. How many tons of clothes were donated by both classes?

    (A) $5\dfrac{13}{15}$

    (B) $5\dfrac{3}{8}$

    (C) $5\dfrac{1}{8}$

    (D) $4\dfrac{13}{15}$

    (E) $4\dfrac{1}{5}$

7. Chris has 7 more baseball cards than Evan. Together they have 45 cards. How many baseball cards does Chris have?

    (A) 45
    (B) 38
    (C) 26
    (D) 19
    (E) 12

8. The students in an eighth-grade class have heights, measured in inches, as follows:

    61, 68, 58, 66, 71, 72, 58, 63

    What is the median height of the class?

    (A) 14
    (B) 63
    (C) 64.5
    (D) 64.6
    (E) 66

9. Which of the following statements is correct?

    (A) $-9 > -2$
    (B) $|-13| < 12$
    (C) $-9 \geq 2$
    (D) $-2 \geq -2$
    (E) $0 < -7$

10. If Caitlin can type 5 pages in 8 minutes, how many pages can she type in 12 minutes?

    (A) 7
    (B) 7.5
    (C) 8
    (D) 8.5
    (E) 9

11. If the temperature dropped from 11° to –8°, how many degrees was the decrease?

    (A) –3
    (B) 3
    (C) 8
    (D) 14
    (E) 19

12. Diana has 4 skirts, 5 blouses, and 3 pairs of shoes. How many combinations of skirts, blouses, and shoes does she have?

    (A) 3
    (B) 4
    (C) 5
    (D) 12
    (E) 60

13. What is 6.7846 rounded to the nearest thousandth?

    (A) 6.7
    (B) 6.78
    (C) 6.784
    (D) 6.785
    (E) 6.8

14. What number is one-half of one-third of thirty-six?

    (A) 6

    (B) 3

    (C) $\dfrac{1}{2}$

    (D) $\dfrac{1}{6}$

    (E) $\dfrac{1}{36}$

15. $3(2-5)^3 - |-12| = ?$

    (A) 93

    (B) 69

    (C) 42

    (D) –69

    (E) –93

ANSWERS AND EXPLANATIONS

1. **(C)**

$$0.16\overline{)25.6} \quad \rightarrow \quad 16\overline{)2560} \;\; ^{160}$$

2. **(D)**

$$\frac{1}{3} = \frac{2}{6}$$

$$\frac{2}{6}n + \frac{1}{6}n = 27$$

$$\frac{3}{6}n = 27$$

$$\frac{1}{2}n = 27$$

$$(2)\left(\frac{1}{2}n\right) = (27)(2)$$

$$n = 54$$

3. **(A)** Use the ratio

$$\frac{\text{favored outcomes}}{\text{all outcomes}}$$

There are 5 dimes, which represent the favored outcomes. There are 15 coins in all which represent all outcomes.

$$\frac{\text{favored outcomes}}{\text{all outcomes}} = \frac{5}{15} = \frac{1}{3}$$

4. **(C)** A regular hexagon has 6 equal sides. If one side is 7 inches long, multiply 7 by 6 to get a perimeter of 42 inches.

5. **(E)** Of means multiply. 29% can be expressed as 0.29 or $\frac{29}{100}$. 29% of 271 can be expressed as 0.29×271.

6. **(A)** To find the combined contribution of the two classes, add $3\frac{1}{5}$ and $2\frac{2}{3}$:

$$3\frac{1}{5} = 3\frac{3}{15}$$
$$+2\frac{2}{3} = 2\frac{10}{15}$$
$$\overline{\phantom{+2\frac{2}{3} = }5\frac{13}{15}}$$

7. **(C)** Let $x =$ the number of cards Evan has and $x + 7 =$ the number of cards Chris has.

$$x + (x + 7) = 45$$
$$2x + 7 = 45$$
$$2x = 38$$
$$x = 19$$

Since Chris is represented by the expression $x + 7$, he has 26 cards.

8. **(C)** The median is the middle term in a series of numbers arranged in ascending order. To find the middle term, array the data from least to greatest:

$$58 \quad 58 \quad 61 \quad 63 \quad 66 \quad 68 \quad 71 \quad 72$$

Notice that there are two numbers in the middle. To find the median, add the two numbers and divide by two:

$$(66 + 63) \div 2 = 64.5$$

9. **(D)** Choice D suggests –2 is greater than **or** equal to –2. Although –2 is not greater than –2, it is equal to –2. Only one of the conditions must be true in order for the statement to be true.

10. **(B)** Use the ratio

$$\frac{\text{pages typed}}{\text{minutes}}$$

$$\frac{5}{8} = \frac{x}{12}$$
$$8x = 60$$
$$x = 7.5$$

11. **(E)** Subtract the lower temperature from the higher temperature:

$$11 - (-8) = 11 + 8 = 19$$

12. **(E)** This problem can be illustrated by using a counting tree:

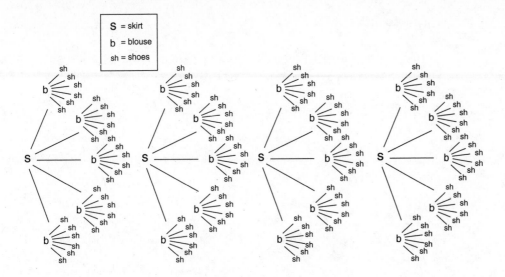

It is more efficient to multiply the number of skirts by the number of blouses by the number of pairs of shoes:

4 (shirts) × 5 (blouses) × 3 (pairs of shoes) = 60 combinations

13. **(D)** Identify the digit in the thousandths place. In this case it is 4. If the digit to its right is 5 or greater, round the thousandths place up. The number, 6, is greater than 5 so round up to 6.785.

14. **(A)**
"Of" means multiply:

$$\frac{1}{2} \times \frac{1}{3} \times 36 = \frac{1}{6} \times 36 = 6$$

15. **(E)** Order of Operations:

PEMDAS
P̲arentheses
E̲xponents
M̲ultiplication
D̲ivision
A̲ddition
S̲ubtraction

Parentheses: $3(2-5)^3 - |-12|$
Exponent: $3(-3)^3 - |-12|$
Multiplication: $3(-27) - |-12|$
Subtraction: $-81 - 12 = -93$

CHAPTER 6

MATH SECTION REVIEW

Math Section Review

INTRODUCTION

For many CBEST-takers, the thought of mastering the Math Section may be a daunting prospect. After all, for most adults, it has probably been several years since they have taken formal math classes. Furthermore, it is quite possible that a prospective CBEST-taker may have struggled with math throughout his or her academic career. Well relax! If you have average everyday math skills, this text will help you pass the test. Even if your math skills need improvement, methodically following the lessons in this book will help you succeed in passing the Math Section.

For most people, all the math knowledge needed to succeed at taking the CBEST was learned in middle school and high school. There is no calculus or trigonometry on the CBEST. In fact, the CBEST covers nothing more advanced than basic high school algebra and geometry.

The successful CBEST-taker is responsible for mastering the following areas:

Geometry:

- Measuring length and perimeter
- Basic knowledge of geometric figures such as squares, rectangles, circles, and triangles
- Basic knowledge of lines, rays, and angles

Arithmetic and algebra:

- Knowledge of fractions, ratios, and decimals
- Transformation of word problems into simple algebraic equations
- Proportions
- Manipulation of algebraic equations with a single variable
- Estimation and rounding
- Converting units of measurement

This text is geared to those test-takers who have not taken a formal math class in several years. If the reader is proficient in math, he or she is invited to start with the Diagnostic Test or any of the three Model Tests. For the rest, this text will refresh those skills that have not been recently tested. Try to follow the sequence of topics throughout this chapter meticulously. This text was developed to help the reader learn important math skills and then build upon them. Each topic will be followed by sample exercises and explanations. Hopefully the reader will appreciate the California-oriented word problems as well as the puzzles and games included to make this review an enjoyable experience.

ARITHMETIC

Positive and Negative Numbers

In our everyday lives, we are faced with positive and negative, or *signed*, numbers. A city near the Arctic Circle might see temperatures so cold they are listed as negative numbers. Each week, when we deposit our paychecks in the bank, we see a net increase in our account. The increase could be viewed as a positive number. It is helpful to use a number line to visualize the relationships among signed numbers:

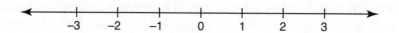

Notice the following:

- All numbers to the right of 0 on the number line are positive.

- All numbers to the left of 0 are negative.

- 0 is neither positive nor negative

- Any number to the left of a number is smaller than that number.

- Any number to the right of a number is larger than that number.

Sample Problem

Which number is larger, –9 or –2?

ANALYSIS

Since –2 is to the right of –9 on the number line, –2 is larger than –9.
It is customary to use inequality signs to denote relationships between numbers

< or > indicates that one number is greater than another.
≤ or ≥ indicates that one number is greater than *or equal to* another number.

It is useful to consider the number being "pointed to" as the smaller number.

Sample Problems

Which of the following statements are true?

(A) $-12 > -24$

(B) $17 < -23$

(C) $7 \geq -5$

(D) $7 \geq 7$

ANALYSIS

A is correct because -12 is to the right of -24 on the number line.

B is not correct because 17 is to the right of -23 on the number line.

C is correct because 7 is greater than or equal to -5.

D is correct. Although 7 is not greater than 7, it is equal to 7. Only one of the conditions, greater than or equal to, needs to be correct for the statement to be true.

EXERCISES FOR SIGNED NUMBERS

1. Which of the following satisfy the inequality $x > -7$?

   (A) -11

   (B) -9

   (C) -8

   (D) -7

   (E) 0

2. Which of the following is a true statement?

   (A) $12 > 13$

   (B) $-9 > -6$

   (C) $8 + 5 < 7 + 6$

   (D) $-8 \geq -2$

   (E) $5 + 5 \leq 6 + 4$

SOLUTIONS TO SIGNED NUMBERS

1. **(E)** On a number line, 0 is to the right of -7.

2. **(E)**

$$5 + 5 = 10 \text{ and } 6 + 4 = 10$$
$$10 \leq 10$$

Number Systems

Depending on its value, a number can be classified in different ways. Below is a list of number systems the CBEST-taker must know.

Natural or Counting Numbers: 1, 2, 3, 4, . . .

Whole Numbers: 0, 1, 2, 3, 4, . . .

Integers: . . . , –2, –1, 0, 1, 2, . . .

Rational Numbers: $-2, \dfrac{1}{2}, 0.625, 0.888, \ldots$

Rational numbers include negative numbers, fractions and decimals. The system of rational numbers contains the following two restrictions:

- If the number is a fraction or decimal, it must terminate. $3.5, 7\dfrac{3}{4}$, and –2.0 are all examples of rational numbers.

- If the number does not terminate, it must repeat a pattern. Examples of this type of rational number include 0.333 . . . and 0.745745. . . . Sometimes, a repeating decimal is shown with a bar listed above it: 0.638638 . . . can be listed as $0.\overline{638}$.

Irrational Numbers: Irrational numbers neither terminate nor repeat a pattern. Examples of irrational numbers include π (pi), which approximately equals 3.14159 . . . , and $\sqrt{17}$, which approximately equals 4.123105. . . .

There are other number systems, such as the imaginary and complex number systems, which will not appear on the CBEST.

EXERCISES FOR NUMBER SYSTEMS

Each number is a set of which number system(s):

1. 8
2. –6
3. 6.7272 . . .
4. $\sqrt{16}$
5. $\sqrt{43}$

SOLUTIONS TO EXERCISES FOR NUMBER SYSTEMS

1. 8 : natural numbers, whole numbers, integers, rational numbers (8, or 8.0, terminates)

2. –6: integers, rational numbers

3. 6.7272 . . . : rational numbers

4. $\sqrt{16}$: $\sqrt{16} = 4$; natural numbers, whole numbers, integers, rational numbers

5. $\sqrt{43}$: $\sqrt{43}$ is approximately equal to 6.5574 . . . ; irrational

Operations in Mathematics

The operations in mathematics should be familiar to all students. They are listed below along with their respective symbols.

Operation	Symbol	Result Is Called
Addition	$+$	Sum
Subtraction	$-$	Difference
Division	$\div$, $\overline{\smash{\big)}}$, $/$	Quotient
Multiplication	$\times$, $\cdot$, $(\ )$	Product

The CBEST-taker must be familiar with all of the symbols for mathematical operations. There are several ways to denote multiplication and division:

$$7 \times 5 = 35 \qquad 9 \cdot 8 = 72 \qquad 3(8) = 24 \qquad (5)(11) = 55$$

$$12 \div 6 = 2 \qquad 15/5 = 3 \qquad 7\overline{)49}^{\,7}$$

Prime and Composite Numbers

A prime number is a number greater than 1 that is divisible solely by one and itself. Examples of prime numbers include:

2, 3, 5, 7, 11, 13, 17, 19, 23, . . . (note that 2 is the only even prime number)

Any number, greater than 1, that is not prime is called a *composite* number. Examples of composite numbers include:

$$4, 6, 8, 9, 12, 14, 15, 16, \ldots$$

Sample Problem

Is 51 a prime number?

ANALYSIS

At first glance, the number seems to have the attributes of a prime number. It's odd and seemingly indivisible by any other number other than 1 and 51. Yet 51 is divisible by 3 and 17:

$$51 \div 3 = 17$$
$$51 \div 17 = 3$$

51 is a not a prime number.

Discerning a prime number can sometimes prove elusive. Because calculator use is not permitted on the CBEST, it would be wise to learn some divisibility rules.

If the Number Is Divisible by	Divisibility Rule
2	The number ends in 0,2,4,6,8, (i.e., it's even).
3	The sum of the digits is divisible by 3.
4	The last two digits are divisible by 4.
5	The number ends in 0 or 5.
9	The sum of the digits is divisible by 9.
10	The number ends in 0.

Sample Problem

Which of the following numbers divide evenly into 2,700?

(A) 2
(B) 3
(C) 4
(D) 5
(E) 9
(F) 10

ANALYSIS

2,700 is divisible by 2 because it ends in 0, an even number.

2,700 is divisible by 3 because $2 + 7 + 0 + 0 = 9$. Since 3 divides evenly into 9, 3 divides evenly into 2,700.

2,700 is divisible by 4 because 4 divides evenly into "00"($0 \div 4 = 0$).

2,700 is divisible by 5 beause it ends in 0.

2,700 is divisible by 9 because $2 + 7 + 0 + 0 = 9$. Since 9 divides evenly into 9, 2,700 is divisible by 9.

2,700 is divisible by 10 because it ends in 0.

All of the above numbers divide evenly into 2,700.

EXERCISES FOR PRIME AND COMPOSITES

> Circle each prime number.
> Place the the corresponding letters, in order, in the blanks below.

Brain Teaser: What six letter word can follow each of the words listed below?

GROUND _ _ _ _ _ _
BELL _ _ _ _ _ _
GREEN _ _ _ _ _ _

H	U	P	L	E	P	M	P	S	E	V	R
8	57	17	21	31	59	108	61	27	29	87	89

_____ _____ _____ _____ _____ _____

SOLUTIONS FOR PRIME AND COMPOSITE NUMBERS

P̲ E̲ P̲ P̲ E̲ R̲
17 31 59 61 29 89

Absolute Value

The absolute value of a number is its distance from 0 on a number line. For example, although an overdrawn checking account may register –$50, it is not possible to say that the dollars are negative. Instead, it is smarter to view the account as $50 away from having 0 dollars. Thus, the absolute value of –50 is 50. Absolute value is denoted by the symbol $|\ |$. Thus, $|-50| = 50$.

Sample Problem

Which of the following statements is/are correct?

(A) $|-2| > 0$
(B) $|-12| = 12$
(C) $|7| < |-9|$
(D) $|-15| = |15|$

ANALYSIS

A is correct because $|-2| = 2$ and $2 > 0$.

B is correct because $|-12| = 12$.

C is correct because $|7| = 7$ and $|-9| = 9$ so $7 < 9$.

D is correct because $|-15| = 15$ and $|-15| = 15$.

Operations with Positive and Negative Numbers

Consider the following:

> Kelsey's checking account was overdrawn in the amount of $35. Another of Kelsey's checking accounts was overdrawn by $10. What is Kelsey's bank balance?

The question requires combining two negative numbers, –35 and –10. In order to combine these numbers, we must first discuss how to add and subtract signed numbers.

To add numbers with the *same* sign, add the absolute values of the numbers and keep the original sign:

$$9 + 5 = |9| + |5| = 9 + 5 = 14$$
$$-12 + -20 = ?$$
$$|-12| + |-20| = 32 \quad \text{Keep the original sign: } -12 + -20 = -32$$

We can now solve the problem about Kelsey and her checking accounts:

$$-10 + -35 \quad = \quad |-10| + |-35| \quad = \quad 10 + 35 = 45$$

Because both numbers are negative, we see that Kelsey is overdrawn by a total of $45 in her two checking accounts. Her current balance is –$45.

When adding numbers with *different* signs, subtract the smaller absolute value from the larger absolute value and keep the sign of the larger absolute value:

$-12 + 15 = |15| - |12| = 3$. Since the sign of 15 is positive, the answer is 3.
$42 + -62 = |-62| - |42| = 20$. Since the sign of –62 is negative, the answer is –20.

When subtracting signed numbers, change the sign of the number being subtracted and *add*:

$$27 - 15 = 27 + (-15) = 12$$
$$27 - (-15) = 27 + (+15) = 42$$

EXERCISES FOR ADDING AND SUBTRACTING SIGNED NUMBERS

Simplify each problem. Place the corresponding letter in each blank.

What time should you visit the dentist?

T	Y	O	H	T	R	T	U	O	H
0	14	–15	–22	3	36	–29	–2	23	–26

$12 + -9$	$-17 + 2$	$15 - (-8)$	$-19 + -10$	$-14 - 12$

$-27 - (-5)$	$17 + -19$	$25 - (-11)$	$-20 - (-20)$	$17 - 3$

SOLUTIONS FOR ADDING AND SUBTRACTING SIGNED NUMBERS

T O O T H
H U R T Y   (2:30)

$12 + -9 = |12| - |-9| = 3$. Since 12 is positive, the answer is 3: T.

$-17 + 2 = |-17| - |2| = 15$. Since -17 is negative, the answer is -15: O.

$15 - (-8) = 15 + (+8) = 23$: O.

$-19 + -10 = |-19| + |-10| = 29$. Since both numbers are negative, the answer is -29: T.

$-14 - 12 = -14 + -12 = |-14| + |-12| = 26$. Since both numbers are negative, the answer is -26: H.

$-27 - (-5) = -27 + (+5) = |-27| - |5| = 22$. Since the larger absolute value is negative, the answer is -22: H.

$17 + -19 = |-19| - |17| = 2$. Since the sign of the larger absolute value is negative, the answer is -2: U.

$25 - (-11) = 25 + (+11) = 36$: R.

$-20 - (-20) = -20 + 20 = |-20| - |20| = 0$: T.

$17 - 3 = 4$: Y.

Multiplying and Dividing Signed Numbers

Consider the following situation:

> In order to help pay some of his college expenses, Corey began a small Internet business in his home. He knew he would not immediately generate a profit, and sure enough, he lost approximately $40 per week for each of the first 7 weeks. How much money did Corey lose before his business began generating a profit?

This problem asks us to multiply a negative number, -40, by a positive number, 7. In order to perform this operation, it is important to learn the rules of multiplying and dividing signed numbers.

Multiplication: Positive × Positive = Positive
Negative × Negative = Positive
Positive × Negative = Negative
Negative × Positive = Negative

Division: Positive ÷ Positive = Positive
Negative ÷ Negative = Positive
Positive ÷ Negative = Negative
Negative ÷ Positive = Negative

Notice that the rules for multiplying and dividing signed numbers are identical. We now have enough information to solve the problem:

$$-40 \times 7 = -280$$

Corey will lose $280 before his business begins to generate a profit.

Sample Problem

$-2 \times -2 \times -3 = ?$

(A) 17
(B) 12
(C) –12
(D) –17
(E) –24

ANALYSIS

Use the rules of multiplying signed numbers by approaching the problem in sections:

$-2 \times -2 = 4$ because a negative multiplied by a negative is a positive.

$4 \times -3 = -12$ because a positive multiplied by a negative is a negative.

$-2 \times -2 \times -3 = -12$. The answer is C.

Sample Problem

$-3 \times -3 \times -3 \times -3 = ?$

(A) –81
(B) –12
(C) 0
(D) 12
(E) 81

ANALYSIS

When two negatives were multiplied, the answer, or *product*, was positive. When three negative numbers were multiplied, the product was negative. What will be the sign when four negative numbers are multiplied?

$$
\begin{array}{cc}
+9 & +9 \\
(-3 \times -3) \times (-3 \times -3) = 81
\end{array}
$$

When an *even* number of negative numbers are multiplied, the answer is *positive*. When an *odd* number of negatives are multiplied, the answer is *negative*.

The same rules apply to dividing signed numbers:

Sample Problems

1. $-56 \div -7 = ?$

2. $-48 \div -4 \div -3 = ?$

ANALYSIS

1. We have two negative numbers. Since two is an even number, the answer is positive:

$$-56 \div -7 = 8$$

2. We have three negative numbers. Since three is an odd number, the answer is negative:

$$-48 \div -4 \div -3 = -4$$

EXERCISES FOR MULTIPLICATION AND DIVISION OF SIGNED NUMBERS

1. $-12 \times -5 =$

2. $-215 \times -3 \times -1 =$

3. $1 \times -1 \times 1 \times 1 \times -1 \times -1 =$

4. $-81 \div 27 =$

5. $-81 \div -3 \div -3 =$

6. $14 \div -2 \div -1 \div -1 \div -7 =$

SOLUTIONS FOR MULTIPLICATION AND DIVISION OF SIGNED NUMBERS

1. 60; even number of negatives

2. -645; odd number of negatives

3. -1; odd number of negatives

4. -3; odd number of negatives

5. -9; odd number of negatives

6. 1; even number of negatives

Exponents

Sample Problem

Express 32 solely as the product of 2's.

ANALYSIS

To solve this problem, we would continuously divide 32 by 2:

$$32 \div 2 = 16$$
$$16 \div 2 = 8$$
$$8 \div 2 = 4$$
$$4 \div 2 = 2$$
$$2 \div 2 = 1$$

Therefore, $2 \times 2 \times 2 \times 2 \times 2 = 32$. However, it is time-consuming to write the same number repeatedly. It is easier to write repeated numbers with an *exponent*. Another name for an exponent is power, as in " 3 to the second power" (3^2). Therefore, 32 can expressed as:

$$2^5$$

We can use our knowledge of signed numbers to solve problems dealing with exponents. Consider the following problem:

Sample Problem

What is the value of $(-3)^3$?

ANALYSIS

Since the exponent is 3, we multiply –3 by itself three times. Since the exponent is an *odd* number, the answer will be a negative number:

$$(-3)^3 = -3 \times -3 \times -3 = -27$$

EXERCISES FOR WORKING WITH EXPONENTS

1. $11^2 = ?$

2. $2^7 = ?$

3. $(-4)^6 = ?$

4. $(-8)^3 = -512$

5. $5^? = 625$

SOLUTIONS TO WORKING WITH EXPONENTS

1. 121; $11 \times 11 = 121$

2. 128; $2 \times 2 \times 2 \times 2 \times 2 \times 2 \times 2 = 128$

3. 4,096; $(-4) \times (-4) \times (-4) \times (-4) \times (-4) \times (-4) = 4,096$ (Since the power is even, the answer will be positive.)

4. 3; $-8 \times -8 \times -8 = -512$ (Since the power is odd, the answer is negative.)

5. 4; $5 \times 5 \times 5 \times 5 = 625$

Squares and Square Roots

The product of two equal factors is called a square. Since $7 \times 7 = 49$, 49 is a square. The number 7 is called the *square root* of 49. The symbol $\sqrt{}$ is called a radical and is used to calculate square roots:

$$\sqrt{49} = 7$$

It is useful to remember a few squares and square roots before taking the CBEST.

$1^2 = 1$	$9^2 = 81$	$20^2 = 400$
$2^2 = 4$	$10^2 = 100$	$30^2 = 900$
$3^2 = 9$	$11^2 = 121$	$40^2 = 1,600$
$4^2 = 16$	$12^2 = 144$	$50^2 = 2,500$
$5^2 = 25$	$13^2 = 169$	
$6^2 = 36$	$14^2 = 196$	
$7^2 = 49$	$15^2 = 225$	
$8^2 = 64$		

$\sqrt{0} = 0$	$\sqrt{49} = 7$	$\sqrt{196} = 14$
$\sqrt{1} = 1$	$\sqrt{64} = 8$	$\sqrt{225} = 15$
$\sqrt{4} = 2$	$\sqrt{81} = 9$	$\sqrt{400} = 20$
$\sqrt{9} = 3$	$\sqrt{100} = 10$	$\sqrt{900} = 30$
$\sqrt{16} = 4$	$\sqrt{121} = 11$	$\sqrt{1600} = 40$
$\sqrt{25} = 5$	$\sqrt{144} = 12$	$\sqrt{2500} = 50$
$\sqrt{36} = 6$	$\sqrt{169} = 13$	

Sample Problem

$\sqrt{131}$ is between which two integers?

(A) 11 and 12
(B) 10 and 11
(C) 9 and 10
(D) 8 and 9
(E) 7 and 8

ANALYSIS

$$\sqrt{121} < \sqrt{131} < \sqrt{144}$$

$$11 < \sqrt{131} < 12$$

$\sqrt{131}$ is between 11 and 12. The correct answer is A.

EXERCISES FOR SQUARES AND SQUARE ROOTS

Simplify each problem.
Place the corresponding letter in each blank.

Why was Mr. Mushroom so popular?

He was a

————	————	————
$\sqrt{81}$	13^2	$\sqrt{1,600}$

————	————	————
14^2	$\sqrt{225}$	$\sqrt{1}$

N   Y   F   U   U   G
40   1   9   169   15   196

SOLUTIONS FOR SQUARES AND SQUARE ROOTS

He was a

<u>F</u> <u>U</u> <u>N</u>
<u>G</u> <u>U</u> <u>Y</u>

$$\sqrt{81} = 9: \quad \textbf{F}$$
$$13^2 = 169: \quad \textbf{U}$$
$$\sqrt{1,600} = 40: \textbf{N}$$
$$14^2 = 196: \quad \textbf{G}$$
$$\sqrt{225} = 15: \quad \textbf{U}$$
$$\sqrt{1} = 1: \quad \textbf{Y}$$

Order of Operations

When reading a book, we read from left to right. Is that always the case in mathematics?

Sample Problem

Simplify the following: $7 + 2 \times 3 = ?$

(A) 27
(B) 13

ANALYSIS

The answer is **B**, 13. This problem probes your knowledge of the *order of operations* in mathematics. When doing any math problem, always proceed in this order:

1. **P**arentheses
2. **E**xponents
3. **M**ultiplication } Equivalent (proceed from left to right)
4. **D**ivision
5. **A**ddition } Equivalent (proceed from left to right)
6. **S**ubtraction

The first letter of each operation has been emphasized to spell the helpful acronym **PEMDAS**. This abbreviation reminds us of the steps involved in the order of operation. Some students prefer the expression **P**lease **E**xcuse **M**y **D**ear **A**unt **S**ally as another method of remembering the order of operations.

Notice that multiplication and division, as well as addition and subtraction, are considered equivalent operations. If a math problem contains solely multiplication and division, or addition and subtraction, simply proceed from left to right.

Let's return to the problem $7 + 2 \times 3$. Multiplication precedes addition, so multiply 2 by 3 and add 7:

$$7 + 2 \times 3 =$$
$$7 + 6 = 13$$

Sample Problem

Simplify the following:

$$5(7-11)^3 - (3-33) \div |-10|$$

ANALYSIS

First, simplify the parentheses:

$$5(-4)^3 - (-30) \div |-10|$$

Next, simplify the exponent:

$$5 \times -64 - (-30) \div |-10|$$

Now do multiplication and division, proceeding from left to right:

$$-320 - (-3)$$

Finally, add or subtract, proceeding from left to right:

$$-320 - (-3) = -320 + 3 = -317$$

EXERCISES FOR ORDER OF OPERATIONS

Solve each problem. Place the corresponding letter in each blank

Why is economic inflation bad for the pillow-stuffing business?

O	U	D	P	N	R	W	S
29	18	343	75	-33	-13	-24	144

Even

$$\overline{7(12-5)^2} \quad \overline{2-(4-7)^3} \quad \overline{12-3\times|-12|} \quad \overline{-17-(-4)^2}$$

goes

$$\overline{12 \div 4 \times 6} \quad \overline{15-3+7(-2+5)^2}$$

SOLUTIONS FOR EXERCISES FOR ORDER OF OPERATIONS

Even

<u>D</u> <u>O</u> <u>W</u> <u>N</u>

goes

<u>U</u> <u>P</u>

$7 (12 - 5)^2 = 7 (-7)^2 = 7 (49) = 343:$ D

$2 - (4 - 7)^3 = 2 - (-3)^3 = 2 - (-27) = 2 + (+27) = 29:$ O

$12 - 3 \times |-12| = 12 - 3 \times 12 = 12 - 36 = -24:$ W

$-17 - (-4)^2 = -17 - 16 = -33:$ N

$12 \div 4 \times 6 = 3 \times 6 = 18:$ U

$15 - 3 + 7 \times (-2 + 5)^2 = 15 - 3 + 7 \times (3)^2 = 15 - 3 + 7 \times 9 = 15 - 3 + 63 = 12 + 63 = 75:$ P

Rounding Numbers and Estimation

The successful test-taker will often use estimation to eliminate incorrect answer choices. However, the CBEST requires you to identify *how* you would estimate a number:

Sample Problem

Which of the following is the best way to estimate $7{,}251 \times 4{,}862$?

(A) $7{,}250 \times 4{,}860$
(B) $7{,}300 \times 4{,}900$
(C) $7{,}000 \times 5{,}000$
(D) $8{,}000 \times 5000$
(E) $8{,}000 \times 4{,}000$

ANALYSIS

Before answering this question, it is important to understand how to round numbers to particular place values. Rounding numbers requires following this sequence of operations:

1. Identify the digit to be rounded.
2. Look at the digit to its right. If it is 5 or more, increase the digit to be rounded by 1. If the digit to the right is less than 5, leave the digit to be rounded as it is.

Let's go back to the sample problem. Since 7,251 and 4,862 have digits in the thousands place, round each number to the nearest thousand:

$$7{,}251 \text{ rounds to } 7{,}000 \qquad 4{,}862 \text{ rounds to } 5{,}000$$

Therefore, the best estimate of $7{,}251 \times 4{,}862$ is $7{,}000 \times 5{,}000$. The correct answer is choice C.

EXERCISES FOR ROUNDING NUMBERS

Round each number to the requested place value. Place the corresponding letter in each blank.

Why did Stockholm Stan put so much sugar in his coffee?

N	D	E	E	W	S
1,990	91,000	90,000	2,000	60	300

He wanted to

" ___ ___ ___ ___ ___ ___ "

307	57	91,234	91,345	1,987	1,991
Hundred	Ten	Ten Thousand	Thousand	Thousand	Ten

it.

SOLUTIONS TO EXERCISES FOR ROUNDING NUMBERS

He wanted to

"S W E D E N"

it.

307 rounds to 300: S
57 rounds to 60: W
91,234 rounds to 90,000: E
91,345 rounds to 91,000: D
1,987 rounds to 2,000: E
1,991 rounds to 1,990: N

FRACTIONS

No less than 20% of the math problems on the CBEST require a solid understanding of fractions. The successful test-taker must be able to add, subtract, multiply, and divide fractions.

What Is a Fraction?

For the purpose of the CBEST, a fraction is the comparison of two integers in the form of x/y. Remember, an integer is the set of numbers : . . . ., –3, –2, –1, 0, 1, 2, 3, ... (i.e., no decimals or fractions). The comparison of integers has many uses.

Comparing a Part to the Whole

Sample Problem

A classroom of twenty students contains thirteen boys. What fraction are girls?

ANALYSIS

Since there are thirteen boys, we assume there must be seven girls (because $20 - 13 = 7$).

Comparing the part to the whole we get:

$$\frac{\text{Part}}{\text{Whole}} = \frac{7}{20}$$

The top portion of a fraction is called the numerator. The bottom section is called the denominator. You can remember that **d** is for **d**enominator and **d**own. The denominator is in the **d**ownward portion of the fraction. The denominator of a fraction can never be 0.

Proper Fractions, Improper Fractions, and Mixed Numbers

When the numerator of a fraction is smaller than the denominator, we call the fraction a *proper fraction*. $\frac{7}{9}, \frac{2}{3}$, and $\frac{13}{84}$ are examples of proper fractions. When the numerator is greater than the denominator, the fraction is called an *improper fraction*. $\frac{11}{4}, \frac{3}{2}$, and $\frac{14}{5}$ are examples of improper fractions. A number that is part integer and part fraction is called a *mixed number*. Numbers such as $2\frac{1}{2}$ and $15\frac{2}{3}$ are examples of mixed numbers.

Simplifying Fractions

Answers involving fractions will be in simplified, or reduced, form. To simplify a fraction, divide the numerator and denominator by the largest number that divides evenly into both. For example, the fraction $\frac{2}{4}$ can be simplified to $\frac{1}{2}$ by dividing the numerator and denominator by 2. In this case, 2 is the largest number that divides evenly into 2 and 4. 2, therefore, is referred to as the *greatest common factor* (GCF):

$$\frac{2}{4} \div \frac{2}{2} = \frac{1}{2}$$

For some problems, it is intuitively easy to find the GCF. There are some problems where the GCF is not readily apparent:

Sample Problem

Reduce $\frac{18}{90}$ into lowest terms.

ANALYSIS

To simplify this fraction, we must find the GCF of 18 and 90. Some students find the "rainbow method" of finding factors a useful visual aid.

Find the factors of 18:

1,2,3,6,9,18

Since $1 \times 18 = 18$, put these factors at the ends of the rainbow (don't forget to draw an arc connecting them). Next, proceed to 2 and 9 and finally 3 and 6. The rainbow method of finding factors helps pair factors, ensuring no factors will be excluded. Furthermore, as the rainbow approaches the center, the list of remaining factors is reduced.

Find the factors of 90:

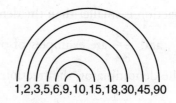

1,2,3,5,6,9,10,15,18,30,45,90

Notice the greatest number to appear in both lists is 18. 18 is the GCF. Divide the numerator and denominator of $\frac{18}{90}$ by 18:

$$\frac{18}{90} \div \frac{18}{18} = \frac{1}{5}$$

The answer is $\frac{1}{5}$.

EXERCISES FOR SIMPLIFYING FRACTIONS

> Reduce each fraction. Place the corresponding letter in each blank.

A Man with Great Vision

R	E	U	S	M	Y	O
$\dfrac{22}{25}$	$\dfrac{1}{5}$	$\dfrac{8}{9}$	$\dfrac{9}{20}$	$\dfrac{18}{25}$	$\dfrac{3}{8}$	$\dfrac{1}{6}$

$\dfrac{18}{40}$	$\dfrac{16}{80}$	$\dfrac{24}{64}$	$\dfrac{36}{50}$	$\dfrac{17}{102}$	$\dfrac{56}{63}$	$\dfrac{88}{100}$

SOLUTIONS FOR SIMPLIFYING FRACTIONS

S E Y M O U R

$$\frac{18}{40} \div \frac{2}{2} = \frac{9}{20}: \quad \textbf{S}$$

$$\frac{16}{80} \div \frac{16}{16} = \frac{1}{5}: \quad \textbf{E}$$

$$\frac{24}{64} \div \frac{8}{8} = \frac{3}{8}: \quad \textbf{Y}$$

$$\frac{36}{50} \div \frac{4}{4} = \frac{18}{25}: \quad \textbf{M}$$

$$\frac{17}{102} \div \frac{17}{17} = \frac{1}{6}: \quad \textbf{O}$$

$$\frac{56}{63} \div \frac{7}{7} = \frac{8}{9}: \quad \textbf{U}$$

$$\frac{88}{100} \div \frac{4}{4} = \frac{22}{25}: \quad \textbf{R}$$

Adding and Subtracting Fractions

We can add or subtract two fractions when the denominators are the same. For example, we can add $\frac{2}{5}$ and $\frac{1}{5}$ because the denominators are both 5:

$$\frac{2}{5} + \frac{1}{5} = \frac{3}{5}$$

Similarly, we can subtract fractions when the denominators are the same:

$$\frac{7}{11} - \frac{2}{11} = \frac{5}{11}$$

Adding and Subtracting Fractions with Different Denominators

Sample Problem

Debra and Iris make jade jewelry. To hold the stones together, they use a fine gold wire. Debra has $\frac{3}{8}$ of a meter of wire and Iris has $\frac{2}{5}$ of a meter. How much gold wire do they have together?

ANALYSIS

The fractions $\frac{3}{8}$ and $\frac{2}{5}$ cannot be added directly because they have different denominators. To add them, we must first find the *lowest common denominator* (LCD). To find the lowest common denominator, it is necessary to first find the *least common multiple* (LCM). The least common multiple of two numbers is found by multiplying each number successively by 1, then 2, and so on:

5: 5, 10, 15, 20, 25, 30, 35, *40*, 45, 50, . . .
8: 8, 16, 24, 32, *40*, 48, . . .

Note that 40 is the first number that appears in both series. Therefore 40 is both the least common multiple as well as the lowest common denominator. Multiply both denominators by the number that gives 40 as the product. **You must multiply both the numerator and the denominator by the same number.**

$$\frac{3}{8} \times \frac{5}{5} = \frac{15}{40}$$
$$+\frac{2}{5} \times \frac{8}{8} = \frac{16}{40}$$
$$\frac{31}{40}$$

Debra and Iris have $\frac{31}{40}$ of a meter of gold wire together.

EXERCISES FOR ADDING FRACTIONS

1. $\frac{2}{9}$
   $+\frac{3}{4}$

2. $\dfrac{2}{7}$
   $+\dfrac{1}{2}$

3. $\dfrac{12}{15} + \dfrac{5}{12} + \dfrac{1}{3} = ?$

4. $\dfrac{7}{12} + \dfrac{3}{16} = ?$

SOLUTIONS FOR ADDING FRACTIONS

1. $\dfrac{2}{9} \times \dfrac{4}{4} = \dfrac{8}{36}$
   $+\dfrac{3}{4} \times \dfrac{9}{9} = \dfrac{27}{36}$
   $\phantom{+\dfrac{3}{4} \times \dfrac{9}{9} = }\dfrac{35}{36}$

2. $\dfrac{2}{7} \times \dfrac{2}{2} = \dfrac{4}{14}$
   $+\dfrac{1}{2} \times \dfrac{7}{7} = \dfrac{7}{14}$
   $\phantom{+\dfrac{1}{2} \times \dfrac{7}{7} = }\dfrac{11}{14}$

3. $\dfrac{2}{15} \times \dfrac{4}{4} = \dfrac{8}{60}$
   $\dfrac{1}{3} \times \dfrac{20}{20} = \dfrac{20}{60}$
   $+\dfrac{5}{12} \times \dfrac{5}{5} = \dfrac{25}{60}$
   $\phantom{+\dfrac{5}{12} \times \dfrac{5}{5} = }\dfrac{53}{60}$

4. $\dfrac{7}{12} \times \dfrac{4}{4} = \dfrac{28}{48}$
   $+\dfrac{3}{16} \times \dfrac{3}{3} = \dfrac{9}{48}$
   $\phantom{+\dfrac{3}{16} \times \dfrac{3}{3} = }\dfrac{37}{48}$

Use the same steps when subtracting fractions with different denominators.

Sample Problem

In a recent fundraising event, the swim team contributed $\frac{2}{7}$ of the school's goal.

The glee club contributed $\frac{3}{8}$ of the goal. How much greater was the glee club's contribution?

ANALYSIS

Find the lowest common denominator.

$$7: 7, 14, 21, 28, 35, 42, 49, \textbf{56}, 63, \ldots$$
$$8: 8, 16, 24, 32, 40, 48, \textbf{56}, 64, \ldots$$

56 is the lowest common denominator.

$$\frac{3}{8} \times \frac{7}{7} = \frac{21}{56}$$
$$-\frac{2}{7} \times \frac{8}{8} = \frac{16}{56}$$
$$\frac{5}{56}$$

The glee club's contribution exceeded the swim team's contribution by $\frac{5}{56}$ of the goal.

EXERCISE FOR SUBTRACTING FRACTIONS

1. $\begin{array}{r} \frac{5}{9} \\ -\frac{3}{8} \end{array}$

2. $\begin{array}{r} \frac{4}{5} \\ -\frac{1}{7} \end{array}$

3. $\frac{7}{8} - \frac{2}{3} = ?$

SOLUTIONS FOR SUBTRACTING FRACTIONS

1. $$\frac{5}{9} \times \frac{8}{8} = \frac{40}{72}$$
    $$-\frac{3}{8} \times \frac{9}{9} = \frac{27}{72}$$
    $$\frac{13}{72}$$

2. $\dfrac{4}{5} \times \dfrac{7}{7} = \dfrac{28}{35}$

  $-\dfrac{1}{7} \times \dfrac{5}{5} = \dfrac{5}{35}$

  $\dfrac{23}{35}$

3. $\dfrac{7}{8} \times \dfrac{3}{3} = \dfrac{21}{24}$

  $-\dfrac{2}{3} \times \dfrac{8}{8} = \dfrac{16}{24}$

  $\dfrac{5}{24}$

Adding and Subtracting Mixed Numbers

Consider the following problem:

Maria wants to increase the length of her daily walk. Yesterday she walked $3\dfrac{1}{5}$ miles. Today she walked $5\dfrac{3}{4}$ miles. How much further did she walk today than yesterday?

(A) $1\dfrac{2}{9}$

(B) $2\dfrac{7}{20}$

(C) $2\dfrac{11}{20}$

(D) $3\dfrac{1}{20}$

(E) $3\dfrac{4}{9}$

Which operation is needed to solve this problem: addition, subtraction, multiplication, or division? Since the difference between the two numbers is required, use subtraction:

$$5\dfrac{3}{4}$$
$$-3\dfrac{1}{5}$$

Next, find the lowest common denominator:

5 : 5, 10, 15, **20**, 25, . . .
4: 4, 8, 12, 16, **20** 24, . . .

The LCD is 20, so the problem is rewritten as:

$$5\frac{3}{4} \times \frac{5}{5} = 5\frac{13}{20}$$

$$-3\frac{1}{5} \times \frac{4}{4} = 3\frac{4}{20}$$

When subtracting mixed numbers, first subtract the fractions, then the whole numbers:

$$5\frac{15}{20}$$
$$-3\frac{4}{20}$$
$$2\frac{11}{20}$$

The answer is C, $2\frac{11}{20}$.

TEST-TAKING STRATEGY

Since the common denominator is 20, eliminate answers A and E, which have different denominators. Round both numbers to the nearest whole number:

$5\frac{3}{4}$ rounds to 6

$3\frac{1}{5}$ rounds to 3

$6 - 3 = 3$

Since $5\frac{3}{4}$ isn't quite 6 and $3\frac{1}{5}$ is slightly larger than 3, the correct answer is the one closest to, but not exceeding, 3. Thus, answer D is also eliminated. If you forget how to do this type of problem, or you are running out of time, use Estimation and Elimination (E & E) to eliminate incorrect answer choices.

Let's go back to Maria, the woman who wanted to increase her walking distance. Suppose the problem appeared this way:

Sample Problem

Maria wants to increase the length of her daily walk. Yesterday she walked $3\frac{7}{8}$ miles. Today she walked $6\frac{1}{3}$ miles. How much farther did she walk today than yesterday?

(A) $2\frac{7}{24}$

(B) $2\frac{11}{24}$

(C) $2\frac{6}{7}$

(D) $3\frac{1}{7}$

(E) $3\frac{11}{24}$

ANALYSIS

First, determine the lowest common denominator, which is 24. Rewrite the problem with 24 in the denominator:

$$6\frac{1}{3} \times \frac{8}{8} = 6\frac{8}{24}$$
$$-3\frac{7}{8} \times \frac{3}{3} = 3\frac{21}{24}$$

There is a twist in this problem. Although $6\frac{1}{3}$ is certainly larger than $3\frac{7}{8}$, $\frac{8}{24}$ is less than $\frac{21}{24}$. What is the next step in the problem?

There are two methods available to continue the calculation. Use the technique that is easier for you.

Method 1. In some subtraction problems, borrowing (also known as *regrouping*) is necessary. 1 can be borrowed from 6 and added to $\frac{8}{24}$:

$$
\begin{array}{c}
6\dfrac{8}{24} \\
-3\dfrac{21}{24}
\end{array}
\quad \rightarrow \quad
\begin{array}{c}
5+1+\dfrac{8}{24} \\
-3\dfrac{21}{24}
\end{array}
$$

Since any number divided by itself equals 1, change 1 to $\frac{24}{24}$:

$$5 + \frac{24}{24} + \frac{8}{24}$$
$$-3\frac{21}{24}$$

Combine like fractions and subtract.

$$5\frac{32}{24}$$
$$-3\frac{21}{24}$$
$$\overline{2\frac{11}{24}}$$

Method 2. It may be easier to convert all mixed numbers into improper fractions before subtracting. In order to convert a mixed number into an improper fraction, perform the following steps:

1. Multiply the denominator of the fraction by the adjacent whole number.
2. Add that sum to the numerator of the fraction.
3. Place the sum over the original denominator.

Some students consider the "horse shoe" method of converting a mixed number into an improper fraction a useful visual aid.

$$6\frac{1}{3} = \qquad 6 \quad \begin{matrix} + & 1 \\ & \rule{1em}{0.4pt} \\ \times & 3 \end{matrix} \quad = \frac{18+1}{3} = \frac{19}{3}$$

$$3\frac{7}{8} = \qquad 3 \quad \begin{matrix} + & 7 \\ & \rule{1em}{0.4pt} \\ \times & 8 \end{matrix} \quad = \frac{24+7}{8} = \frac{31}{8}$$

Find common denominators and subtract the improper fractions:

$$\frac{19}{3} \times \frac{8}{8} = \frac{152}{24}$$

$$-\frac{31}{8} \times \frac{3}{3} = \frac{93}{24}$$

$$\frac{59}{24}$$

Reconvert the answer to a mixed number when necessary:

$$\frac{59}{24} = 59 \div 24 = \qquad 2\frac{11}{24} = 2\frac{11}{24}$$

$$24\overline{)\ 59}$$
$$\underline{-48}$$
$$11$$

The answer is B, $2\frac{11}{24}$.

TEST-TAKING STRATEGY

Knowing the common denominator is 24 eliminates answers C and D. Using E & E (estimation and elimination), round to the nearest whole number:

$$6\frac{1}{3} \text{ rounds to } 6$$

$$3\frac{7}{8} \text{ rounds to } 4$$

$$6 - 4 = 2$$

The answer E, $3\frac{1}{20}$, is too large. Answers C, D, and E have been eliminated prior to doing the problem.

EXERCISES FOR SUBTRACTING MIXED NUMBERS—PART ONE

1. $4\frac{3}{8}$

   $-2\frac{1}{6}$

2. $17\frac{3}{5}$

   $-9\frac{1}{11}$

3. $9\dfrac{7}{12}$

$-2\dfrac{3}{7}$

SOLUTIONS FOR SUBTRACTING MIXED NUMBERS—PART ONE

1. $4\dfrac{3}{8} \times \dfrac{3}{3} = 4\dfrac{9}{24}$

$-2\dfrac{1}{6} \times \dfrac{4}{4} = 2\dfrac{4}{24}$

$\phantom{-2\dfrac{1}{6} \times \dfrac{4}{4} = }2\dfrac{5}{24}$

2. $17\dfrac{3}{5} \times \dfrac{11}{11} = 17\dfrac{33}{55}$

$-\ 9\dfrac{1}{11} \times \dfrac{5}{5} = \ 9\dfrac{5}{55}$

$\phantom{-\ 9\dfrac{1}{11} \times \dfrac{5}{5} = }8\dfrac{28}{55}$

3. $9\dfrac{7}{12} \times \dfrac{7}{7} = 9\dfrac{49}{84}$

$-2\dfrac{3}{7} \times \dfrac{12}{12} = 2\dfrac{36}{84}$

$\phantom{-2\dfrac{3}{7} \times \dfrac{12}{12} = }7\dfrac{13}{84}$

EXERCISES FOR SUBTRACTING MIXED NUMBERS—PART TWO

Change each mixed number into an improper fraction.

1. $2\dfrac{7}{8}$

2. $3\dfrac{1}{5}$

3. $5\dfrac{5}{6}$

Change each improper fraction into a mixed number.

4. $\dfrac{14}{3}$

5. $\dfrac{21}{5}$

6. $\dfrac{17}{7}$

7. Subtract: $13\dfrac{3}{7} - 5\dfrac{1}{2}$

SOLUTIONS FOR SUBTRACTING MIXED NUMBERS—PART TWO

1. $\dfrac{8 \times 2 + 7}{8} = \dfrac{23}{8}$

2. $\dfrac{5 \times 3 + 1}{5} = \dfrac{16}{5}$

3. $\dfrac{6 \times 5 + 5}{6} = \dfrac{35}{6}$

4. $\begin{array}{r} 4\frac{2}{3} \\ 3\overline{)\,14} \\ \underline{-12} \\ 2 \end{array}$
5. $\begin{array}{r} 4\frac{1}{5} \\ 5\overline{)\,21} \\ \underline{-20} \\ 1 \end{array}$
6. $\begin{array}{r} 2\frac{3}{7} \\ 7\overline{)\,17} \\ \underline{-14} \\ 3 \end{array}$

7. $13\frac{3}{7} \times \frac{2}{2} = 13\frac{6}{14}$

$-5\frac{1}{2} \times \frac{7}{7} = 5\frac{7}{14}$

$\downarrow$

$12 + 1 + \dfrac{6}{14}$

$- \qquad 5\dfrac{7}{14}$

$\downarrow$

$12 + \dfrac{14}{14} + \dfrac{6}{14}$

$- \qquad 5\dfrac{7}{14}$

$\downarrow$

$12\dfrac{20}{14}$

$\underline{-5\dfrac{7}{14}}$

$7\dfrac{13}{14}$

Here is another typical CBEST problem.

Sample Problem

If two boogie boards weigh $4\frac{2}{3}$ and $7\frac{9}{20}$ pounds, respectively, what is their total weight?

(A) $10\frac{7}{23}$

(B) $11\frac{5}{60}$

(C) $12\frac{5}{60}$

(D) $12\frac{7}{60}$

(E) $12\frac{7}{40}$

ANALYSIS

In this problem, two mixed numbers, $4\frac{2}{3}$ and $7\frac{9}{20}$, must be added. First, determine the LCD is 60.

Rewrite the problem with common denominators:

$$4\frac{2}{3} \times \frac{20}{20} = 4\frac{40}{60}$$
$$+7\frac{9}{20} \times \frac{3}{3} = 7\frac{27}{60}$$

Add the whole numbers and the fractions:

$$4\frac{40}{60}$$
$$+7\frac{27}{60}$$
$$\overline{11\frac{67}{60}}$$

Note the improper fraction in the answer. When $\frac{2}{3}$ and $\frac{9}{20}$ are added, $\frac{67}{60}$ is the sum.

Convert $\dfrac{67}{60}$ into a mixed number:

$$\frac{67}{60} = 60\overline{\smash{)}\begin{array}{r}1\frac{7}{60}\\ 67\\ -60\\ \hline 7\end{array}}$$

Add $1\dfrac{7}{60}$ to the sum of the whole numbers:

$$11 + 1 + \frac{7}{60} = 12\frac{7}{60}$$

The answer is D, $12\dfrac{7}{60}$.

TEST-TAKING STRATEGY

Knowing the common denominator is 60 eliminates A and E. Using E&E, we get the following:

$$\text{Round } 4\frac{2}{3} \text{ to } 5$$

$$\text{Round } 7\frac{9}{20} \text{ to } 7$$

$$5 + 7 = 12$$

Answer choice B, $11\dfrac{5}{60}$, can quickly be eliminated.

EXERCISES FOR ADDING MIXED NUMBERS

1. $\quad 12\dfrac{2}{5}$
   $+13\dfrac{5}{8}$

2. $\quad 9\dfrac{7}{12}$
   $+ 1\dfrac{5}{8}$

SOLUTIONS FOR ADDING MIXED NUMBERS

1. $12\dfrac{2}{5} \times \dfrac{8}{8} = 12\dfrac{16}{40}$

   $+13\dfrac{5}{8} \times \dfrac{5}{5} = 13\dfrac{25}{40}$

   $\qquad\qquad\qquad 25\dfrac{41}{40}$

   $25\dfrac{41}{40} = 25 + \dfrac{40}{40} + \dfrac{1}{40} = 25 + 1 + \dfrac{1}{40} = 26\dfrac{1}{40}$

2. $9\dfrac{7}{12} \times \dfrac{2}{2} = 9\dfrac{14}{24}$

   $+1\dfrac{5}{8} \times \dfrac{3}{3} = 1\dfrac{15}{24}$

   $\qquad\qquad\qquad 10\dfrac{29}{24}$

   $10\dfrac{29}{24} = 10 + \dfrac{24}{24} + \dfrac{5}{24} = 10 + 1 + \dfrac{5}{24} = 11\dfrac{5}{24}$

Multiplying and Dividing Fractions

When multiplying fractions, multiply the numerators and the denominators:

$$\frac{2}{7} \times \frac{3}{11} = \frac{6}{77}$$

Sometimes it's easier to *cross-cancel* by dividing numerators and denominators by common factors. Notice how much easier it is to cross-cancel rather than to wait until the end to simplify the answers.

$$\frac{7}{15} \times \frac{5}{14} = \frac{35}{210}$$

$$\frac{35}{210} \div \frac{35}{35} = \frac{1}{6}$$

With cross-canceling, divide 7 and 14 by 7 and 5 and 15 by 5:

$$\frac{\overset{1}{\cancel{7}}}{\underset{3}{\cancel{15}}} \times \frac{\overset{1}{\cancel{5}}}{\underset{2}{\cancel{14}}} = \frac{1}{6}$$

EXERCISES FOR MULTIPLYING FRACTIONS

1. $\dfrac{2}{7} \times \dfrac{3}{5}$

2. $\dfrac{3}{8} \times \dfrac{16}{19}$

3. $\dfrac{14}{21} \times \dfrac{5}{21}$

3. $\dfrac{9}{16} \times \dfrac{4}{27}$

SOLUTIONS FOR MULTIPLYING FRACTIONS

1. $\dfrac{2}{7} \times \dfrac{3}{5} = \dfrac{6}{35}$

2. $\dfrac{3}{\cancel{8}_{1}} \times \dfrac{\cancel{16}^{2}}{19} = \dfrac{6}{19}$

3. $\dfrac{\cancel{14}^{2}}{\cancel{25}_{5}} \times \dfrac{\cancel{5}^{1}}{\cancel{21}_{3}} = \dfrac{2}{15}$

4. $\dfrac{\cancel{9}^{1}}{\cancel{16}_{4}} \times \dfrac{\cancel{4}^{1}}{\cancel{27}_{3}} = \dfrac{1}{12}$

MULTIPLYING MIXED NUMBERS

Multiplying mixed numbers uses the same steps, but first each mixed number must be converted into an improper fraction:

$$4\dfrac{2}{3} \times 5\dfrac{2}{7} = ?$$
$$4\dfrac{2}{3} = \dfrac{14}{3}$$
$$5\dfrac{2}{7} = \dfrac{37}{7}$$
$$\dfrac{14}{3} \times \dfrac{37}{7} = ?$$

Cross-cancel and multiply:

$$\frac{\overset{2}{\cancel{14}}}{3} \times \frac{37}{\underset{1}{\cancel{7}}} = \frac{74}{3}$$

Convert into a mixed number:

$$\frac{74}{3} = 3{\overline{\smash{\big)}\,74}} \; 24\frac{2}{3}$$

$$\begin{array}{r} 24\frac{2}{3} \\ 3{\overline{\smash{\big)}\,74}} \\ \underline{-6} \\ 14 \\ \underline{-12} \\ 2 \end{array}$$

Sample Problem

Naomi has to lay six rugs, side by side, in the hallway. Each rug is $5\frac{2}{3}$ feet long. What will be the total length of the rugs?

(A) 31 feet

(B) 32 feet

(C) $33\frac{1}{3}$ feet

(D) 34 feet

(E) $36\frac{2}{3}$ feet

ANALYSIS

First convert both $5\frac{2}{3}$ and 6 into improper fractions. The integer 6 can be converted into the improper fraction $\frac{6}{1}$.

$$5\frac{2}{3} = \frac{17}{3}$$
$$6 = \frac{6}{1}$$

Cross-cancel and multiply:

$$\frac{17}{\cancel{3}_1} \times \frac{\cancel{6}^2}{1} = 34$$

The answer is D, 34 feet.

TEST-TAKING STRATEGY

Using E & E, answer E is eliminated. $5\frac{2}{3}$ is slightly less than 6, so the answer cannot be more than 36.

EXERCISES FOR MULTIPLYING MIXED NUMBERS

1. $3\frac{1}{3} \times 2\frac{1}{2} = ?$

2. $7\frac{1}{7} \times 1\frac{2}{5} = ?$

3. $4\frac{2}{7} \times 5\frac{3}{10} = ?$

SOLUTIONS FOR MULTIPLYING MIXED NUMBERS

1. $3\frac{1}{3} \times 2\frac{1}{2} = \frac{\cancel{10}^5}{3} \times \frac{5}{\cancel{2}_1} = \frac{25}{3} = 8\frac{1}{3}$

2. $7\frac{1}{4} \times 1\frac{2}{5} = \frac{\cancel{50}^{10}}{\cancel{7}_1} \times \frac{\cancel{7}^1}{\cancel{5}_1} = 10$

3. $4\frac{2}{7} \times 5\frac{3}{10} = \frac{\cancel{30}^3}{7} \times \frac{53}{\cancel{10}_1} = \frac{159}{7} = 22\frac{5}{7}$

When dividing by a fraction, first find the *reciprocal* of the second fraction and change the division sign into a multiplication sign (*invert and multiply*). The reciprocal of a fraction is the fraction with the numerator and denominator reversed. For example, the reciprocal of $\frac{2}{3}$ is $\frac{3}{2}$, while the reciprocal of $\frac{6}{1}$ (or just plain 6) is $\frac{1}{6}$.

> ### Sample Problem

What is the quotient of $\frac{3}{8}$ and $\frac{7}{24}$?

(A) $\frac{7}{64}$

(B) $\frac{2}{3}$

(C) $\frac{6}{7}$

(D) $\frac{9}{7}$

(E) $\frac{12}{7}$

ANALYSIS

A quotient is the answer to a division problem so divide $\frac{3}{8}$ by $\frac{7}{24}$:

$$\frac{3}{8} \div \frac{7}{24}$$

Invert the second fraction and multiply:

$$\frac{3}{8} \times \frac{24}{7}$$

Cross-cancel:

$$\frac{3}{\cancel{8}_1} \times \frac{\cancel{24}^3}{7} = \frac{9}{7}$$

The correct answer is D, $\frac{9}{7}$.

> ### Sample Problem:

What is the quotient of $7\frac{2}{3}$ and $1\frac{1}{2}$?

(A) $4\frac{1}{9}$

(B) $5\frac{1}{9}$

(C) $5\dfrac{2}{9}$

(D) $6\dfrac{1}{3}$

(E) $6\dfrac{2}{9}$

ANALYSIS

Convert both mixed numbers into improper fractions:

$$7\dfrac{2}{3} = \dfrac{23}{3} \qquad 1\dfrac{1}{2} = \dfrac{3}{2}$$

Invert and multiply:

$$\dfrac{23}{3} \times \dfrac{2}{3} = \dfrac{46}{9}$$

Convert $\dfrac{46}{9}$ into a mixed number:

$$\begin{array}{r} 5\frac{1}{9} \\ 9\overline{)46} \\ \underline{-45} \\ 1 \end{array}$$

The answer is B, $5\dfrac{1}{9}$.

EXERCISES FOR DIVIDING FRACTIONS

1. $\dfrac{11}{14} \div \dfrac{2}{7} = ?$

2. $\dfrac{3}{8} \div 1\dfrac{1}{4} = ?$

3. $2\dfrac{3}{8} \div 5\dfrac{7}{12} = ?$

4. If a 6-pound cake is sliced into pieces weighing $\dfrac{3}{8}$ of a pound each, how many pieces will there be?

SOLUTIONS FOR DIVIDING FRACTIONS

1. $\dfrac{11}{14} \div \dfrac{2}{7} = \dfrac{11}{\cancel{14}_{7}} \times \dfrac{\cancel{7}^{1}}{2} = \dfrac{11}{4} = 2\dfrac{3}{4}$

2. $\dfrac{3}{8} \div 1\dfrac{1}{4} = \dfrac{3}{8} \div \dfrac{5}{4} = \dfrac{3}{\cancel{8}_{2}} \times \dfrac{\cancel{4}^{1}}{5} = \dfrac{3}{10}$

3. $2\dfrac{3}{8} \div 5\dfrac{7}{12} = \dfrac{19}{8} \div \dfrac{67}{12} = \dfrac{19}{\cancel{8}_{2}} \times \dfrac{\cancel{12}^{3}}{67} = \dfrac{57}{134}$

4. $\dfrac{6}{1} \div \dfrac{3}{8} = \dfrac{\cancel{6}^{2}}{1} \times \dfrac{8}{\cancel{3}_{1}} = 16$

DECIMALS

Decimal problems comprise about 20% of the CBEST math questions. You must have a working knowledge of decimals to pass the Math Section of the CBEST.

What Is a Decimal?

A decimal is the number to the right of the decimal point. In the number 4.73, the number to the right of the decimal point, 73, is a decimal.

Place Value

Each place value in a decimal represents a fraction of ten or some multiple of ten. Look at the following number below:

64.75219

6   10s (tens)

4   1s (ones)

•

7   $\frac{1}{10}$ (tenths)

5   $\frac{1}{100}$ (hundredths)

2   $\frac{1}{1,000}$ (thousandths)

1   $\frac{1}{10,000}$ (ten thousandths)

9   $\frac{1}{100,000}$ (hundred thousandths)

The 7 in the first decimal place represents $\frac{7}{10}$, the five represents $\frac{5}{100}$, and so on.

This decimal could be rewritten as the sum of fractions:

$$60 + 4 + \frac{7}{10} + \frac{5}{100} + \frac{2}{1,000} + \frac{1}{10,000} + \frac{9}{100,000}$$

Or as a mixed number:

$$64\frac{75219}{100000}$$

Sample Problem

In the number 8,942.3578, what fraction is represented by the number 7?

(A) 7

(B) $\dfrac{7}{10}$

(C) $\dfrac{7}{100}$

(D) $\dfrac{7}{1,000}$

(E) $\dfrac{7}{10,000}$

ANALYSIS

Since the 7 is in the thousandths place, the seven represents the fraction $\dfrac{7}{1,000}$. The answer is D, $\dfrac{7}{1,000}$.

Rounding Decimals

When rounding a decimal to a particular place value, inspect the digit to the immediate right of that place value. If the digit to the right is 5 or greater, round up. If the number is less than 5, round down.

Sample Problem:

The number for pi (π) begins 3.1415926 . . . . Round pi to the nearest hundredth.

(A) 3.14
(B) 3.15
(C) 3.141
(D) 3.142
(E) 3.1416

ANALYSIS

First, identify the number in the hundredths place. The number is 4. Since the number to its right, 1, is less than 5, round down. The answer is A, 3.14.

TEST-TAKING STRATEGY

Answer choices C, D, and E all offer answers beyond the hundredths place and can be eliminated.

EXERCISES FOR ROUNDING DECIMALS

Round each decimal to the nearest tenth.

1. 9.82
2. 3.67
3. 5.98

Round each decimal to the nearest hundredth.

4. 17.087
5. 217.411
6. 0.586

Round each decimal to the nearest thousandth.

7. 9.1932
8 27.4036
9. 54.5455

SOLUTIONS FOR ROUNDING DECIMALS

1. 9.8

2. 3.7

3. 6.0 or 6

4. 17.09

5. 217.41

6. 0.59

7. 9.193

8. 27.404

9. 54.546

Adding and Subtracting Decimals

To add or subtract decimals, align the decimal points and perform the indicated operation:

$$8.5 + 7.54 + 3.892 =$$

$$
\begin{array}{r}
8.5 \\
7.54 \\
+3.892 \\
\hline
19.932
\end{array}
$$

$$13.27 - 9.62 =$$

$$
\begin{array}{r}
13.27 \\
-9.62 \\
\hline
3.65
\end{array}
$$

Zero place holders are useful visual aids.

Sample Problem

Xavier has 60 pounds of modeling clay to distribute to several classrooms. The first-grade class needs 7.7 pounds, while the fifth-grade class has requested 14.67 pounds. If Xavier allots both classes what they need, how much modeling clay will he have available for the other classes?

(A) 22.37 pounds
(B) 32.37 pounds
(C) 37.36 pounds
(D) 37.63 pounds
(E) 38.21 pounds

ANALYSIS

Solving this problem requires two steps. First, find the total clay needed by the first- and fifth-grade classes:

$$
\begin{array}{r}
7.70 \\
+14.67 \\
\hline
22.37
\end{array}
$$
Adding a zero place holder is helpful.

Subtract the total from 60:

$$
\begin{array}{r}
60.00 \\
-22.37 \\
\hline
37.63
\end{array}
$$
Adding zero place holders is helpful.

The answer is D, 37.63 pounds.

TEST-TAKING STRATEGY

Round each of the numbers to the nearest whole number:

7.7 rounds to 8
14.67 rounds to 15

60 − (8 + 15) =
60 − 23 = 37

Since the answer should be close to 37, eliminate answers A and B.

EXERCISES FOR ADDING AND SUBTRACTING DECIMALS

Add or subtract. Place the corresponding letter in each blank.

What happened when the karate expert saluted the president?

E	T	N	C	U	K	K	O	O	D
0.11	33.188	2.1	1.88	13.97	31	140.158	9.42	15.089	11.32

HE

_____ _____ _____ _____ _____ _____ _____

12.6   7 − 4.9   15   3.08   15.1   0.1 + 0.01   17.9
+18.4   + 0.089   −1.2   17.42   − 6.58
                                                        +107.638

HIMSELF

_____ _____ _____

3.8   18 − 4.03   16 + 2.8 + 14.388
+5.62

SOLUTIONS FOR ADDING AND SUBTRACTING DECIMALS

HE

<u>K</u> <u>N</u> <u>O</u> <u>C</u> <u>K</u> <u>E</u> <u>D</u>

<u>H</u> <u>I</u> <u>M</u> <u>S</u> <u>E</u> <u>L</u> <u>F</u>

<u>O</u> <u>U</u> <u>T</u>

```
  12.6
 +18.4
  31.0      : K

   7.0
  −4.9
   2.1      : N

  15.000
 + 0.089
  15.089    : O

   3.08
  −1.20
   1.88     : C

  15.100
  17.420
+107.638
 140.158    : K

   0.10
  +0.01
   0.11     : E

  17.90
 − 6.58
  11.32     : D

   3.80
  +5.62
   9.42     : O

  18.00
 − 4.03
  13.97     : U

  16.000
   2.800
 +14.388
  33.188    : T
```

Multiplying Decimals

Sample Problem

Surfin' Sam needs 4.5 gallons of gas to fill up his motorcyle. The price of gas today is $3.31 per gallon. To the nearest cent, how much will it cost him to fill up his tank?

(A) $7.81
(B) $8.85
(C) $14.89
(D) $14.90
(E) $15.05

ANALYSIS

Since each one of the 4.5 gallons costs $3.31, multiply 4.5 by 3.31 (ignore the $ until the end of the problem). To multiply numbers that have one or more decimal places, do the following:

1. Multiply the two numbers as though they were whole numbers.
2. Count the number of decimal places in both numbers.
3. Move the decimal point that many places to the left in your answer.

$$\begin{array}{r} \$3.31 \\ \times \ 4.5 \end{array} \qquad \text{Think:} \qquad \begin{array}{r} 331 \\ \times \ \ 45 \\ \hline 14{,}895 \end{array}$$

Since $3.31 has two numbers to the right of the decimal point and 4.5 has one number to the right of the decimal point, move the decimal point a total of three places to the left:

$$14{,}895 \quad \text{becomes} \quad 14.895$$

Since the problem requires an answer rounded to the nearest cent, look at the number to the right of 9, the number in the one cents place. The number to the right of 9 is 5, so round up. Therefore, $14.895 rounds up to $14.90. The answer is D, $14.90.

TEST-TAKING STRATEGY

Use E&E to eliminate answer choices. Round 3.31 and 4.5 to the nearest whole number:

3.31 rounds down to 3; 4.5 rounds up to 5. Since $3 \times 5 = 15$, answers A and B can be eliminated.

EXERCISES FOR MULTIPLYING DECIMALS

Find each product.

1. 4.8×2.7
2. 17.55×3.6
3. 3.051×2.3

SOLUTIONS FOR MULTIPLYING DECIMALS

1.
$$\begin{array}{r} 4.8 \\ \underline{\times 2.7} \end{array}$$
Think:
$$\begin{array}{r} 48 \\ \underline{\times 27} \\ 1,296 \end{array}$$
Move the decimal point two places to the left: 12.96.

2.
$$\begin{array}{r} 17.55 \\ \underline{\times \;\; 3.6} \end{array}$$
Think:
$$\begin{array}{r} 1,755 \\ \underline{\times \quad 36} \\ 63,180 \end{array}$$
Move the decimal point three places to the left: 63.180 or 63.18.

3.
$$\begin{array}{r} 3.051 \\ \underline{\times \;\; 2.3} \end{array}$$
Think:
$$\begin{array}{r} 3,051 \\ \underline{\times \quad 23} \\ 70,173 \end{array}$$
Move the decimal point four places to the left: 7.0173.

Dividing Decimals

Sample Problem

What is the quotient of 0.962 and 0.26?

(A) .037
(B) 0.37
(C) 3.7
(D) 37
(E) 370

ANALYSIS

The quotient is the answer to a division problem, so divide 0.962 by 0.26. In order to divide a number by a decimal, follow these steps:

1. Move the decimal point in the divisor (in this case 0.26) as many places to the right as necessary to form a whole number.
2. Move the decimal in the dividend (in this case 0.962) an equal number of places to the right.
3. Divide.

$$0.26\overline{)0.962}$$

becomes

$$26\overline{)96.2}^{3.7}$$

If the dividend contains a decimal, place another decimal point above it in the space where the quotient appears. The answer to this problem is C, 3.7.

TEST-TAKING STRATEGY

Notice that all the answers contain a 3 followed by a 7. You do not have to finish this problem. Once you have decided the largest number in the quotient is in the one's place, immediately select choice C. No other answer begins in the one's place.

Adding Zero Place Holders

When dividing by decimals, it may be necessary to add zero place holders in the dividend:

$$14.4 \div 0.12 = ?$$

Move the decimal in the divisor two places to the right. As the same is done in the dividend, a lack of place values becomes apparent. Add as many zeroes as necessary to move the decimal point as required:

$$0.12\overline{)14.4} \quad \rightarrow \quad 12\overline{)1,440}^{120}$$

The answer is 120.

Try a problem that requires knowledge of decimals and fractions.

Sample Problem

Anita Job wants work. She is scheduled to interview for a teaching position in Los Angeles this afternoon, but her car is in the shop for repairs. Anita has decided to take a cab to the district office for the interview. The cab company uses the following fee schedule:

First $\frac{1}{4}$ mile: $2.75

Each additional $\frac{1}{4}$ mile: $1.40

If Anita's fare was $20.95 (excluding gratuity), how far did she travel in the cab?

(A) 3 miles

(B) $3\frac{1}{4}$ miles

(C) $3\frac{1}{2}$ miles

(D) 13 miles

(E) 14 miles

ANALYSIS

To solve this problem, subtract the cost of the first quarter mile from the fare:

$$\$20.95 - \$2.75 = \$18.20$$

Divide $18.20 by $1.40, the cost of each additional $\frac{1}{4}$ mile. Remember to move the decimal point two places to the right in both the divisor and the dividend:

$$1.40\overline{)18.20} \quad \rightarrow \quad \overset{13}{140\overline{)1,820}}$$

Add 1 to our quotient, which represents the first quarter mile that cost $2.75. Thus Anita has traveled fourteen quarter miles. To find the total distance in miles, divide 14 by 4, the number of quarter miles in one mile.

$$\begin{array}{r} 3\frac{2}{4} = 3\frac{1}{2} \\ 4\overline{)14} \\ \underline{-12} \\ 2 \end{array}$$

The answer is C, $3\frac{1}{2}$ miles.

TEST-TAKING STRATEGY

Answer D is a trap: 13 is the number of *quarter miles* Anita traveled before adding the more expensive first quarter mile. Answer E is a trap: 14 is the number of *quarter miles* Anita actually traveled. All of the answers are listed in miles, so answers D and E can be eliminated.

EXERCISES FOR DIVIDING DECIMALS

1. $3.926 \div 0.26$

2. $6.634 \div 6.62$

3. $0.00217 \div 0.31$

4. Kallie Fornya wants to relocate to San Diego for a teaching position. The fee schedule for the moving company is as follows:

   First 100 pounds transported: $11.65
   Each 100 pounds thereafter: $7.75

   If her cost to relocate was $375.90, how many pounds were transported?

SOLUTIONS FOR DIVIDING DECIMALS

1. $0.26\overline{)3.926}$ $\rightarrow$ $26\overline{)392.6}$ with quotient 15.1

2. $6.2\overline{)6.634}$ $\rightarrow$ $62\overline{)66.34}$ with quotient 1.07

3. $0.31\overline{)0.00217}$ $\rightarrow$ $31\overline{)0.217}$ with quotient 0.007

4. Subtract the cost of first 100 pounds:

$$\$375.90 - \$11.65 = \$364.25$$

Divide:

$7.75\overline{)375.90}$ $\rightarrow$ $775\overline{)37,590}$ with quotient 47 hundred pounds

Kallie transported 4,800 pounds. (Don't forget to add back the first 100 pounds).

Converting Decimals into Fractions

Some questions may require converting a decimal into a fraction.

Sample Problem

Arrange these numbers from least to greatest:

$$\frac{2}{5}, 0.24, \frac{1}{3}$$

ANALYSIS

One way to solve this problem is to convert the decimal, 0.24, into a fraction. A common denominator would then be found so the fractions could be arranged in order. To convert a decimal into a fraction, find the place value of the last digit:

$0.2\underline{4}$ The 4 is in the hundredth's place ($\frac{1}{100}$'s)

Rewrite the decimal as a fraction:

$$0.24 = \frac{24}{100}$$

Simplify:

$$\frac{24}{100} \div \frac{4}{4} = \frac{6}{25}$$

Since the lowest common denominator of 3, 5, and 25 is 75, rewrite the fractions:

$$\frac{2}{5} = \frac{30}{75} \qquad \frac{6}{25} = \frac{18}{75} \qquad \frac{1}{3} = \frac{25}{75}$$

Arrange the fractions from least to greatest:

$$\frac{18}{75}, \frac{25}{75}, \frac{30}{75}$$

Remember to convert the fractions to original form:

$$0.24, \frac{1}{3}, \frac{2}{5}$$

EXERCISES FOR CONVERTING DECIMALS INTO FRACTIONS

Change each decimal into a simplified fraction. Place the corresponding letter in each blank.

A Good Name for a Teacher

A	B	I	O	R	T	O	K
$\frac{11}{500}$	$\frac{63}{100}$	$\frac{4}{5}$	$\frac{16}{25}$	$\frac{6}{25}$	$\frac{3}{8}$	$\frac{483}{500}$	$\frac{7}{8}$

_____	_____	_____	_____
24	0.8	0.375	0.022

_____	_____	_____	_____
0.63	0.64	0.966	0.875

SOLUTIONS FOR CONVERTING DECIMALS INTO FRACTIONS

$$\underline{R} \quad \underline{I} \quad \underline{T} \quad \underline{A}$$

$$\underline{B} \quad \underline{O} \quad \underline{O} \quad \underline{K}$$

$0.24 = \dfrac{24}{100} \div \dfrac{4}{4} = \dfrac{6}{25}$: **R**

$0.8 = \dfrac{8}{10} \div \dfrac{2}{2} = \dfrac{4}{5}$: **I**

$0.375 = \dfrac{375}{1,000} \div \dfrac{125}{125} = \dfrac{3}{8}$: **T**

$0.022 = \dfrac{22}{1,000} \div \dfrac{2}{2} = \dfrac{11}{500}$: **A**

$0.63 = \dfrac{63}{100}$: **B**

$0.64 = \dfrac{64}{100} \div \dfrac{4}{4} = \dfrac{16}{25}$: **O**

$0.966 = \dfrac{966}{1,000} \div \dfrac{2}{2} = \dfrac{483}{500}$: **O**

$0.875 = \dfrac{875}{1,000} \div \dfrac{125}{125} = \dfrac{7}{8}$: **K**

Converting Fractions into Decimals

To convert a fraction into a decimal, divide the numerator by the denominator:

$$\frac{3}{4} = \quad 4\overline{)3.00}^{\,0.75} \qquad \frac{17}{25} = 25\overline{)17.00}^{\,0.68}$$

Sample Problem

Arrange the following numbers from least to greatest:

$$\frac{3}{8}, 0.39, \frac{17}{68}$$

ANALYSIS

Solve this problem by converting both fractions into decimals:

$$\frac{3}{8} = 0.375$$

$$\frac{17}{68} = \frac{1}{4} = 0.25$$

Arrange the decimals from least to greatest:

$$0.25, \ 0.375, \ 0.39$$

Convert the decimals into their original form:

$$\frac{17}{68}, \frac{3}{8}, 0.39$$

EXERCISES FOR CONVERTING FRACTIONS INTO DECIMALS

Convert each fraction into a decimal.

1. $\dfrac{29}{40}$

2. $\dfrac{17}{85}$

3. $\dfrac{2}{9}$

4. Alice wants premium digital cable installed into her home. Her current monthly cable bill is $\dfrac{1}{8}$ of her weekly take-home pay. The monthly cost for premium cable will represent $\dfrac{6}{25}$ of her pay. As a portion of her weekly paycheck, how much greater is the premium cable bill than the basic cable bill? (Leave your answer in decimal form.)

SOLUTIONS FOR CONVERTING FRACTIONS INTO DECIMALS

1. $\dfrac{29}{40} = 29 \div 40 = 0.725$

2. $\dfrac{17}{85} = \dfrac{1}{5} = 1 \div 5 = 0.2$

3. $\dfrac{2}{9} = 2 \div 9 = 0.222$

4. Convert each fraction into a decimal:

$$\frac{6}{25} = 6 \div 25 = 0.240$$

$$\frac{1}{8} = 1 \div 8 = 0.125$$

Subtract:

$$
\begin{array}{r}
0.240 \\
-0.125 \\
\hline
0.115
\end{array}
$$

ALGEBRA

Imagine a balancing scale with each side containing 6 nickels. Does the scale balance? What happens when one nickel is removed from one of the sides? What happens when one nickel is removed from *each* side? The scale stays balanced when equal weights remain on each side. The image of a balancing scale helps envision the fundamentals of algebra.

Sample Problem

What number is missing below?

$$8 + 5 = 6 + ?$$

(A) 4
(B) 5
(C) 6
(D) 7
(E) 8

ANALYSIS

Since $8 + 5 = 13$, find a number, when added to 6, that will also equal 13. The statement $8 + 5 = 6 + ?$ "balances" when 7 is substituted for the missing value.

Variables and Algebraic Expressions

In algebra, letters or symbols are used to represent unknown quantities. These letters or symbols are called *variables*. The letters x and n are commonly used, though other letters may serve as variables:

$$\text{rate} \times \text{time} = \text{distance}$$

$$r \times t = d$$

The perimeter of a rectangle is found by adding both widths and both lengths:

$$P = 2l + 2w$$

A quantity that contains a variable is called an *algebraic expression.* Variables are useful for modeling algebraic expressions.

Sample Problem

Jenny has 7 more blouses than Emily. If Emily has n blouses, how many blouses does Jenny have?

(A) $n - 7$

(B) $n + 7$

(C) $7n$

(D) $\dfrac{7}{n}$

(E) n^7

ANALYSIS

"7 more than" means addition. If a friend has \$8 more than you, and you have \$12, then your friend has \$20 because $12 + 8 = 20$. Similarly, if Emily has n blouses, and Jenny has 7 more than Emily, then Jenny must have $n + 7$ blouses. The answer is B.

The CBEST-taker will frequently be asked to translate English phrases into algebraic expressions. There are key words that help fashion an algebraic expression:

Key Words	Operation
increased by	addition
added to	addition
more than	addition
decreased by	subtraction
less than	subtraction
times	multiplication
double, triple, etc.	multiplication
split, cut, grouped, shared	division

It would also be wise to review the results of mathematical operations:

Operation	Result
multiplication	product
division	quotient
addition	sum
subtraction	difference

Earlier, it was noted that the symbols for multiplication include ×, ·, and ( )( ). When using variables, multiplication can take another form:

3 times a number *n*

3*n* means or

the product of 3 and *n*

or

3 multiplied by *n*

In the term 3*n*, the number 3 is referred to as the *coefficient* of *n*.

The use of parentheses in algebraic expressions means "the quantity of." The expression:

$$3(n + 7)$$

should be read as "three times the quantity of *n* plus 7."

EXERCISES FOR ALGEBRAIC EXPRESSIONS

Express each phrase with an algebraic expression.

1. The sum of 5 and a number *n*.

2. The product of 2 and *r*.

3. The quotient of *n* and 6.

4. Seven times the quantity of *m* and 4.

5. *x* increased by 7.

6. *n* decreased by the quantity of 8 and three times *n*.

7. The difference of twice a number *c* and 4.

8. The quotient of *r* squared and 5.

9. The product of 8 and the quantity of *n* plus *f*.

SOLUTIONS FOR EXERCISES FOR ALGEBRAIC EXPRESSIONS

1. $5 + n$

2. $2r$

3. $\dfrac{n}{6}$ or $n \div 6$

4. $7(m + 4)$

5. $x + 7$

6. $n - (8 + 3n)$

7. $2c - 4$

8. $r^2 \div 5$ or $\dfrac{r^2}{5}$

9. $8(n + f)$

Combining Like Terms

Algebraic expressions can be simplified by combining like terms. Just as $7 + 8$ can be simplified to 15, so, too, can $7n + 8n$ be simplified to $15n$. $7n$ and $8n$ are like terms because they have the same variable raised to the same power. (Any variable, such as n, can be also thought of as n^1 or n to the first power.)

Sample Problem

What is the sum of $3r - 11 + 2r - 11r^2$?

(A) $5r^2 - 11 - 11r^2$
(B) $5r - 11 - 11r^2$
(C) $16r - 11$
(D) $16r^2 - 11$
(E) -17

ANALYSIS

The only like terms in this problem are $3r$ and $2r$. Although $11r^2$ has the variable r, its power, 2, is not the same as the power of $3r$ and $2r$. Therefore,

$$3r - 11 + 2r - 11r^2 = 5r - 11 - 11r^2$$

The answer is B.

Sample Problem

Simplify:

$$2x + x = ?$$

(A) 2
(B) $2x$
(C) $2x^2$
(D) $3x$
(E) $3x^2$

ANALYSIS

The answer is D, *3x.* It is important to note that when the coefficient of a variable is not written, it is assumed to be 1:

$$2x + x = 2x + 1x = 3x$$

EXERCISES FOR COMBINING LIKE TERMS

1. $5x + 6x = ?$

2. $3x^2 + 2x + 2x^2 + 4x = ?$

3. $-12(x^2 - 4) - 2x^2 - 6 = ?$

4. $5x + 2y = ?$

5. $2\frac{1}{5}x + x + 3\frac{2}{3}x = ?$

SOLUTIONS FOR EXERCISES FOR COMBINING LIKE TERMS

1. $11x$

2. $5x^2 + 6x$

3. $-12(x^2 - 4) - 2x^2 - 6 = -12x^2 + 48 - 2x^2 - 6 = -14x^2 + 42$

4. $5x + 2y$ (*x* and *y* are not like terms)

5. $6\frac{13}{15}x$

Equations

An equation is a mathematical statement that indicates two algebraic expressions are equal. The following are examples of equations:

$$x + 6 = 12$$
$$2x - 5 = 3x + 2$$
$$5x^2 + 2y^2 = 7 - 3x$$

The CBEST-taker is responsible for solving equations containing only *one* variable.

Consider the first example, $x + 6 = 12$. It takes little effort to conclude the solution is $x = 6$ because $6 + 6 = 12$. However, the solution to the equation $-3x - 15 = -73$ is not so readily apparent. There are rules in algebra, however, that facilitate the search for answers.

The key to solving an equation is to isolate the variable. In the problem $x + 6 = 12$, the final statement isolates the variable:

$$x + 6 = 12$$
$$x = 6$$

Equations are solved by following two rules:

1. To isolate a variable, perform the opposite operation(s).
2. Any manipulation of an equation must occur equivalently on both sides of the equal sign.

Consider the first example, $x + 6 = 12$, and apply the two rules:

$$x + 6 = 12$$
$$x + 6 - 6 = 12 - 6$$
$$x = 6$$

Since 6 was added to x in the original equation, *subtract* 6 from *both* sides.

Sample Problem

$$\frac{x}{6} = 6$$

(A) 1
(B) 6
(C) 12
(D) 36
(E) 96

ANALYSIS

Since x is being divided by 6, multiply both sides of the equation by 6:

$$\frac{x}{6} = 6$$
$$6\left(\frac{x}{6}\right) = 6(6)$$
$$x = 36$$

The answer is D, 36.

EXERCISES FOR EQUATIONS

Solve each equation.

1. $x + 8 = 38$

2. $x - 15 = -97$

3. $2x = 68$

4. $-17x = -85$

5. $x \div 11 = 14$

6. $\dfrac{x}{-5} = 71$

SOLUTIONS FOR EXERCISES FOR EQUATIONS

1. $x + 8 = 38$
    $x + 8 - 8 = 38 - 8$
    $x = 30$

2. $x - 15 = -97$
    $x - 15 + 15 = -97 + 15$
    $x = -82$

3. $2x = 68$
    $\dfrac{2x}{2} = \dfrac{68}{2}$
    $x = 34$

4. $-17x = -85$
    $\dfrac{-17x}{-17} = \dfrac{-85}{-17}$
    $x = 5$

5. $x \div 11 = 14$
    $(x \div 11)(11) = 14(11)$
    $x = 154$

6. $\dfrac{x}{-5} = 71$
    $-5\left(\dfrac{x}{-5}\right) = 71(-5)$
    $x = -355$

More Advanced Equations

Solving certain equations may require several steps. Consider the equation $2x - 9 = 15$. In order to isolate the variable, add 9 and divide by 2:

$$2x - 9 + 9 = 15 + 9$$
$$2x = 24$$
$$\dfrac{2x}{2} = \dfrac{24}{2}$$
$$x = 12$$

When solving equations with multiple steps, the sequence of operations is:

1. Combine like terms
2. Addition or subtraction
3. Multiplication or division

Sample Problem

Solve for *n*:

$$7n + 8 - 5n - (-3) = 14$$

ANALYSIS

Combine like terms: $\qquad\qquad\qquad 2n + 11 = 14$
Subtract 11 from both sides: $\qquad 2n + 11 - 11 = 14 - 11$
Simplify: $\qquad\qquad\qquad\qquad\quad 2n = 3$

Divide both sides by 2: $\qquad\qquad \dfrac{2n}{2} = \dfrac{3}{2}$

Simplify: $\qquad\qquad\qquad\qquad\quad n = \dfrac{3}{2}$ or 1.5

More Advanced Equations

The more advanced equations on the CBEST contain one or both of the following:

1. Equations with variables on both sides of the equal sign
2. Equations containing fractions or decimals

When solving equations, the goal is to isolate the variable. This is true even when variables are on both sides of the equal sign.

Sample Problem

Solve for *n*:

$$5n - 11 = 2n + 4$$

(A) 1
(B) 2
(C) 3
(D) 4
(E) 5

ANALYSIS

First, subtract 2*n* from both sides of the equation:

$$5n - 11 - 2n = 2n + 4 - 2n$$

Combine like terms:

$$3n - 11 = 4$$

Add 11 to both sides:

$$3n - 11 + 11 = 4 + 11$$

Combine like terms:

$$3n = 15$$

Divide each side by 3:

$$\frac{3n}{3} = \frac{15}{3}$$
$$n = 5$$

Check the solution:

$$\overset{?}{5(5) - 11 = 2(5) + 4}$$
$$\overset{?}{25 - 11 = 14}$$
$$14 = 14 \ \checkmark$$

The answer is E, 5.

TEST-TAKING STRATEGY

If time is running out, try a plug-and-check strategy. Quickly substitute answer choices into the equation to see which one is correct.

EXERCISES FOR EQUATIONS

Solve each equation. Place the corresponding letter in each blank.

A Baseball Term and an Insect's Father

Y	O	L	P	F	M	P	R
0	$\frac{-1}{11}$	7	1	$\frac{-8}{5}$	$\frac{-2}{3}$	-5	$\frac{-5}{8}$

_____ _____ _____

$10n - 5 = 2n + 3$ $-12n + 6 = 7 - n$ $-2(10 + 2n) = 5 + n$

_____ _____ _____

$14 - (-2n) = 6 - 3n$ $7 - n = n - 7$ $6n - 4 = 5n - 4$

SOLUTIONS TO EXERCISES WITH EQUATIONS

$$\underline{P} \quad \underline{O} \quad \underline{P}$$
$$\underline{F} \quad \underline{L} \quad \underline{Y}$$

$$10n - 5 = 2n + 3$$
$$8n = 8$$
$$n = 1:$$ P

$$-12n + 6 = 7 - n$$
$$-11n = 1$$
$$n = \frac{-1}{11}:$$ O

$$-2(10 + 2n) = 5 + n$$
$$-20 - 4n = 5 + n$$
$$-25 = 5n$$
$$-5 = n.$$ P

$$14 - (-2n) = 6 - 3n$$
$$14 + 2n = 6 - 3n$$
$$5n = -8$$
$$n = \frac{-8}{5}:$$ F

$$7 - n = n - 7$$
$$14 = 2n$$
$$7 = n.$$ L

$$6n - 4 = 5n - 4$$
$$n - 4 = -4$$
$$n = 0:$$ Y

Equations with Decimals or Fractions

The CBEST features equations with decimals or fractions. To solve equations containing decimals, follow the basic rules of solving equations.

Sample Problem

Solve for m:

$$0.2m - 11 = 0.05m - 6.5$$

(A) 0.3
(B) 3
(C) 30
(D) 300
(E) 3,000

Isolate the variable on one side of the equation:

$$0.2m - 11 - .05m = .05m - 6.5 - .05m$$

Combine like terms:

$$0.15m - 11 = -6.5$$

Add 11 to both sides:

$$0.15m - 11 + 11 = -6.5 + 11$$

Combine like terms:

$$0.15m = 4.5$$

Divide both sides by 0.15:

$$\frac{0.15m}{0.15} = \frac{4.5}{0.15}$$
$$m = 30$$

The answer is C, 30.

Solving equations with fractions requires using *reciprocals*. The reciprocal of a fraction is found by reversing the numbers in the numerator and the denominator. The product of a fraction and its reciprocal always equals 1.

The following fractions are paired with their reciprocals:

$$\frac{1}{2}, \frac{2}{1} \text{ (or simply 2)} \qquad \frac{3}{5}, \frac{5}{3} \qquad \frac{-8}{9}, \frac{-9}{8}$$

The reciprocal of $3\frac{1}{3}$ is $\frac{3}{10}$ because $3\frac{1}{3} = \frac{10}{3}$ and $\frac{10}{3} \times \frac{3}{10} = 1$.

To solve equations whose coefficients are fractions, multiply both sides by the reciprocal.

Sample Problem

Solve for *n*:

$$\frac{7}{9}n = \frac{14}{27}$$

(A) 3

(B) 2

(C) $\frac{3}{2}$

(D) $\frac{2}{3}$

(E) $\frac{2}{9}$

ANALYSIS

Multiply both sides of the equation by $\frac{9}{7}$, the reciprocal of $\frac{7}{9}$:

$$\left(\frac{9}{7}\right)\left(\frac{7}{9}n\right)=\left(\frac{14}{27}\right)\left(\frac{9}{7}\right)$$

Cross-cancel and multiply:

$$\frac{9}{7}\times\frac{7}{9}n=\frac{\overset{2}{\cancel{14}}}{\underset{3}{\cancel{27}}}\times\frac{\overset{1}{\cancel{9}}}{\underset{1}{\cancel{7}}}$$

$$n=\frac{2}{3}$$

The answer is D, $\frac{2}{3}$.

EXERCISES FOR EQUATIONS WITH FRACTIONS OR DECIMALS

1. $0.4x=-24$

2. $\frac{2}{3}x=12$

3. $2\frac{2}{3}x=1\frac{7}{9}$

4. $7-2.4n=-12+3.6n$

5. $4\frac{1}{5}n-\frac{12}{15}=\frac{1}{5}$

SOLUTIONS FOR EXERCISES WITH FRACTIONS OR DECIMALS

1. $0.4x=-24$

$$\frac{0.4x}{0.4}=\frac{-24}{0.4}$$

$$x=-60$$

2. $$\frac{2}{3}x=12$$

$$\left(\frac{3}{2}\right)\left(\frac{2}{3}x\right)=12\left(\frac{3}{2}\right)$$

$$x=18$$

3. $$2\frac{2}{3}x = 1\frac{7}{9}$$

$$\frac{8}{3}x = \frac{16}{9}$$

$$\frac{3}{8}\left(\frac{8}{3}x\right) = \left(\frac{16}{9}\right)\left(\frac{3}{8}\right)$$

$$x = \frac{2}{3}$$

4. $$7 - 2.4\,n = -12 + 3.6n$$

$$7 - 2.4n + 2.4n = -12 + 3.6n + 2.4n$$

$$7 = -12 + 6n$$

$$7 + 12 = -12 + 6n + 12$$

$$19 = 6n$$

$$\frac{19}{6} = \frac{6n}{6}$$

$$n = \frac{19}{6}$$

5. $$4\frac{1}{5}n - \frac{12}{15} = \frac{1}{5}$$

$$4\frac{1}{5}n - \frac{12}{15} + \frac{12}{15} = \frac{1}{5} + \frac{12}{15}$$

$$4\frac{1}{5}n = 1$$

$$\frac{21}{5}n = 1$$

$$\frac{5}{21}\left(\frac{21}{5}n\right) = 1\left(\frac{5}{21}\right)$$

$$n = \frac{5}{21}$$

Word Problems with Algebra

The CBEST will test your ability to solve word problems using Algebra. The topics are varied but fall into these four categories:

- Relative quantity problems
- Distance problems
- Geometric measurement problems
- Number problems

Regardless of the category, use a four-step strategy when solving word problems:

1. Define the variable.
2. Construct an equation that models the problem.
3. Solve the equation
4. Answer the question

The following are examples of word problems from the four categories.

Relative Quantities

Rachel is eight years older than Karen. The sum of their ages is 42. How old is Rachel?

(A) 17
(B) 24
(C) 25
(D) 42
(E) 59

ANALYSIS

1. Define the variable:

$$\text{Let } x = \text{Karen's age}$$
$$x + 8 = \text{Rachel's age}$$

2. Construct an equation:

$$x + (x + 8) = 42$$

3. Solve the equation:

$$x + (x + 8) = 42$$
$$2x + 8 = 42$$
$$2x = 34$$
$$x = 17$$

4. Answer the question: Rachel's age is $x + 8$. Since $x = 17$, Rachel's age is 25. The answer is C, 25.

TEST-TAKING STRATEGY

Although you must solve for the variable, the solution for the variable is not always the solution to the problem. In this problem, the value for x, 17, is also listed as an answer choice. The question, however, required the value for $x + 8$, which is 25.

Distance Problem

An airplane traveled the 440-mile distance from Bakersfield, California, to Las Vegas, Nevada, in $1\frac{1}{4}$ hours. In miles per hour, what was the airplane's average speed?

(A) 480
(B) 440
(C) 352
(D) 350
(E) 320

ANALYSIS

In distance problems, use the formula rate × time = distance.

1. Define the variable:

$$\text{Let } r = \text{the airplane's average speed}$$

2. Construct an equation:

$$(r)\left(1\frac{1}{4}\right) = 440$$

3. Solve the equation:

$$\left(1\frac{1}{4}\right)(r) = 440$$

$$\frac{5}{4}r = 440$$

$$\left(\frac{4}{5}\right)\left(\frac{5}{4}r\right) = (440)\left(\frac{4}{5}\right)$$

$$r = 352$$

4. Answer the question: Since r is the airplane's average speed, the answer is C, 352 miles per hour.

Geometric Measurement Problem

The length of a rectangle is 4 inches longer than the width. The perimeter of the rectangle is 56 inches. What is the length of the rectangle?

(A) 16
(B) 12
(C) 8
(D) 4
(E) 2

ANALYSIS

Draw a diagram to visualize the problem:

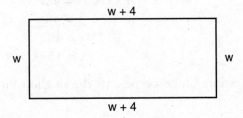

1. Define the variable:

$$\text{Let } w = \text{the rectangle's width}$$
$$w + 4 = \text{the rectangle's length}$$

2. Construct an equation: The perimeter of a rectangle is calculated by adding the two widths and the two lengths.

$$2w + 2(w + 4) = 56$$

3. Solve the equation:

$$2w + 2(w + 4) = 56$$
$$2w + 2w + 8 = 56$$
$$4w + 8 = 56$$
$$4w = 48$$
$$w = 12$$

4. Answer the question: Since the length is 4 inches longer than the width, its measure is $12 + 4 = 16$. The answer is A, 16 inches.

Number Problem

The sum of three consecutive integers is 48. What is the smallest of the three integers?

(A) 14
(B) 15
(C) 16
(D) 17
(E) 18

ANALYSIS

1. Define the variable:

Let x = first consecutive integer
$x + 1$ = second consecutive integer
$x + 2$ = third consecutive integer

2. Construct an equation:

$$x + (x + 1) + (x + 2) = 48$$

3. Solve the equation:

$$x + (x + 1) + (x + 2) = 48$$
$$3x + 3 = 48$$
$$3x = 45$$
$$x = 15$$

4. Answer the question: Since x repesents the smallest integer, the answer is B, 15.

TEST-TAKING STRATEGY

The answer choices on the CBEST are either in ascending or descending order. In the problem above, the answers proceed from least to greatest. Try a plug-and-check strategy and always start with choice C.

Substituting the value of C, 16, we get

$$16 + 17 + 18 \overset{?}{=} 48$$

Since $16 + 17 + 18 > 48$, try B, 15, the next largest number:

$$15 + 16 + 17 \overset{?}{=} 48$$
$$48 = 48 \checkmark$$

EXERCISES FOR WORD PROBLEMS

1. The California Pizza Palace sold 264 pizzas on a particular day. The number of pizzas sold during the day shift exceeded those sold in the evening by 42. How many pizzas were sold during the evening shift?

   (A) 84
   (B) 111
   (C) 153
   (D) 264
   (E) 308

2. Two cars began driving in opposite directions. One car drove 10 miles per hour faster than the other. After 5 hours, the cars were 440 miles apart. What was the speed of the slower car?

   (A) 29 mph
   (B) 39 mph
   (C) 49 mph
   (D) 59 mph
   (E) 69 mph

3. The sides of a certain pentagon are equal in length. The perimeter of the pentagon is equal to the perimeter of a square with side length 5 inches. How long is one of the sides of the pentagon?

   (A) 20
   (B) 15
   (C) 12
   (D) 5
   (E) 4

4. Five times a certain number, increased by 13, is 78. What is the number?

   (A) 78
   (B) 75
   (C) 65
   (D) 26
   (E) 13

SOLUTIONS TO EXERCISES FOR WORD PROBLEMS

1. **(B)**

$$\text{Let } x = \text{pizzas sold during the evening shift}$$
$$x + 42 = \text{pizzas sold during the day shift}$$
$$x + (x + 42) = 264$$
$$2x + 42 = 264$$
$$2x = 222$$
$$x = 111$$

The evening shift sold 111 pizzas.

2. **(B)** Use the formula rate × time = distance.

$$\text{Let } x = \text{speed of the slower car}$$
$$x + 10 = \text{speed of the faster car}$$

Since the slower car's distance is its rate, x, multiplied by its time, 5 hours, its distance is $5x$.

The faster car traveled at a speed of $x + 10$ and its time was also 5 hours. Therefore the faster car's distance was $5(x + 10)$. The sum of the distances was 440.

$$5x + 5(x + 10) = 440$$
$$5x + 5x + 50 = 440$$
$$10x + 50 = 440$$
$$10x = 390$$
$$x = 39$$

The slower car traveled 39 miles per hour.

3. **(E)** The perimeter of the square, 20 inches, is found by adding the four equal sides (or multiplying 5 by 4). A pentagon has five sides.

$$\text{Let } n = \text{one side of the pentagon}$$
$$5n = 20$$
$$n = 4$$

One side of the pentagon measures 4 inches.

4. **(E)**

$$\text{Let } x = \text{the number}$$
$$5x + 13 = 78$$
$$5x = 65$$
$$x = 13$$

The number is 13.

Ratios and Proportions

Each day, people use ratios and proportions in their lives. Speed limits and sale prices are examples of ratios. Using maps and recipes requires knowledge of proportions. The CBEST will probe your knowledge of these concepts.

Ratios

Ratios are mathematical expressions that compare quantities. For example, if Class A has 11 students and Class B has 14 students, the ratio of the students in Class A to Class B is 11 to 14. This ratio can be expressed three ways:

(A) $\dfrac{11}{14}$

(B) $11 : 14$

(C) 11 to 14

ANALYSIS

If Class A had 12 students, the ratio, $\dfrac{12}{14}$, would be expressed in lowest terms:

$$\frac{12}{14} \div \frac{2}{2} = \frac{6}{7}$$

One common use of ratios is found at the supermarket.

Sample Problem

Kyra noticed that a one-pound bag of candy cost $1.60 and a six-ounce bag cost $.90. Which is the better deal?

ANALYSIS

Notice the weights, pounds and ounces, are not the same. To accurately compare prices, choose identical units of weight. Since 1 pound = 16 ounces, rewrite the second ratio as

$$\frac{\$1.60}{1 \text{ lb}} = \frac{\$1.60}{16 \text{ oz}}$$

Now compare ratios:

$$\frac{\$1.60}{16} = \$.10 \text{ per ounce}$$

$$\frac{\$.90}{6} = \$.15 \text{ per ounce}$$

The one-pound bag is the better deal.

EXERCISES FOR RATIOS

State each ratio in simplest form.

1. 3 hours : 36 minutes

2. $$\frac{\$108}{2 \text{ stereo speakers}}$$

3. 1 mile to 8 feet

4. Which is the better deal? What is the ratio of the greater cost to the lesser cost?

Deal #1: $\frac{1}{2}$ gallon of milk for $2.40

Deal #2: 1 cup of milk for $.36

SOLUTIONS TO EXERCISES FOR RATIOS

1. 1 hour = 60 minutes
   3 hours : 36 minutes = 180 minutes : 36 minutes = 5:1

2. $\dfrac{\$108}{2 \text{ speakers}} = \dfrac{54}{1}$

3. 1 mile = 5,280 feet
   1 mile to 8 feet = 5,280 feet to 8 feet = 660 to 1

4. 1 cup = 8 ounces   1 gallon = 128 ounces

$$\frac{\$2.40}{\frac{1}{2} \text{ gallon}} = \frac{\$2.40}{64 \text{ ounces}} = \frac{\$2.40}{8 \text{ cups}}$$

$.30 per cup

Since the single cup serving is $.36, deal # 1 is less expensive.

The ratio of the greater cost to the lesser cost is $\dfrac{36}{30}$, which simplifies to $\dfrac{6}{5}$.

Proportions

When two ratios are equal to each other, the resulting expression is called a *proportion*.

The following are examples of proportions:

$$\frac{1}{2} = \frac{3}{6} \qquad \frac{2}{3} = \frac{10}{15} \qquad \frac{7}{10} = \frac{7,000}{10,000}$$

To verify the equivalence of a proportion, multiply the two outer terms (extremes) and the two inner terms (means). If they are equal, the proportion is correct.

$$\begin{array}{ccc} \text{(Extreme)} & \underline{2} & = & \underline{3} & \text{(Mean)} \\ \text{(Mean)} & 4 & & 6 & \text{(Extreme)} \end{array}$$

$$2 \times 6 = 3 \times 4$$

$$12 = 12$$

Proportions can be used to calculate unknown values.

Sample Problem

The El Centro City Council has planned a street fair for the Spring. Expecting a turnout of 700 people, the city manager authorized spending $12,000 to fund the event. As the day of the street fair approached, it became apparent that the actual turnout would be 1,050 people. How much more money should be authorized to fully fund the event?

(A) $6,000
(B) $9,000
(C) $12,000
(D) $18,000
(E) $24,000

ANALYSIS

Use a proportion to solve this problem.

$$\frac{\text{funding}}{\text{attendees}} : \quad \frac{12,000}{700} = \frac{x}{1,050}$$

Cross-multiply and solve:

$$700x = 12,600,000$$
$$x = 18,000$$

Since $12,000 was already allocated for the street fair, an additional $6,000 will be needed. The answer is A.

EXERCISES FOR PROPORTIONS

Solve each proportion.

1. $\dfrac{8}{15} = \dfrac{40}{x}$

2. $\dfrac{7}{5} = \dfrac{x}{11}$

3. $\dfrac{20}{27} = \dfrac{x}{11}$

4. A man whose height measures 6 feet casts a shadow 7.5 feet. What will be the length of the shadow cast by a nearby flag pole whose height is 20 feet?

5. A map of San Diego County has a scale of 1 inch = 8 miles. If the distance on the map between Spring Valley and Alpine is 4.5 inches, what is the actual distance?

SOLUTIONS FOR EXERCISES FOR PROPORTIONS

1. $\dfrac{8}{15} = \dfrac{40}{x}$

   $8x = 600$

   $x = 75$

2. $\dfrac{7}{5} = \dfrac{x}{11}$

   $77 = 5x$

   $x = \dfrac{77}{5}$ or 15.4

3. $\dfrac{20}{27} = \dfrac{x}{81}$

   $27x = 1,620$

   $x = 60$

4. Use the ratio $\dfrac{\text{height}}{\text{shadow}}$.

   $\dfrac{6}{7.5} = \dfrac{20}{x}$

   $6x = 150$

   $x = 25$

5. Use the ratio $\dfrac{\text{map distance}}{\text{actual distance}}$.

$$\frac{1}{8} = \frac{4.5}{x}$$
$$x = 36$$

PERCENTS

Roughly 15% of CBEST math problems require an understanding of percents. Knowing how to use percentages is an important test-taking skill.

What Is a Percent?

Literally, percent means "part of a hundred." A percent compares quantities as parts of a hundred.

Percents as Proportions

Sample Problem

A history teacher at Chula Vista High School realized that 23 of his 50 students speak both English and Spanish. What percent of his students are bilingual?

ANALYSIS

Percents can be computed as proportions in the form of:

$$\frac{\text{part}}{\text{whole}} = \frac{x}{100}$$

Try this problem as a proportion:

$$\frac{23}{50} = \frac{x}{100}$$

Cross-multiply and set the products equal to each other:

$$\frac{23}{50} = \frac{x}{100}$$
$$50x = 2,300$$

Divide each side by 50 to isolate the variable:

$$\frac{50x}{50} = \frac{2,300}{50}$$
$$x = 46$$

46% of the students in the history teacher's class are bilingual.

Percents as Decimals

The same percentage problem can be performed using decimals instead of fractions. Since 23 of the 50 students are bilingual, divide 23 by 50:

$$50\overline{)23.00} \quad 0.46$$

To convert the decimal, 0.46, into a percent, multiply by 100:

$$0.46 \times 100 = 46\%$$

Note: Once the fraction is converted into a decimal, it may be easier to move the decimal point two places to the right to compute the percentage:

$$0.46 = 46\%$$

EXERCISES FOR PERCENTS AS DECIMALS AND PROPORTIONS

Convert each fraction into a percent. Place the corresponding letter in each blank.

Why is it unkind to calculate an average?

E	T	G	M	H	I	A	N	N
20%	17.5%	26%	6%	83.3%	76%	36%	37.5%	28%

It's a

_____ _____ _____ _____

$\dfrac{3}{50}$ $\dfrac{7}{35}$ $\dfrac{9}{25}$ $\dfrac{3}{8}$

_____ _____ _____ _____ _____

$\dfrac{7}{40}$ $\dfrac{5}{6}$ $\dfrac{19}{25}$ $\dfrac{7}{25}$ $\dfrac{13}{50}$

to do.

SOLUTIONS FOR PERCENTS AS DECIMALS AND PROPORTIONS

It's a

<u>M</u> E A <u>N</u>

<u>T</u> <u>H</u> <u>I</u> N <u>G</u>

to do.

$\dfrac{3}{50} = \dfrac{x}{100}$

$50x = 300$

$x = 6\%$: M

$\dfrac{7}{35} = \dfrac{1}{5}$

$\dfrac{1}{5} = \dfrac{x}{100}$

$5x = 100$

$x = 20\%$: E

$\dfrac{9}{25} = \dfrac{x}{100}$

$25x = 900$

$x = 36\%$: A

$\dfrac{3}{8} = \dfrac{x}{100}$

$8x = 300$

$x = 37.5\%$: N

$\dfrac{7}{40} = 7 \div 40 = 0.175 = 17.5\%$: T

$\dfrac{5}{6} = 5 \div 6 = .833\ldots = 83.\overline{3}\%$: H

$\dfrac{19}{25} = 19 \div 25 = 0.76 = 76\%$: I

$\dfrac{7}{25} = 7 \div 25 = 0.28 = 28\%$: N

$\dfrac{13}{50} = 13 \div 50 = 0.26 = 26\%$: G

Percent Increase and Decrease

Sample Problem

The cost of a gallon of gas in Santa Cruz was $3.20 yesterday. Today, it has soared to $3.80. What percent increase is today's price compared to yesterday's price?

ANALYSIS

To solve this problem, use the formula:

$$\frac{\text{increase in price}}{\text{original price}} = \frac{x}{100}$$

Calculate the increase in price by subtracting yesterday's price from today's price:

$$\$3.80 - \$3.20 = \$.60$$

Place the numbers into the formula:

$$\frac{0.60}{3.20} = \frac{x}{100}$$

Cross-multiply:

$$(0.60)(100) = 3.20x$$
$$60 = 3.20x$$

Solve:

$$\frac{60}{3.20} = \frac{3.20x}{3.20}$$
$$x = 18.75$$

The gas price today has increased 18.75% over its price yesterday.

Sample Problem

McDoogle's Burger Shack has a sale price on double cheesesburgers every Tuesday. Normally $2.00, the Tuesday sale price is $1.25. What percent is the Tuesday discount?

ANALYSIS

We use the following formula to calculate the percent discount:

$$\frac{\text{decrease in price}}{\text{original price}} = \frac{x}{100}$$

Find the decrease in price:

$$\$2.00 - \$1.25 = \$.75$$

Set up a proportion, cross-multiply, and solve:

$$\frac{0.75}{2.00} = \frac{x}{100}$$
$$2x = 75$$
$$x = 37.5$$

The Tuesday discount for a double cheeseburger at McDoogle's is 37.5%.

EXERCISES FOR PERCENTAGE INCREASE AND DECREASE

1. Last year, the Sacramento Kings basketball team shot 1,470 free throws. This year they shot 1,371. To the nearest tenth, what percentage was the decrease in free throws?

   (A) 4.2%
   (B) 6.7%
   (C) 6.8%
   (D) 7.0%
   (E) 9.4%

2. Irish pop star, Angie O'Plasty, just released a CD. Record stores buy the CDs for $9.00 per unit and then sell them for $16.00. To the nearest tenth, what percentage is the store's markup? (Hint: Markup is the difference between the cost and the sale price.)

   (A) 44%
   (B) 52.1%
   (C) 56.3%
   (D) 77.7%
   (E) 77.8%

SOLUTIONS FOR PERCENTAGE INCREASE AND DECREASE

1. **(B)** 6.7%. Find the difference in free throws:

$$1,470 - 1,371 = 99$$

$$\frac{decrease}{original} = \frac{x}{100}$$

Use the 3 divisibility rule:

$$\frac{99}{1470} \div \frac{3}{3} = \frac{33}{490}$$

$$\frac{33}{490} = \frac{x}{100}$$
$$490x = 3,300$$
$$x = 6.73$$

Round to the nearest tenth: 6.7%.

2. **(E)** 77.8%. Find the markup:

$$\$16 - \$9 = \$7$$

$$\frac{\text{increase}}{\text{original}} = \frac{x}{100}$$

$$\frac{7}{9} = \frac{x}{100}$$

$$9x = 700$$

$$x = 77.77...\%$$

Round to the nearest tenth: 77.8%.

Interest Problems

Interest is the money a bank pays for keeping one's money. The *interest rate* is listed as a percentage. Use the formula $I = PRT$, where

> I = interest, the money a bank pays for keeping one's money
> P = principal, the lump sum placed in an account
> R = rate, the interest rate expressed as a percent
> T = time, usually expressed in years

Sample Problem

Wilma Kidslearn, a second-grade teacher, can invest in her school district's Certificate of Deposit (CD) account for a year at a rate of 4.3%. She can also invest at her local bank at a rate of 7.1%, but for only 9 months. Wilma has $1,575 to invest. Which investment is more lucrative? How much more will she earn with the better investment?

ANALYSIS

Using the formula $I = PRT$, compare the two investments:

> School Account : $I = 0.1575 \times 0.043 \times 1 = \$67.73$
> Local bank investment: $1575 \times 0.071 \times 0.75 = \$83.87$

Subtract the smaller return from the larger return:

$$\$83.87 - \$67.73 = \$16.14$$

Wilma will earn more with the investment at her local bank. She will earn $16.14 more from the local bank CD than from her school district's CD.

Notice how much easier it was to express the percentages as decimals rather than as fractions. Would it have been preferable to multiply 1,575 by $\frac{43}{1,000}$ and $\frac{71}{1,000}$?

Also, whenever time is presented in terms of months, it must be reexpressed as years. Wilma could only invest in the bank CD for 9 months. Since there are 12 months in a year, place $\frac{9}{12}$, or $\frac{3}{4}$, into the interest formula. It is often easier to express that fraction as a decimal ($\frac{3}{4} = .75$).

EXERCISES FOR INTEREST PROBLEMS

1. $I = ?$
   $P = \$1,800$
   $R = 4.5\%$
   $T = 1.5$ years

2. $I = \$105$
   $P = \$437.50$
   $R = 8\%$
   $T = ?$

3. $I = \$240$
   $P = ?$
   $R = 15\%$
   $T = 4$

4. Pham wants to earn at least $250 in interest this year. If she invests $1,500 at 9.5% for 10 months, will she reach her goal?

SOLUTIONS FOR INTEREST PROBLEMS

1. $I = PRT$
   $I = 1,800(0.045)(1.5)$
   $I = \$121.50$

2. $I = PRT$
   $105 = (437.50)(0.08)(T)$
   $105 = 35T$
   $3 = T$

3. $I = PRT$
   $240 = P(0.15)\ (4)$
   $240 = 0.6P$
   $\$400 = P$

4. Pham will not reach her goal.
   $I = PRT$
   $I = (1,500)(.095)(0.83)$
   $I = \$118.75$

Fractions, Percents, and Decimals

There are usually a few problems on the CBEST that require converting percents into fractions and decimals.

Sample Problem

Arrange the following from least to greatest:

$$\frac{2}{7}, 31\%, 0.26, 2.4 , \frac{5}{8}$$

(A) $31\%, 0.26, \frac{2}{7}, \frac{5}{8}, 2.4$

(B) $\frac{2}{7}, 2.4, .26, 31\%, \frac{5}{8}$

(C) $2.4, \frac{2}{7}, 0.26, \frac{5}{8}, 31\%$

(D) $0.26, \frac{2}{7}, 31\%, \frac{5}{8} , 2.4$

(E) $31\%, \frac{2}{7}, 0.26, \frac{5}{8}, 2.4$

ANALYSIS

It is difficult to compare percentages to fractions and decimals. The quickest way to perform this problem is to convert each of the numbers into decimals:

$$\frac{2}{7} = 0.286$$

$$31\% = 0.31$$

$$0.26 = 0.26$$

$$2.4 = 2.4$$

$$\frac{5}{8} = 0.625$$

The correct order becomes obvious:

$$0.26, \frac{2}{7}, 31\%, \frac{5}{8}, 2.4$$

The correct answer is D.

TEST-TAKING STRATEGY

Use E&E to reduce choices. Decide which of the values are greater than $\frac{1}{2}$ and which ones are smaller. Since $\frac{5}{8}$ and 2.4 are more than $\frac{1}{2}$ while the rest are less than $\frac{1}{2}$, any answer choice that does not have $\frac{5}{8}$ and 2.4 in the last two places can

be ignored. Choices B and C can quickly be eliminated.

Memorizing a few conversions will pay dividends when taking the CBEST. The following chart will be helpful.

Fraction	Percentage	Decimal
$\frac{1}{100}$	1%	0.01
$\frac{1}{50}$	2%	0.02
$\frac{1}{25}$	4%	0.04
$\frac{1}{20}$	5%	0.05
$\frac{1}{10}$	10%	0.1
$\frac{1}{9}$	11.11 . . . %	0.11 . . .
$\frac{1}{8}$	12.5%	0.125
$\frac{1}{6}$	16.66 . . . %	0.166 . . .
$\frac{1}{5}$	20%	0.20
$\frac{1}{4}$	25%	0.25
$\frac{1}{3}$	33.33 . . . %	0.333 . . .
$\frac{1}{2}$	50%	0.50
$\frac{1}{1}$	100%	1.0

Use this table to quickly figure out other values.

Sample Problem

Convert $\frac{5}{8}$ to a percent.

ANALYSIS

Since $\frac{1}{8}$ is 12.5%, multiply 12.5% by 5 to get 62.5%.

EXERCISES FOR FRACTIONS, PERCENTAGES, AND DECIMALS

Arrange from least to greatest.

1. $\frac{5}{7}$, 0.68, $\frac{2}{3}$, 71%, 0.814

2. $\frac{8}{5}$, $2\frac{2}{3}$, 147%, 1.717, $\frac{7}{11}$

3. In 2006, teachers were encouraged to ensure their students passed the California High School Exit Exam (CAHSEE). A three-day excursion to Ensenada, Baja California, was promised to the teacher who garnered the highest pass rate. The top three finishers achieved these pass rates:

   Teacher A: $\frac{11}{16}$ of the class passed

   Teacher B: 0.69 of the class passed
   Teacher C: 74.2% of the class passed.

   Which teacher went to Ensenada?

SOLUTIONS FOR FRACTIONS, PERCENTAGES, AND DECIMALS

1. Convert each number into a decimal:

   $\frac{5}{7} = 0.714$

   $0.68 = 0.68$

   $\frac{2}{3} = 0.66\ldots$

   $71\% = 0.71$

   $0.814 = 0.814$

   $0.66\ldots, 0.68, 0.71, 0.714, 0.814$

   $\frac{2}{3}, 0.68, 71\%, \frac{5}{7}, 0.814$

2. Convert each number into a decimal:

$$\frac{8}{5} = 1.6$$

$$2\frac{2}{3} = 2.66\ldots$$

$$147\% = 1.47$$

$$1.717 = 1.717$$

$$\frac{7}{11} = 0.6363\ldots$$

$$0.6363\ldots, 1.47, 1.6, 1.717, 2.66\ldots$$

$$\frac{7}{11}, 147\%, \frac{8}{5}, 1.717, 2\frac{2}{3}$$

3. Convert each number into a decimal:

$$\frac{11}{16} = 0.6875$$

$$0.69 = 0.69$$

$$74.2\% = 0.742$$

Teacher C wins the trip to Ensenada.

STATISTICS AND PROBABILITY

The CBEST will test your ability to analyze statistics and compute probability. Test-takers are not expected to have advanced knowledge in these areas.

Statistics

A batting average and a semester grade are familiar examples of statistics. Other statistical concepts that appear on the CBEST include the median, mode, and range.

The Mean

The mean, or average, is the sum of a series of numbers divided by the number of terms. Each semester, students receive grades based on their averages.

Sample Problem

Sally has received grades of 85, 68, and 99 on her last three tests. What is her average grade?

(A) 72
(B) 78
(C) 83
(D) 84
(E) 88

ANALYSIS

Find Sally's average grade by adding the scores and dividing the sum by 3:

$$85 + 68 + 99 = 252$$
$$252 \div 3 = 84$$

The answer is D, 84.

The Median

The median is the middle term in a set of numbers that have been arranged in ascending or descending order. In the group of consecutive integers (−2, −1, 0, 1, 2), 0, is the median because 0 is the middle term. If two terms are in the middle, the average of those terms is the median.

Sample Problem

The temperatures in Redondo Beach during the first six days in July were as follows:

7/1 : 84   7/2 : 88   7/3: 76   7/4 : 78   7/5 : 86   7/6: 80

What was the median temperature for that time period?

(A) 76
(B) 79
(C) 80
(D) 82
(E) 83

ANALYSIS

Find the middle term by arraying the numbers from least to greatest:

76, 78, 80, 84, 86, 88

Since there are two terms in the middle, 80 and 84, find their mean:

$$80 + 84 = 164$$
$$164 \div 2 = 82$$

The answer is D, 82.

The Mode

The mode of a set of numbers is the term that appears most frequently. There can be more than one mode in a set of data.

Sample Problem

The temperatures in Redondo Beach for the first ten days of July were as follows:

7/1 : 84   7/2 : 88   7/3 : 76   7/4 : 78   7/5 : 86
7/6 : 80   7/7 : 78   7/8 : 84   7/9: 80   7/10 : 84

What is the mode of these temperatures?

(A) 76
(B) 78
(C) 80
(D) 82
(E) 84

ANALYSIS

Arrange the data from least to greatest:

76   78   78   80   80   84   84   84   86   88

Since 84 appears the most frequently, it is the mode. The answer is E.

The Range

The range of a set of data is the difference between the highest and lowest values. In the problem above, the lowest temperature was 76 while the highest was 88. To find the range, subtract 76 from 88:

$$88 - 76 = 12$$

The range of the temperatures was 12.

EXERCISE FOR MEAN, MEDIAN, MODE, AND RANGE

Mr. Tanaka, the AP U.S. history teacher, gave his students a mock AP exam. The scores were as follows:

74   68   90   84   86   80   42   79   68   83

What were the mean, median, mode, and range of the scores in his class?

SOLUTIONS FOR MEAN, MEDIAN, MODE, AND RANGE

Array the data from least to greatest:

42   68   68   74   79   80   83   84   86   90

To find the mean, add the numbers and divide by 10:

$$(42 + 68 + 68 + 74 + 79 + 80 + 83 + 84 + 86 + 90) \div 10 = 75.4$$

The median is the number in the middle. Since there are two numbers in the middle, find their mean:

$$(79 + 80) \div 2 = 79.5$$

The mode is the value that occurs most frequently. Since 68 occurs most frequently, 68 is the mode.

The range is the lowest score subtracted from the highest score:

$$90 - 42 = 48$$

Interpreting Data from Charts

The CBEST will test your ability to assess data provided in charts and tables. No more than two questions will refer to any particular data set.

Sample Problem

Elinor was preparing for the big swim meet with cross-town rival, Eureka High School. Her times for the 100-yard freestyle were as follows:

Date	Time (in seconds)
3/1	60
3/2	58.6
3/2	59.4
3/3	57.1
3/5	55.8
3/6	55

(A) What was the percent decrease between Elinor's time on 3/1 and 3/6?

(B) What is the difference between Elinor's shortest time and her mean time?

ANALYSIS

Elinor's 3/1 time was 60 seconds. Her 3/6 time was 55 seconds. To find the percentage decrease, use the formula:

$$\frac{\text{decrease}}{\text{original}} = \frac{x}{100}$$

$$60 - 55 = 5$$

$$\frac{5}{60} = \frac{1}{12} = \frac{x}{100}$$

$$100 = 12x$$

$$8.33... = x$$

Elinor's time decreased by 8.3%.

To find the difference between Elinor's shortest time and her mean time, find the mean of the values:

$$(60 + 58.6 + 59.4 + 57.1 + 55.8 + 55) \div 6 = 57.65$$

Subtract 55 from the mean time:

$$57.65 - 55 = 2.65$$

The difference between Elinor's mean time and her shortest time was 2.65 seconds.

Stanine Scores

When you graduated from college, were you number one in your class? Were you in the top 10%? Top quarter? These are various ways to rank students according to their levels of achievement. Another way to rank students is according to a *stanine score.* Short for "standard nine," the stanine system ranks students into nine categories. For example, a student whose test scores ranked in stanine 7 has better scores than a student whose stanine rank is 5. Stanine scores rate the bottom 4% of a data set as a stanine of 1, the next 7% as a stanine of 2, and so on. Review the table below to find the distribution of stanine scores.

Percentage:	4%	7%	12%	17%	20%	17%	12%	7%	4%
Stanine:	1	2	3	4	5	6	7	8	9

Students who scored in stanine 5 are viewed as being in the median range of scores. All other scores are either above or below the median.

Sample Problem

When Josh received his CAHSEE score, he noticed his stanine score was 7. What can Josh conclude about his performance on the CAHSEE?

(A) He scored 77.7% on the CAHSEE.
(B) Only two students earned a higher score than he.
(C) A stanine score of 7 and 3 mean the same thing.
(D) He scored in the top half of all test-takers.
(E) A score in stanine 7 is the highest possible score.

ANALYSIS

Scores in stanine 5 represent the median, or middle, range of scores. Since Josh scored in stanine 7, he can conclude that his score fell within the top half of all test-takers. The answer is D.

Probability

There will be some questions on the CBEST that test your knowledge of probability. The types of probability problems fall into two categories, counting problems and outcome problems.

Counting Problems

Counting problems require the test-taker to assess the number of possible combinations available, given certain data. Meal choices and wardrobe selections are typical subjects of such questions.

Sample Problem

Jimmy enjoys the sandwich selection at his favorite restaurant. The restaurant features roast beef, turkey, or pastrami sandwiches. Each sandwich comes with a choice of the following side orders: french fries, cole slaw, or potato salad. In addition, the meal comes with a drink. The beverage choices are soft drinks or coffee. How many different combinations of sandwich, side order, and beverage are available to Jimmy?

ANALYSIS

This problem can be illustrated by using a tree diagram to show the combinations:

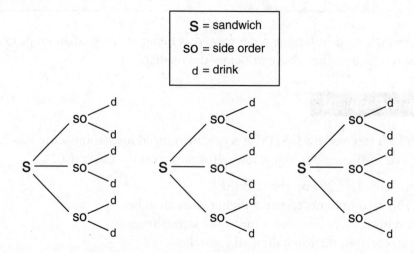

The quickest way to solve this problem, however, is to multiply the number of sandwich choices by the number of side orders and beverages:

$$3 \text{ (sandwiches)} \times 3 \text{ (side orders)} \times 2 \text{ (beverages)} = 18 \text{ combinations}$$

Outcome Problems

Outcome problems assess your ability to compute the likelihood of a certain outcome occurring, given a data set. All probabilities are expressed as some number that is greater than or equal to 0 and less than or equal to 1 ($0 \leq x \leq 1$).

To solve an outcome problem, use the following ratio:

$$\frac{\text{favorable outcomes}}{\text{all outcomes}}$$

Sample Problem

Hank has 3 white socks, 4 black socks, and 5 brown socks in his drawer. If he draws a sock at random, what is the probability it will be brown or white?

ANALYSIS

Since the favorable outcomes include brown or white socks, find the number of each:

brown socks = 5
white socks = 3
all socks = 12

$$\frac{\text{favorable outcomes}}{\text{all outcomes}} = \frac{5+3}{12} = \frac{8}{12} = \frac{2}{3}$$

There is a $\frac{2}{3}$ probability that Hank will draw a brown or white sock.

EXERCISES FOR PROBABILITY

1. Sheila has 7 blouses, 6 skirts, and 5 pairs of shoes. How many different combinations of blouses, skirts, and shoes does she have?

2. A pair of dice, each with six sides, is rolled. What is the probability that the sum of the dice will be a prime number?

SOLUTIONS FOR EXERCISES FOR PROBABILITY

1. 210 combinations.

   7 (blouses) × 6 (skirts) × 5 (pairs of shoes) = 210

2. 5/12. There are 12 different outcomes possible when a pair of dice are rolled. Between 2 and 12 (the sum of two die cannot be 1), the prime numbers are 2, 3, 5, 7, and 11. Remember, 2 is the only even prime number.

   $$\frac{\text{favored outcomes}}{\text{all outcomes}} = \frac{5}{12}$$

"ENOUGH INFORMATION" AND PROCESS PROBLEMS

If you drove for 6 hours, what time did you arrive at your destination? Common sense indicates you could calculate your arrival time if you knew your departure time. For example, if you left at 8:00 A.M. and drove for 6 hours, your arrival time would be 2:00 P.M. The departing time was the missing information needed to answer the question. There will be several problems on the CBEST that ask you to conclude what constitutes "enough information" to solve a problem. Further, there will be similar problems that require you to identify the process necessary to answer a particular question.

"Enough Information" Problems

The fastest way to correctly answer an "enough information" problem is to draw on your common sense. In the problem above, common sense indicated a departure time was needed to calculate the arrival time. In these types of problems, try to step back and assess what additional information is needed.

Sample Problem

Starting at 7 A.M., Amy ran 6 miles at an average rate of 7 minutes per mile. She then biked for another 6 miles and went home. At what time did she arrive at her home?

What additional information is necessary to answer this question?

(A) The time she began the bike portion of her trip.
(B) The weather conditions that day.
(C) Her level of fatigue during the last two miles of the bike portion of the trip.
(D) Her departure time.
(E) The average speed she traveled on her bike.

ANALYSIS

Draw on your common sense as each answer choice is considered.

Choice A is incorrect. Amy's bike portion of the trip began after she finished running. Since her running rate was 7 minutes per mile, it can be concluded she began the bike portion 42 minutes into the trip, or at 7:42 A.M. We still do not know, however, how long the bike portion lasted.

Choice B is incorrect. There is no information in this problem to indicate that weather conditions impeded any part of her traveling.

Choice C is incorrect. Any fatigue would have been factored into her average rate of speed. She may have started quickly and slowed somewhat due to fatigue. However, her average rate for the first 6 miles was 7 minutes per mile.

Choice D is incorrect. Her departure time, 7 A.M., was given in the problem.

Choice E is correct. If it was known, for example, that the average speed Amy traveled on her bike was 15 miles per hour (or 4 minutes per mile), we could make the following calculations:

At 7 A.M., Amy began her trip. She ran six 7-minute miles which took her 42 minutes. She biked for six 4-minute miles, which took her 24 minutes. Add the two times together to get 66 minutes. 66 minutes after 7:00 A.M. is 8:06 A.M.

Process Problems

Most of the problems on the CBEST require you to calculate an answer. In some problems, the answer is the calculation.

Sample Problem

Sabrina was showing her brother how to solve a percent problem. To find 17% of 673, she showed him the following calculation:

$$673 \times \frac{17}{100}$$

What would have been another way to calculate this problem?

(A) 673×1.7

(B) $673 \div \dfrac{17}{100}$

(C) $673 \div 0.17$

(D) 673×0.17

(E) $673 + 17$

ANALYSIS

Of means multiply. 17% also equals 0.17. Therefore, another calculation that could be used would be 673×0.17. The answer is D, 673×0.17.

Some process problems are more complex.

Sample Problem:

Jake bought 4 Hawaiian shirts for $15 each. The next day he returned to the store, exchanged the shirts for 3 others that were on sale for $11. Anticipating how much his refund would be, he used the calculation:

$$(4 \times 15) - (3 \times 11)$$

What other calculation could he have used?

(A) $3(15 - 11) + 15$

(B) $3(15 - 11) + 11$

(C) $(15 + 11) \times 3$

(D) $4(15 - 11) + 3$

(E) $3(15 - 11) + 4$

ANALYSIS

Choice A implies that Jake would receive triple the difference between the costs of the shirts plus the entire cost of one of the more expensive shirts. The answer is A.

TEST-TAKING STRATEGY

Don't waste too much time on this problem if the answer is not apparent. Jake's initial calculation was correct, so his refund should have been:

$$(4 \times 15) - (3 \times 11) = \$27$$

The correct answer should also equal 27. Since the numbers in this problem are not very large, quickly calculate which alternative also equals 27. In choice A, $3(15 - 11) + 15 = 27$.

EXERCISES FOR "ENOUGH INFORMATION" AND PROCESS PROBLEMS

1. Ervin needs to drive from Long Beach to Santa Barbara which is 95 miles away. If gasoline costs $2.89 per gallon, how much will the trip cost him?

   What additional information is necessary to answer the question?

   (A) Weather conditions the day of the trip
   (B) The number of gallons of gasoline his car holds
   (C) The time needed to travel 95 miles
   (D) The number of miles his car can travel on a gallon of gasoline
   (E) The cost of a gallon of gasoline

2. Steve had $97.00 in his bank account. He withdrew $45.00 from the account, all in $5 and $10 denominations.

   Which of the following facts can be concluded from the information above?

   (A) The number of $5 bills Steve received
   (B) The number of $10 bills Steve received
   (C) Steve's bank balance after the withdrawal
   (D) The sum of the number of $5 and $10 bills Steve received
   (E) The withdrawal fee charged by the bank

3. Denise has to divide $7\frac{2}{3}$ yards of saltwater taffy among the 27 students in her third-grade class. She uses the calculation:

$$7\frac{2}{3} \div 27$$

   What other calculation could she have used?

   (A) $\frac{23}{3} \times 27$

   (B) $27 \div 7\frac{2}{3}$

   (C) $7\frac{2}{3} \times \frac{1}{27}$

   (D) 8×30
   (E) $27 \div 7$

"ENOUGH INFORMATION" AND PROCESS PROBLEM SOLUTIONS

1. **(D)** Suppose Ervin's car could travel 19 miles for every gallon of gasoline. He would divide 95, his distance, by 19 to get the number of gallons he needs for the trip. He then could multiply that number by $2.89, the cost of a gallon of gas, to find his cost for the trip.

2. **(C)** Since Steve had $97.00 in his account and withdrew $45.00, it can be concluded that he had $52.00 remaining in his account.

3. **(C)** To divide a number by a fraction, multiply by the reciprocal (invert and multiply):

$$7\frac{2}{3} \div 27 = 7\frac{2}{3} \div \frac{27}{1} = 7\frac{2}{3} \times \frac{1}{27}$$

MEASUREMENT AND PERIMETER

The successful CBEST-taker must demonstrate an understanding of units of measurement. Converting minutes to seconds, for example, is an important test-taking skill. This section will discuss units of measure as they pertain to the CBEST. A discussion of geometric shapes and perimeter will follow.

Measurement

Each day, people are faced with units of measure. Arriving on time for an 8:00 AM class demands wise use of time. Purchasing two pounds of tomatoes requires knowledge of weight. The following areas of measurement will appear in problems on the CBEST:

- Time

- Weight

- Fluid measures

- Distance

CBEST-takers are only responsible for knowing U.S. standard measures. Liters, meters, and other metric measures will not appear on the test.

Units of Measure

Time
52 weeks = 1 year
12 months = 1 year
1 week = 7 days
1 day = 24 hours
1 hour = 60 minutes
1 minute = 60 seconds

Weight
1 ton = 2,000 pounds
1 pound = 16 ounces

Fluid Measures
1 gallon = 4 quarts	1 gallon = 128 ounces
1 quart = 2 pints	1 quart = 32 ounces
1 pint = 2 cups	1 pint = 16 ounces
1 cup = 8 ounces	

Distance Measures
1 mile = 5,280 feet	
1 yard = 3 feet	1 yard = 36 inches
1 foot = 12 inches	

Measurement Conversions

There are two rules for converting units of measure:

- When converting larger units into smaller units, use multiplication.

- When converting smaller units into larger units, use division.

Sample Problem

How many feet equal $10\frac{1}{2}$ yards?

(A) $13\frac{1}{2}$

(B) 30

(C) $30\frac{1}{2}$

(D) 31

(E) $31\frac{1}{2}$

ANALYSIS

This question requires converting larger units, yards, into smaller units, feet. Since the conversion proceeds from larger units to smaller units, use multiplication:

$$1 \text{ yard} = 3 \text{ feet}$$

$$10\frac{1}{2} \times 3 = 31\frac{1}{2} \text{ feet}$$

The answer is choice E.

Sample Problem

How many minutes are equal to 3,780 seconds?

(A) 226,800
(B) 3,780
(C) 63
(D) 62
(E) 18

ANALYSIS

Answering this question requires converting smaller units, seconds, into larger units, minutes. Therefore, use division to arrive at the correct solution:

$$1 \text{ minute} = 60 \text{ seconds}$$
$$3,780 \div 60 = 63$$

The answer is choice C.

EXERCISES FOR MEASUREMENT CONVERSION

1. 17 inches equal how many feet?

   (A) 3
   (B) $2\frac{11}{12}$
   (C) $1\frac{7}{12}$
   (D) $1\frac{5}{12}$
   (E) $1\frac{1}{2}$

2. Janet needs to arrive at an appointment by 10:00 A.M. Prior to the appointment, she will go to the gym for 70 minutes. The drive to the appointment lasts 22 minutes. What time should she arrive at the gym?

   (A) 8:22
   (B) 8:24
   (C) 8:26
   (D) 8:28
   (E) 9:00

3. What unit is most suited to measure the weight of a bag of cement?

   (A) Pounds
   (B) Ounces
   (C) Tons
   (D) Feet
   (E) Quarts

4. How many yards are in 2 miles?

   (A) 760
   (B) 1,760
   (C) 2,760
   (D) 3,200
   (E) 3,520

SOLUTIONS TO EXERCISES FOR MEASUREMENT CONVERSION

1. **(D)** Use division to convert smaller units into larger:

$$17 \div 12 = 1\frac{5}{12}$$

2. **(D)** Add the length, in minutes, of the gym visit and the drive:

$$\begin{array}{r} 70 \text{ minutes} \\ +22 \text{ minutes} \\ \hline 92 \text{ minutes} \end{array}$$

Convert minutes to hours:

$$1 \text{ hour} = 60 \text{ minutes}$$
$$92 \div 60 = 1 \text{ hour } 32 \text{ minutes}$$

Subtract 1 hour 32 minutes from 10:00

10 hour 0 minutes		9 hours 60 minutes
−1 hour 32 minutes	=	−1 hour 32 minutes
		8 hours 28 minutes or 8:28

3. **(A)** Choices D and E can be eliminated as they are not measures of weight. The weight of a bag of cement may be the same as the weight of a small child. Using pounds as a unit of measure is appropriate for humans and bags of cement.

4. **(E)** Find the number of feet in 2 miles:

$$1 \text{ mile} = 5{,}280 \text{ feet}$$
$$2 \times 5{,}280 = 10{,}560$$

Divide 10,560 by 3, the number of feet in a yard:

$$10{,}560 \div 3 = 3{,}520$$

Perimeter

The perimeter of a figure is the distance measured around that figure. A fence, for example, demarcates the perimeter of the field it surrounds. There will be a few perimeter problems on the CBEST.

Sample Problem

What is the perimeter of a square with a side measuring 12 feet?

(A) 12
(B) 24
(C) 36
(D) 48
(E) 144

A square has 4 equal sides. Calculate the perimeter by multiplying a side length, 12, by 4:

$$12 \times 4 = 48$$

The answer is choice D, 48.

The successful CBEST-taker should be familiar with a few geometry terms.

Lines and Line Segments

A line is a figure that connects two points. A line extends infinitely in two directions.

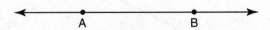

The figure above can be represented as $\overleftrightarrow{AB}$ or $\overleftrightarrow{BA}$.

A line segment also connects two points but has definite endpoints.

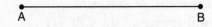

The figure above can be represented as $\overline{AB}$ or $\overline{BA}$.

Rays

A ray is a figure that connects two points. Unlike a line or a line segment, a ray has *one* endpoint.

The above figure can be represented as $\overrightarrow{AB}$. It *cannot* be represented as $\overrightarrow{BA}$.

Collinear and Noncollinear Points

Collinear points are three or more points that lie on the same line.

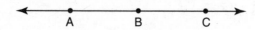

Noncollinear points are three or more points that do not lie on the same line.

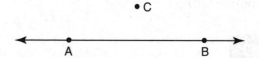

Planes

Planes are figures that extend infinitely in two directions. A minimum of three non-collinear points are needed to determine a plane.

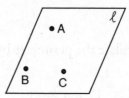

The figure above can be represented as plane *l* or plane *ABC*.

Angles

Two rays that share a common endpoint form an angle. In the figure below, ray $\overrightarrow{AB}$ and $\overrightarrow{AC}$ form an angle.

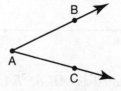

The figure above can be represented as $\angle BAC$ or $\angle CAB$. Point *A*, the point in the middle, is referred to as the vertex of the angle.

Three types of angles will appear on the CBEST:

- **Obtuse angles**: Obtuse angles have measures less than 180° but greater than 90°. ∠*DEF* is an obtuse angle.

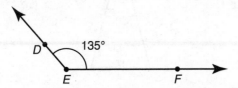

- **Right angles**: Right angles measure exactly 90°. ∠MPR is a right angle.

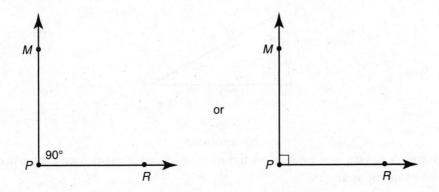

or

- **Acute angles**: Acute angles measure less than 90° but greater than 0°. ∠*STU* is an acute angle.

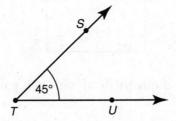

Polygons

CBEST-takers need to be familiar with certain geometric shapes. The general term for these shapes is polygon which literally means "many sides."

    Triangle: A triangle is a series of segments connecting three noncollinear points. Triangles can be categorized by their side lengths:

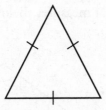

Equilateral
Three equal sides

Isosceles
Two equal sides

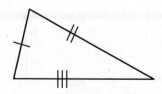

Scalene
No equal sides

Square: A square is a four-sided figure (also called a quadrilateral) with equal sides and four right angles.

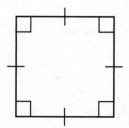

Rectangle: A rectangle is a quadrilateral with two pairs of equal sides and four right angles.

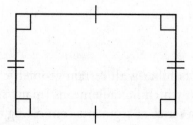

Regular polygon: A regular polygon is a figure with a minimum of three sides whose sides and angles have equal measures. Below are some regular polygons that may appear on the CBEST:

Pentagon: A five-sided figure

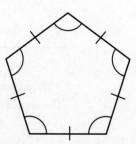

Hexagon: A six-sided figure

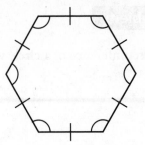

Octagon: An eight-sided figure

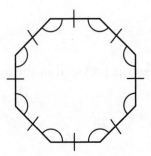

Circles and Circumference

Review the following diagram.

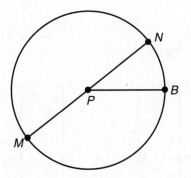

Point P is called the *center* of the circle. The expression ⊙ *P* refers to a circle with a center *P*.

$\overline{MN}$ is called a *diameter* of the circle. A diameter is a segment that passes through the center of the circle. The endpoints of a diameter lie on the circle.

$\overline{PB}$ is called a *radius* of the circle. A radius is a segment with one endpoint at the circle's center and the other on the circle.

The measure around a circle is called the *circumference*. There are two formulas available to calculate the circumference of a circle:

$$2 \times \pi \times \text{radius } (2\pi r)$$

or

$$\pi \times \text{diameter } (\pi D)$$

The symbol π (pronounced PIE) is approximately equal to 3.14 or $\frac{22}{7}$.

> **Sample Problem**

What is the circumference of a circle with a diameter measuring 4 feet?

(A) 11
(B) 12
(C) 12.56
(D) 12.65
(E) 13.15

ANALYSIS

Since the diameter is provided in the problem, use the formula πD:

$$3.14 \times 4 = 12.56$$

The answer is C, 12.56.

Challenging Perimeter Problems

Some of the perimeter problems require deducing measures not explicitly given.

> **Sample Problem**

Find the perimeter of the figure below:

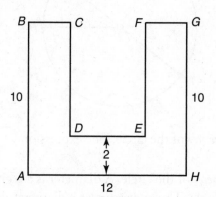

(A) 120
(B) 60
(C) 30
(D) 15
(E) 12

ANALYSIS

Note that the measures $\overline{BC}$, $\overline{DE}$, $\overline{FG}$, $\overline{CD}$, and $\overline{FE}$ are not provided in the figure. Each, however, can be deduced from the information available. For example, the sum of the lengths of $\overline{BC}$, $\overline{DE}$, and $\overline{FG}$ are equal to the length of $\overline{AH}$, which is 12. $\overline{CD}$ and $\overline{FE}$ must each equal 8 since both are 2 less than $\overline{BA}$, which is 10.

Add the missing segments and calculate the perimeter:

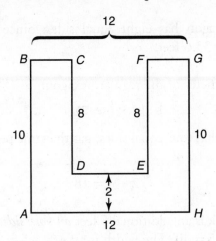

$$10 + 12 + 8 + 8 + 10 + 12 = 60$$

The answer is B, 60.

EXERCISES FOR PERIMETERS

1. A regular octagon has a side length measuring 4.2 feet. What is its perimeter?

   (A) 33.6
   (B) 33
   (C) 32.6
   (D) 32
   (E) 30

2. A square and a regular hexagon have equal perimeters. If the length of one side of the hexagon is 12, what is the length of the side of the square?

   (A) 6
   (B) 12
   (C) 15
   (D) 18
   (E) 21

3. A swimming pool is 30 feet long and 12 feet wide. Surrounding the pool is a patio deck whose width measures 5 feet. What is the perimeter of the outside of the patio deck?

   (A) 84
   (B) 96
   (C) 104
   (D) 124
   (E) 480

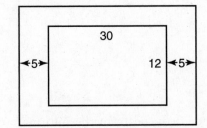

SOLUTIONS TO EXERCISES FOR PERIMETERS

1. **(A)** A regular octagon has eight equal sides. Since each side is 4.2 feet, multiply $8 \times 4.2 = 33.6$ feet.

2. **(D)** Find the perimeter of the regular hexagon:

$$12 \times 6 = 72$$

The square, which has four equal sides, has the same perimeter as the hexagon. Therefore, divide 72 by 4:

$$72 \div 4 = 18$$

3. **(D)** The patio deck is an additional 5 feet *on both sides*. Thus, the patio's deck length is $30 + 5 + 5 = 40$. The width is $12 + 5 + 5 = 22$.

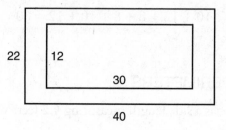

$$40 + 40 + 22 + 22 = 124$$

CHAPTER 7

WRITING SECTION REVIEW

Writing Section Review

In the third section of the CBEST, you are required to write two essays to demonstrate that you can clearly and logically express yourself in writing. By taking less time for the reading and math sections or by taking the CBEST in multiple test sessions, test-takers can have more than 60–90 minutes to write these two essays. However, if you intend to sit for the test only once and finish all three sections, you must prepare yourself to write two good essays in about 30–45 minutes each. (These strategies will also help if you are planning to take the new CSET for Multiple Subjects writing subtest. In this chapter, you will find

1. Strategies to maximize your essay planning and writing time

2. Specific qualities that the scorers will look for

3. Tips on how to write with those qualities

4. Explanation of the grading scale used by the essay scorers

5. Examples of papers that illustrate the grading scale

6. Sample practice topics

As a prospective California or Oregon public school employee, you undoubtedly know how important it is for students to be able to communicate well.

Understanding the qualities of clear and effective written communication is a big part of being able to teach those skills to students.

Take a look at this part of the CBEST from a new perspective. If *you* were scoring the following essay, what score would you assign it? As mentioned in Chapter 1, essays receive scores of 4 (pass), 3 (marginal pass), 2 (marginal fail), 1 (fail), and 0 (nothing written). Details will be presented later, but essentially, the essay scorers look for

- Clarity (The paper is understandable and logical.)
- Focus (The paper maintains its focus on the main point being explained.)

- Development (The paper has substance; it has reasoning, supporting details, and examples.)

- Correctness (The paper is written in conventional English.)

Given this background, read and assign a score (4, 3, 2, or 1) to Essay #1.

PROMPT

"Freedom is like steam, useless unless confined," according to Woodrow T. Wilson. To what extent do you agree or disagree with his observation? Provide specific reasoning and examples in defense of your position.

Essay #1

The idea expressed by former president Woodrow Wilson that "freedom is like steam, useless unless contained" is very true. This idea can be verified by examination of our life cycle. We might be born free, and perhaps remain entirely free for a very short while, but as we age we become more productive and fulfilled as we negotiate limitations, as we are "contained."

Never are we more free then we are as young children. Most societies and socioeconomic classes are very tolerant of the natural behaviors of young children. Children vocalize when they are uncomfortable, hungry, or bored, and their needs are met. Slightly older children may express displeasure by crying or hitting or biting and still they are not harshly dealt with (at least at first). This is like the uncontained steam—except to the single child, it has no use and can be, in fact, harmful to others.

There comes a time when children must learn to live and work within a group. By the time children are school aged, they are expected to know certain rules of etiquette such as saying "please" and "thank you," not interrupting conversations, showing restraint when they are angry or upset, and generally being respectful of others, especially adults.

As teens and young adults, people become more familiar with the possibilities within their constraints. By this stage, people are familiar with a system of morals, laws, and social system. These systems place limits on the behaviors of those who live under them. We have justice built right into our legal system so that even those who would not let morals guide them must abide by the rules (laws) or pay the price. Laws limit how fast we can drive, ordinances limit how loud our music can be at night. Most people abide by these rules because their desire for safety and amiable existence with others has a higher priority than their own ego-driven needs. Morals limit our behaviors in times of anger, greed, and lust. We recognize that uncontained anger or lust leads to violence and debasement.

Now, social systems limit our freedoms, as well, but I believe this kind of "containment" is often nonproductive. In many groups, society determines what brand we buy, where we shop, eat, or dance. Society teaches us many of our customs and traditions. As a result, not many people will get up and sing along at an opera or dance at the symphony, while not many remain seated at a Brooks and Dunn concert. For adults, the limitations loose some of their strength, but the limits of laws and morals are still there. Mature adults are more confident in themselves, and so they can relax in their adherence to societal expectations. For example, if Grandpa is tired, he may excuse himself to go to bed early even if there is company in the house. Or I can stand up and sing along at an opera—well, maybe at a performance of the "Messiah."

Wilson's idea may at first seem very negative until one considers the true definition of absolute "freedom." A society could not exist if at every moment of stress or pique its adults continued to bite or hit or scratch others as they might have in early childhood.

Your score for Essay #1: _____

Explain your reasons for giving this score. How do you rate its clarity, focus, development, and correctness? _____

_____

_____

Now read and score Essay #2, written from the same prompt.

Essay #2

To the statement by Woodrow Wilson, "Freedom is like steam, useless unless confined" I agree I feel that we are slaves to society and the way it works. We need to work to survive We will be thrown on the streets without money. If we disobey the rules of society we are thrown in prison So in many ways if we don't work with society, we will be thrown out of society.

We live in a system of money. We cannot live in this world pleasently without money. Everyone has the duty of working except for those who are supported financially. If someone in the household doesn't bring money in, you can end up on the streets. They are a lot of homeless people out their who were abandoned by society. There are other ways we aren't really free

If we disobey the rules of society or the government we are thrown in prison So we are slaves of society. We are contained by the law. Freedom only goes so far.

I look at other countries and compared to them we have more freedom but in some ways we are chained as well by moral values also.

So we are slaves to different things in this world Money enslaves us along with working Rules keep us restraint Morally we don't have complete freedom from guilt

Your score for Essay #2: _____

Explain your reasons for giving this score. How do you rate its clarity, focus, development, and correctness?_____

_____

_____

SCORING STANDARDS FOR CBEST ESSAYS

The people who read your CBEST essays are English teachers from secondary schools and college campuses across the nation. They are trained to read and score CBEST essays uniformly, again, based on a four-point scale.

4 = Pass
3 = Marginal pass
2 = Marginal fail
1 = Fail

The CBEST scorers read "holistically," which means while assessing your essay they take into account all aspects of the writing at the same time. Additionally, they do not mark on your essays; they don't tally "pluses" and "minuses" to come up with your score. Instead, the CBEST scorers are trained to assess essays on six standards, which correlate to our streamlined four:

Clarity
Focus
Development
Correctness

Details about the CBEST scorers' six standards are given later in this chapter. When scoring holistically, taking into account the "whole" essay, scorers do not enumerate or selectively weigh particular features of the writing. This means that

- Your essay is assessed for its overall quality of thinking and writing, as described in the CBEST standards. They do not focus on a single weakness or minor errors that do not distract from their ability to read easily through the essay.

- Your essay is read in its entirety; it is not judged based on the first or second paragraph alone.
- Your essays are scored without written notes or comments marked on the paper.
- Your essay is not judged on its length.
- Whether you agree or disagree with the prompt statement is up to you and is not a factor in the scoring of the essay.

Instead, your essay is scored on the evidence that you can write with

1. **Clarity.** The clear and logical CBEST essay conveys its meaning transparently with ideas arranged in a logical order. The essay addresses every aspect of the topic mentioned in the prompt. And precise words are used appropriately.

2. **Focus.** Even without a lot of time to reread and edit, CBEST test-takers are expected to compose essays which do not veer from the point. The point is expressed in the essay's thesis statement and is followed by paragraphs with relevant topic sentences. Those topic sentences and the paragraphs' development directly and overtly support the thesis statement.

3. **Development.** Prospective California and Oregon public school teachers must demonstrate their critical thinking abilities, especially their ability to reason logically. Therefore, while generalizations are appropriate for an essay's thesis statement and topic sentences, the rest of the essay is expected to be detailed, containing relevant, specific support. High-scoring essays contain reasoning and examples that provide a rich explanation of the general idea expressed in each topic sentence. Without this kind of depth, the reader doesn't really learn anything or isn't really convinced of your statements.

4. **Correctness.** As detailed above in the discussion about the editing stage, your paragraphs are expected to be clear and convincing on their own, without the need for your audience to "rewrite" your sentences into comprehensible English. Writing problems such as choppy sentences, imprecise language, and serious errors in sentence structure, grammar, or punctuation distract the reader from understanding your ideas.

Given these understandings, we can proceed to a reassessment of the previous sample essays.

EXPLANATION OF ACTUAL SCORES FOR ESSAYS #1 AND #2

Essay #1 would be scored a 4 or pass, and Essay #2 would be scored a 2 or marginal fail.

Essay #1 uses language and sentence structure that is *clear to read*. It is *logical* in that it takes the idea of limits on absolute freedom and divides it based on stages of human development. It maintains its *focus* on that idea, agreeing with the quote and substantiating that agreement with examples of the idea that young children are ego-centrically oriented and society expects nothing more, but as young adults and beyond, society imposes restraints in the attempt to provide social stability. This "4" paper also has *substance*, especially as it moves beyond simple chronology of stages of development and adds that society's restraints on social conformity go too far and are not *useful*. Furthermore, the paper is mostly *correct*; it has only a few incorrect words or punctuation, and these do not detract from the reader's ability to understand the ideas.

Essay #2, on the other hand, is harder to follow because it is *not clear* why the writer agrees with the quotation. It *lacks focus* as it moves around between saying that Americans have more freedom than other countries and saying our freedom is limited by how much money we have. In addition, there are *very few details or examples*, and the paper has *many misspelled words and grammatical mistakes*, making it difficult to understand.

Now, how do your scores compare to the ones above? If you gave the same scores or were one point away, you've done very well! The rest of this chapter will help you clarify and refine your ability to meet the expectations of the Writing Section of the CBEST. Since it is a timed test, effective used of your time is critical.

STRATEGIES TO MAXIMIZE YOUR ESSAY PLANNING AND WRITING TIME

In a timed situation, writers often "jump the gun," starting to scribble out their paragraphs as soon as they've read the writing prompt (topic) and chosen their subject. But this approach often leads to essays that lack clarity and logic. The CBEST essay graders know that writers have a limited amount of time to compose their essays; nevertheless, they expect a short, meaningful composition. PLANNING your essays will help ensure they are *meaningful*.

Maximizer #8—Planning Stage

Proportion your planning and writing time effectively. For most writers, the effective strategy is to use 20% of the allotted time for jotting down and organizing notes, 60% for writing, and the last 20% for editing the essay. Thus, for a 45-minute essay, you take about 10 minutes for planning, 20 minutes for writing, and about 15 minutes for editing.

Planning

Have at least two #2 pencils at hand. (The CBEST requires pencil, not ink.) Read the prompt thoroughly, slowly, underlining key words and phrases so that you are sure you comprehend the intent.

After underlining, place a number above each of the different parts of the prompt so that you can later check your plan to ensure you have covered all parts. As presented in Chapter 1, you will be writing two different types of essays.

The Type I essay asks writers to *describe and analyze a personal experience.* For example,

> *"Everyone says forgiveness is a lovely idea, until they have something to forgive,"* *according to C. S. Lewis. Write about one such situation where forgiveness was hard* *to give. Why did forgiveness seem difficult? Was forgiveness given? Accepted? If not,* *what was the outcome and why?*

The Type II essay asks writers to *explain their position on an idea or issue.* For example,

> *"Freedom is like steam, useless unless confined," according to Woodrow T. Wilson. To* *what extent do you agree or disagree with his observation? Provide specific reason-* *ing and examples in defense of your position.*

Maximizer #9—Prewriting Stage

When you are writing in the Writing Section, you are not allowed extra paper or resources like dictionaries in the test-taking area. So once you are sure you understand the topic, use the white space on the page containing the prompt for brief map, brainstorm, or sketch outline.

Here is an example of a map or cluster plan for the Type I essay prompt above:

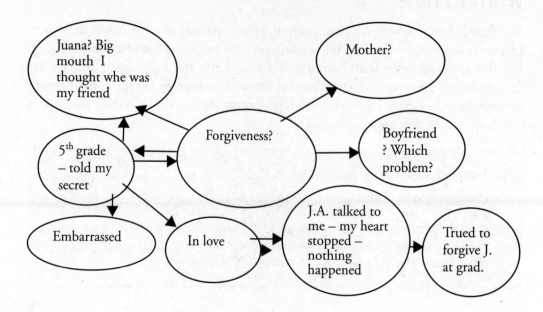

Here are examples of brainstorming and sketch outline for the Type I and Type II essay prompts:

EXAMPLES

Who have I forgiven?→→mother being so strict
                       Boyfriend
                       Juana's big mouth

Forgiveness hard? yes↑

Juana and me
[#1] 5th grade—I was "in love" with Johnny Angel she told my
     secret to his best friend
     Johnny actually spoke to me! Maybe sneered, to tell the truth
[#3] Totally embarrassed & cried at home
     Afraid he's make fun of me w/ everyone
[#4] I cut Juana out of my life—I hated her—she had betrayed
     my trust
     I had everyone on my "side" she was ostracized & I was
     sympathized with
[#2] When J. came up to me I immediately know Juana had
     revealed my secret
[#5] It was hard to give up my anger yet I did at 6th grade
     graduation day. She could have cared less.

<u>Agree</u>

limits on freedom laws
physical capabilities
consequences

true freedom = anarchy
commandments/morals
laws — national, state
          local

rules and conduct by age
  ☐2 per society
  ☐1 per peers
  ☐2—1 per environment —

Thesis: more rules/expectations as we age

Children—allowed to cry, bit, hit—at least at first
        We know they can't control themselves
        Then they learn from role models—please and thank you
Teens—learn limits to freedom but they try to push the boundaries
        Learn laws about driving, drinking, playing loud music
        Also learn to be controlled by advertising and their peers
Adults—can overcome the group pressure but remain "contained"
    by laws and morals because they know it helps society

<u>Disagree</u>

freedom of ideas
freedom as a concept
freedom of will/thoughts

Notice all that has been accomplished on this one sheet of paper: The writers have written down many ideas (where they won't disappear, as they sometimes do if test-takers try to keep their plans in their heads) and made numbered, sketch outlines of the best points.

Although you only have one page to write out and connect ideas, there is still much that can be accomplished which will guide the actual writing of the essay.

Maximizer #10—Address every Aspect in the Prompt

Review the prompt after you have brainstormed, mapped, or written your sketch outline. Number the parts of the prompt and as a cross-reference, apply those numbers to your main ideas to spot any gaps. For example, there are four parts to the "forgiveness" prompt. *1) describe the forgiveness situation, 2) explain why forgiveness was difficult, 3) describe why forgiveness was or was not accepted, and then 4) analyze the significance of the forgiveness event.* Do not speed through the directions; do not let yourself become anxious, which will only diminish your reasoning and writing power.

Clarity

To be easily understood, a writer's main points must be ordered in a way that makes sense to the audience. Typically, the points can be arranged by

- Time
- importance (usually from least to most important point)
- types of categories
- comparison and contrast
- cause to effect
- problem to solution

Can you tell how the writers of the essays above arrange their best points? In the sample for a Type I essay, the writer has arranged the points:

_____

_____

In the sample for a Type II essay, the writer has arranged the points:

_____

_____

Yes, both essays are arranged according to time. The Type I essay example above will be arranged in chronological (time) order from the initial event to the final event when the writer gave forgiveness. The Type II essay example will be arranged based on stages of development from childhood through adulthood. Time order is not the only appropriate arrangement of main point for CBEST essays; other organizational strategies will be demonstrated in future examples.

However, to continue with our first examples, you can tell that the resulting essays will have

- *Clarity* because the writer will be able to concentrate on expressing the ideas already captured on paper
- *Focus* because the writer has developed and scrutinized the plan for the essay, ensuring that it stays true to the main idea and the prompt
- *Development* because meaningful substance for the reader has already been planned

Based on the brainstorming, sketch outline, or map, the essay can be crafted in approximately 20–30 minutes.

> **Maximizer #11—Writing Stage**
>
> Write the essay only once, without skipping lines or leaving side margins. You will revise directly on that draft.

Although CBEST test-writers are not given any particular essay length requirement, essays scored as a 3 or 4 are usually between four and six paragraphs in length. The first paragraph usually functions as the introduction, and the final paragraph creates closure through a conclusion.

So how do you get from a sketch outline to a full draft?

First, begin the introduction paragraph with something intriguing or contemporary. This paragraph can be as short as three or four sentences, but it is too abrupt to simply open with the main idea (thesis statement) alone. Effective beginnings are often accounts of current events, statistics, short anecdotes, or questions *relevant to the topic*. For example:

Introduction Paragraph for Type I Essay:

> *Actress Angelina Jolie finally forgave her former husband Billy Bob Thornton. At one time she was extremely bitter over his inability to appreciate her devotion to humanitarian causes. Today, she claims Thornton as a life-long friend. Like Jolie, I was bitterly angry with a good friend, but I was ultimately able to forgive.*

Notice how this introduction contains a reference to a contemporary figure (Angelina Jolie). The reference is relevant because she was involved in "forgiving," which is the designated topic. After the beginning, the introduction paragraph must include a thesis statement. This thesis statement embodies the overall point of the essay. For example, in the introduction paragraph presented above, the thesis is:

> *Like Jolie, I was bitterly angry with a good friend, but I was ultimately able to forgive.*

After writing the fleshed out introduction paragraph, begin writing the body of the essay, creating topic sentences that convey the major points planned during the prewriting. (A topic sentence, which articulates the general ideas of the paragraph, usually appears at the beginning of each body paragraph, allowing the reader to know the point of the paragraph in advance.) Each of the key points should be developed into its own paragraph, in the already established logical order. At this point, transitions between ideas in each paragraph should be included, as well.

The first topic sentence for the Type I essay begun above could be

> *In fifth grade, I shared a heart-felt secret with my best friend, Juana.*

The next paragraph could begin with a topic sentence like:

> *I'll never forget the feeling of mortification that struck deep into my young heart when Johnny strolled over as I stood by the bus stop, locked eyes with me, and said, "So I heard you like me?"*

After this paragraph, the next topic sentence could read:

> *For a year I refused to acknowledge Juana's existence and therefore many of my friends shunned her also; I never considered forgiving her, as "lovely" as that gesture might have been.*

Finally, the body paragraph's most important key point can be expressed as:

Finally, at graduation day in sixth grade I felt extremely sentimental, yet when I saw Juana in her white dress, I still had to force myself to do what was right and speak to her.

The concluding paragraph must leave the CBEST scorer with a strong sense of your ability to complete an essay meaningfully. It doesn't require a topic sentence, or even a (perhaps boring) repetition of the thesis statement. But you are expected to be able to show the significance of your experience. An example for the above essay is:

Funny, Juana wasn't overjoyed when I spoke with her, yet I know that if I hadn't done that, I would have many regrets. Now, my childhood memories are not marred by the presence of an egotistically cruel retaliation for being hurt. Yes, that's all it was, simple and cruel. I didn't really care that Johnny Angel knew my feelings; in fact, I was glad, even if nothing came of it. Nevertheless, letting go of that anger-driven power, the power to hurt another human being, was very hard. I liked having that power. I'm proud of having given it up.

> **Maximizer #12—Editing Stage**
> After the entire essay has been written in the time you've allotted, without skipping spaces or leaving extra-wide margins, you have the remainder of your time to review the paragraphs and make corrections and stylistic

The CBEST scorers expect that words are correctly spelled, punctuation and grammar are correct, and sentences are complete, not fragments. You would be wise to assess your personal strengths and weaknesses in these areas and acquire an English handbook or tutoring help if you have doubts about your ability to write clear, clean English.

When spending the last 10–15 minutes on the essay, you should take a deep breath, perhaps give yourself a minute to relax, then refocus and make improvements directly on the written paragraphs. CBEST graders know that writers have no extra paper, so they expect neat line-outs and legible corrections written above the lines. Notice the emphasis on neat and legible, though. An essay that is hard to read is in jeopardy of receiving a low score.

This is also the case for poor handwriting. If necessary, practice your handwriting so that it is readable, not too large, not too small. You might also ask a friend to read something you've handwritten to find out if, indeed, a stranger can easily comprehend your handwriting.

To edit for *use of appropriate language*, go through your essay *twice*. First, from beginning to end to look for places to improve the clarity, focus, development, and correctness.

EXAMPLES OF COMMON CORRECTIONS
BASED ON THE FOUR STANDARDS

Clarity
CLEARY EXPRESSED IDEAS

DO write: *Our social system is based on the getting and spending of money.*

DON'T write: We live in a system of money.

LOGICAL ORDER OF IDEAS

DO write: *"We might be born free, and perhaps remain entirely free for a short while, but as we age we become more productive and fulfilled as we negotiate our limitations.*

DON'T write: "We are more productive and fulfilled as we age, but when we are born we are free and remain free for a short while, then as we are older we negotiate our limitations.

PRECISE WORDING

DO write: *Limitations prevent people from taking unfair advantage of situations.*

DON'T write: Without the distinction of crossing the line, people would push to see what they can get away with.

DO write: *We will be thrown out of society if we do not work with it.*

DON'T write: So in many ways if we don't work with society, we will be thrown out of society.

APPROPRIATE TONE AND STYLE

DO write: *Without a steady income, people face the danger of becoming homeless.*

DON'T write: If someone in the household doesn't bring money in, you can end up on the street.

DON'T speed through the directions; don't let yourself become anxious, which will only diminish your reasoning and writing power.

Focus
ESSAY STAYS ON TRACK

DO take time with the brainstorm, map, or sketch outline and analyze it. Ask yourself: Do the main points directly and obviously support the thesis? In addition, even after you have followed your plan, read the essay to find places where it may have gone off track. For example:

Thesis: We have laws and personal morals that confine us.

Topic Sentence #1: Each state within the country has its own laws that one must abide by.

Topic Sentence #2: Personal morals also keep people from true freedom.

DON'T rush into writing before making a plan.

TOPIC SENTENCES DIRECTLY RELATED TO
THE THESIS STATEMENT

DO think of the topic sentences and thesis statement as an equation: Topic Sentence #1 + Topic Sentence #2 + Topic Sentence #3 = Thesis statement. For example:

Each state within the country has its own laws that one must abide by + Personal morals also keep people from true freedom = We have laws and personal morals that confine us.

DON'T make wild or exaggerated thesis statement claims, especially those that contain the words *never* or *always*. For example: If we disobey the rules of society or the government, we are thrown in prison.

DON'T leave in points that you realize are not relevant to "proving" the thesis statement. Remember that it's acceptable to line out words and sentences as you revise.

ABUNDANT AND APPROPRIATE SUPPORT

DO take time to plan the details, examples, and reasoning; when your mind is in the planning mode, it's easier to come up with good material. When editing, read for places that still need more examples or details.

DON'T submit an essay containing only generalizations.

Development

CAREFUL REASONING

DO scrutinize your sketch outline and, later, the full essay, asking: Where are the logical flaws?"

"Does this really make sense?

DON'T assume all your initial or first draft ideas are reasonable and usable.

GENERALIZATIONS ELABORATED IN DETAIL

DO imagine that you are writing to convince the reader of your ideas. The reader can't enter your mind, so all that you remember and all that you have reasoned must appear on the paper. For example:

There comes a time when children must learn to live and work within a group. By the time children are school-aged, they are expected to know certain rules of etiquette such as saying "please" and "thank-you," not interrupting conversations, showing restraint when they are angry or upset, and generally being respectful of others, especially adults.

DON'T write as if the essay were a journal or letter, to be read only by you or your close friends.

Correctness

SMOOTH SENTENCES AND SEQUENCING

DO check for appropriate pronoun agreement and sequencing of verb tense. For example: *Each state within the country has its* (not *their*) *own laws that one must abide by.*

DON'T confuse the reader with inappropriate word tense. For example: *In the late 1800s, people vary widely in their understanding of science.*

APPROPRIATE LANGUAGE

DO write: *Slightly older children may express displeasure by crying or hitting or biting, and still they are not punished harshly.*

DON'T write: Older children show they are mad by acting out, and still there is no reaction.

DO write: *As a result, not many people will get up and sing along at an opera or dance at the symphony . . .*

DON'T write: As a result, people won't get up and sing along at an opera or rock out at the symphony.

CORRECT MECHANICS

DO save time to make corrections to spelling, grammar, and mechanics like punctuation. Review these rules thoroughly before taking the test.

DON'T fail to apportion your time, leaving yourself without adequate time to catch spelling, grammar, and punctuation errors, like

1. Slang
2. Misspellings
3. Need for transition words or phrases
4. Wordiness or redundancy
5. Words omitted
6. Unnecessary use of passive voice
7. Contractions

> **QUICK REMINDERS**
>
> **Your**: a possessive pronoun, as in *I would like to borrow your coat.*
>
> **You're**: the contraction of *you are* or *you were.*
>
> **Whose**: a pronoun, as in *We will vote for the student whose behavior best represents the ideals of our club.*
>
> **Who's**: a contraction of *who is.*
>
> **Its**: a pronoun, as in *The dog wagged its tail.*
>
> **It's**: a contraction of *it is*, as in *It's raining outside.*
>
> **To**: meaning "toward," as in *The train traveled to San Jose before arriving in San Francisco.*
>
> **Too**: meaning "excessive" or "additional," as in *There are too many onions in the stew.*

Then go through the essay a second time. The second read-through is best done *from the end to the beginning.* That is, read the last sentence, then the next-to-last, and so forth. When concentrating on grammar and punctuation, you can avoid distractions when editing in this fashion. Check and correct

1. Subject–verb agreement errors
2. Pronoun errors
3. Omitted commas, or unnecessary commas

4. Fragment sentences

5. Semicolons and apostrophes

The essay need not be 100% correct to receive a passing score, but writing flaws that make it difficult for the scorer to quickly understand your sentences will bring down your score.

Again, we are using four standards in explaining how you can best demonstrate your **writing** ability, that is, how to (1) be clear and logical, (2) be focused, (3) think deeply, and (4) write correctly. Below are the more technical criteria of the CBEST essay scorers.

ESSAY SCORERS' GRADING SCALE IN DETAIL

The CBEST scorers actually use six standards, which are

1. **Rhetorical force.** This refers to how clear and logically, how forcefully, you make the case in your essay.

2. **Organization.** This refers to the logical arrangement of your ideas.

3. **Support and development.** This means there are specifics and supporting ideas to provide depth to your ideas.

4. **Usage.** This means using careful and precise words.

5. **Structure and conventions.** This means adhering to the rules for paragraph structure, sentence structure, and mechanics.

6. **Appropriateness.** This refers to writing directly about the assigned topic with formal language and style.

These six scoring standards are really for the scorers, not the writers. They are too cumbersome for test-takers to learn or dwell on, and we hope you agree that our four are more useful. Again, CFDC: Clear, Focused, Deep thinking, Correctness.

1. Be **clear** and logical
2. Be **focused**
3. Show **deep thinking**
4. Write **correctly**

SAMPLE PAPERS

Type II Essay

"Freedom is like steam, useless unless confined," according to Woodrow T. Wilson. To what extent do you agree or disagree with his observation? Provide specific reasoning and examples in defense of your position.

ESSAY RATED 4

Everyone wants freedom, but watch out! The idea expressed by former president Woodrow Wilson that "freedom is like steam, useless unless contained" is very true. This idea can be verified by examination of our life cycle. We might be born free, and perhaps remain entirely free for a very short while, but as we age we become more productive and fulfilled as we negotiate limitations, as we are "contained."

Never are we more free then we are as young children. Most societies and socioeconomic classes are very tolerant of the natural behaviors of young children. Children vocalize when they are uncomfortable, hungry, or bored, and their needs are met. Slightly older children may express displeasure by crying or hitting or biting and still they are not harshly dealt with (at least at first). This is like the uncontained steam except to the single child, it has no use and can be, in fact, harmful to others.

There comes a time when children must learn to live and work within a group. By the time children are school aged, they are expected to know certain rules of etiquette such as saying "please" and "thank you," not interrupting conversations, showing restraint when they are angry or upset, and generally being respectful of others, especially adults.

As teens and young adults, people become more familiar with the possibilities within their constraints. By this stage, people are familiar with a system of morals, laws, and social system. These systems place limits on the behaviors of those who live under them. We have justice built right into our legal system so that even those who would not let morals guide them must abide by the rules (laws) or pay the price. Laws limit how fast we can drive, ordinances limit how loud our music can be at night. Most people abide by these rules because their desire for safety and amiable existence with others has a higher priority than their own ego-driven needs. Morals limit our behaviors in times of anger, greed, and lust. We recognize that uncontained anger or lust leads to violence and debasement.

Now, social systems are very strong vehicles for containing our freedom, as well. And I believe this kind of "containment" is often nonproductive. In many groups, society determines what brand we buy, how we decorate the outside of our homes, where we shop, eat or dance. Society teaches us many of our customs and traditions. As a result, not many people will get up and sing along at an opera or dance at the symphony, while not many remain seated at a Brooks and Dunn concert. For adults, the chains of society loose some of their strength, but the limits of laws and morals are still there. Mature adults are more confident in themselves and so they can relax in their adherence to societal expectations. For example, if grandpa is tired, he may excuse himself to go to bed early even if there is company in the house. Or I can stand up and sing along at an opera—well, maybe at a performance of the "Messiah."

Wilson's idea may at first seem very negative until one considers the true definition of absolute "freedom." A society could not exist if at every moment of stress or pique its adults continued to bite or hit or scratch others as they might have in early childhood.

ESSAY RATED 3

The United States of America is known as the land of the free. America has three major documents that outline these freedoms, and these documents give Americans the right to live life as they want. Yet although the constitution, Bill of Rights, and the Amendments give people freedom, this freedom is not unlimited. Woodrow Wilson states that "Freedom is like steam, useless unless confined." Wilson has a good point. We have laws and personal morals that confine us.

Each state within the country has their own laws that one must abide by. Laws are made for the safety of the people. If there were true freedom, all laws would be cast aside and all crimes go unpunished Laws are made to uphold the rights and freedoms of people, even when some say they are unjust Anyone who tries to circumvent all laws by speeding on the freeway, robbing gas stations, assaulting pedestrians, or shop lifting, all for their personal gain, will eventually be stopped However, laws aren't the only way that complete freedom is contained

Personal morals also keep people from true freedom They keep people from breaking the law or selfishly taking advantage of other people Parents and other adults, as positive role models, instill these morals into children Morals "contain" people when they have the urge to speed on the freeway because they know they may cause an accident and hurt or kill others, which is wrong Morals also "contain" people when they have the urge to shoplift an item from a store because they know it is wrong

Laws and personal morals are factors which keep people from achieving true freedom How terrible? Wilson was right when he said that freedom that is unlimited is "useless." In fact, it's worse than useless. It's dangerous.

ESSAY RATED 2

To the statement by Woodrow Wilson, "Freedom is like steam, useless unless confined" I agree I feel that we are slaves to society and the way it works. We need to work to survive We will be thrown on the streets without money. If we disobey the rules of society we are thrown in prison So in many ways if we don't work with society, we will be thrown out of society.

We live in a system of money. We cannot live in this world pleasently without money. Everyone has the duty of working except for those who are supported financially. If someone in the household doesn't bring money in, you can end up on the streets. They are a lot of homeless people out their who were abandoned by society. There are other ways we aren't really free

If we disobey the rules of society or the government we are thrown in prison. So we are slaves of society. We are contained by the law. Freedom only goes so far.

I look at other countries and compared to them we have more freedom but in some ways we are chained as well by moral values also.

So we are slaves to different things in this world. Money enslaves us along with working. Rules keep us restraint. Morally we don't have complete freedom from guilt.

ESSAY RATED 1

"Freedom" is hard to determine. I believe everyone is born with a free will meaning everyone is free to make their own decessions, however, there are consequences for choices we make that break laws. For instance we have the freedom to vote, to speak freely and wear what we please, but guidelines are placed. Some jobs may require one to wear ties and dress shoes daily. One can choose to wear it ot not, but ulitmitly will pay the price for note following the requirements. I do not believe true "freedom" exists.

But one mustent look at regulations as a negative thing. Without the distinction of crossing the line people would push to see what they can get away with. Speaking freely is a great gift, however, if one man slanders another man consequences will be layed upon those who break the law. The reason why we have laws is ultimately for the protection of people. One thing that cannot be taken away from a person is thier freedom to choose obeying the law or not.

PRACTICE

Now it's your turn. Time yourself and allow no more than 45 minutes for each practice essay below. Write in pencil so that you can erase and edit. Follow the strategies in this chapter.

This is a Type I essay, requiring a response describing a remembered experience: *Sometimes success is harder to accept than failure. Write about one such situation you faced when success brought its own difficulties. What brought on your success? What difficulties accompanied it? What did you learn from this?*

_____

_____

_____

_____

_____

_____

_____

_____

_____

_____

_____

_____

_____

_____

_____

_____

_____

_____

_____

_____

_____

_____

This is a Type II essay, requiring an expository response: "A friend in power is a friend lost." Do you agree or disagree with this statement by Henry Brooks Adams? Support your ideas with reasoning and examples.

_____

_____

_____

_____

_____

_____

_____

_____

_____

_____

_____

_____

_____

_____

_____

_____

_____

_____

_____

_____

_____

_____

_____

_____

_____

_____

_____

_____

_____

Now rate the two essays you have written; then seek another opinion, perhaps from a friend or tutor, for a second rating. You might compare your essays to those about forgiveness that were rated 1–4 in the beginning of this chapter.

In general, as we have said,

The **4** is a well-organized essay that clearly communicates its message, touching on all parts of the prompt.

The **3** is adequately organized and communicates its message without significant confusion.

The **2** is not well organized and/or has ineffective support, and its ability to communicate is marred by distracting errors.

The **1** is poorly organized and may have serious logical flaws, imprecise language, and many mechanical errors.

Use our standards and place a check in the appropriate boxes in the table below.

- Clarity (The paper is understandable and logical.)
- Focus (The paper doesn't digress from the main point being explained.)
- Development (The paper has substance; it has details, reasons, and examples.)
- Correctness (The paper is written in correct English.)

My Type I Essay

	4 (Good)	3 (Adequate)	2 (Needs Work)	1 (Poor)
Clarity				
Focus				
Development				
Correctness				

My Type II Essay

	4 (Good)	3 (Adequate)	2 (Needs Work)	1 (Poor)
Clarity				
Focus				
Development				
Correctness				

If you, or others who have read your essays, rated them as "needs work" and "poor," your next steps are to reread this chapter, take notes, and then rewrite your two essays in accordance with your improved understanding of the expectations of CBEST essays rated 3 and 4.

If you, or others who have read your essays, rated them mainly in the "good" and "adequate" columns, they have been judged to be in the passing range.

Next, you should write several more practice essays, followed by self-rating, before taking the exam. You can create your own prompts that are in the Type I or Type II style based on any subject that does not require specialized knowledge.

CHAPTER 8

MODEL EXAMS

Model Exam 1: Reading
ANSWER SHEET

1 Ⓐ Ⓑ Ⓒ Ⓓ Ⓔ	14 Ⓐ Ⓑ Ⓒ Ⓓ Ⓔ	27 Ⓐ Ⓑ Ⓒ Ⓓ Ⓔ	39 Ⓐ Ⓑ Ⓒ Ⓓ Ⓔ
2 Ⓐ Ⓑ Ⓒ Ⓓ Ⓔ	15 Ⓐ Ⓑ Ⓒ Ⓓ Ⓔ	28 Ⓐ Ⓑ Ⓒ Ⓓ Ⓔ	40 Ⓐ Ⓑ Ⓒ Ⓓ Ⓔ
3 Ⓐ Ⓑ Ⓒ Ⓓ Ⓔ	16 Ⓐ Ⓑ Ⓒ Ⓓ Ⓔ	29 Ⓐ Ⓑ Ⓒ Ⓓ Ⓔ	41 Ⓐ Ⓑ Ⓒ Ⓓ Ⓔ
4 Ⓐ Ⓑ Ⓒ Ⓓ Ⓔ	17 Ⓐ Ⓑ Ⓒ Ⓓ Ⓔ	30 Ⓐ Ⓑ Ⓒ Ⓓ Ⓔ	42 Ⓐ Ⓑ Ⓒ Ⓓ Ⓔ
5 Ⓐ Ⓑ Ⓒ Ⓓ Ⓔ	18 Ⓐ Ⓑ Ⓒ Ⓓ Ⓔ	31 Ⓐ Ⓑ Ⓒ Ⓓ Ⓔ	43 Ⓐ Ⓑ Ⓒ Ⓓ Ⓔ
6 Ⓐ Ⓑ Ⓒ Ⓓ Ⓔ	19 Ⓐ Ⓑ Ⓒ Ⓓ Ⓔ	32 Ⓐ Ⓑ Ⓒ Ⓓ Ⓔ	44 Ⓐ Ⓑ Ⓒ Ⓓ Ⓔ
7 Ⓐ Ⓑ Ⓒ Ⓓ Ⓔ	20 Ⓐ Ⓑ Ⓒ Ⓓ Ⓔ	33 Ⓐ Ⓑ Ⓒ Ⓓ Ⓔ	45 Ⓐ Ⓑ Ⓒ Ⓓ Ⓔ
8 Ⓐ Ⓑ Ⓒ Ⓓ Ⓔ	21 Ⓐ Ⓑ Ⓒ Ⓓ Ⓔ	34 Ⓐ Ⓑ Ⓒ Ⓓ Ⓔ	46 Ⓐ Ⓑ Ⓒ Ⓓ Ⓔ
9 Ⓐ Ⓑ Ⓒ Ⓓ Ⓔ	22 Ⓐ Ⓑ Ⓒ Ⓓ Ⓔ	35 Ⓐ Ⓑ Ⓒ Ⓓ Ⓔ	47 Ⓐ Ⓑ Ⓒ Ⓓ Ⓔ
10 Ⓐ Ⓑ Ⓒ Ⓓ Ⓔ	23 Ⓐ Ⓑ Ⓒ Ⓓ Ⓔ	36 Ⓐ Ⓑ Ⓒ Ⓓ Ⓔ	48 Ⓐ Ⓑ Ⓒ Ⓓ Ⓔ
11 Ⓐ Ⓑ Ⓒ Ⓓ Ⓔ	24 Ⓐ Ⓑ Ⓒ Ⓓ Ⓔ	37 Ⓐ Ⓑ Ⓒ Ⓓ Ⓔ	49 Ⓐ Ⓑ Ⓒ Ⓓ Ⓔ
12 Ⓐ Ⓑ Ⓒ Ⓓ Ⓔ	25 Ⓐ Ⓑ Ⓒ Ⓓ Ⓔ	38 Ⓐ Ⓑ Ⓒ Ⓓ Ⓔ	50 Ⓐ Ⓑ Ⓒ Ⓓ Ⓔ
13 Ⓐ Ⓑ Ⓒ Ⓓ Ⓔ	26 Ⓐ Ⓑ Ⓒ Ⓓ Ⓔ		

MODEL EXAM 1: READING

Use the answer sheet preceding this sample test; then turn to the key at the end of the chapter to check your answers.

> Read the passage below; then answer the four questions that follow.

Clever Hans was a horse which stamped his hoof the correct number of times when his master said a number. Hans and his master went about the German countryside early in the century demonstrating Clever Hans' ability to count. This was not an act of <u>charlatanism</u> because Hans' master believed Hans could indeed count. Eventually, it was demonstrated that Hans could count only if his master performed with him and only if Hans could see his master.

(1) Hans was actually stamping his hoof as long as his master maintained a tense stance. (2) When Hans got to the correct number of stamps, his master unconsciously would relax a bit and take a breath. (3) _____. (4) The positive reinforcement came from the affectionate approval, including lumps of sugar perhaps, given to Hans by his master when Hans was successful. (5) _____, Hans' master realized what was going on, and horse and master retired to their farm.

1. Which of the following is the best meaning of the word <u>charlatanism</u> as it is used in the first paragraph of the passage?

   (A) con artistry
   (B) spiritualism
   (C) tomfoolery
   (D) indignation
   (E) desperation

2. Which sentence, if inserted as Sentence 3, would be most consistent with the writer's purpose and intended audience?

   (A) Hans' master really thought he had taught his horse to count.
   (B) A similar incident happened with a harbor seal in New England.
   (C) Hans' clever behavior was the result of conditioning.
   (D) Isn't that amazing?
   (E) Animals often have such close contact with humans.

3. Which word or phrase, inserted at the beginning of Sentence 5 in the second paragraph, would best help the reader understand the sequence of the writer's ideas?

(A) On the other hand
(B) However
(C) Eventually
(D) In contrast
(E) Therefore

4. Which of the following best organizes the main topics addressed in this passage?

(A) I. Influence of conditioning on animals
    II. How Hans' master conditioned Hans

(B) I. Clever Hans' performances
    II. How Hans' master unconsciously conditioned Hans

(C) I. Animals who perform tricks
    II. Revealing the trick behind Clever Hans

(D) I. Animals conditioned by humans
    II. Horse and harbor seal

(E) I. How Hans' master conditioned Hans
    II. Revealing the trick behind Clever Hans

Read the passage below; then answer the five questions that follow.

---

(1) Helen Keller was almost 7 years old when Annie Sullivan came to Helen's home in Alabama to teach her. (2) _____in Helen Keller's book, these events are recounted in great detail by Helen, and the book also contains extracts from the letters of Annie Sullivan to Mrs. Hopkins, a friend from the Perkins School for the Blind. (3) But when Annie wrote the letters, Mrs. Hopkins no longer worked at Perkins School where Sullivan had been trained. (4) During the time recounted in the book, Sullivan spent all of her days attempting to provide Keller with an understanding that people, even people who are deaf, can communicate with each other. It took many months for Sullivan to convey to Keller that motions Sullivan was making in her palm represented things in her world. (5) _____ the early chapters are relevant to the question of what it is like to be without language. (6) The book is fascinating as a document of the power of the human mind.

5. Which words or phrases, if inserted in order into the blanks in the passage, would help the reader understand the sequence of the writer's ideas?

   (A) In contrast, In fact,
   (B) In fact, In addition,
   (C) Likewise, Therefore,
   (D) Similarly, In sum,
   (E) None of the above

6. Which of the following inferences may be drawn from the information presented in the passage?

   (A) Helen Keller lived her early life without language.
   (B) Mrs. Hopkins was Annie Sullivan's real mother.
   (C) Annie Sullivan wrote letters to Helen Keller.
   (D) Annie Sullivan wanted Helen Keller to go to Perkins Institution.
   (E) Annie Sullivan told everything she knew about Helen Keller in her book.

7. Which of the sentences numbered in the passage expresses an opinion, rather than a fact?

   (A) 2
   (B) 3
   (C) 4
   (D) 5
   (E) 6

8. Which of the following numbered sentences is *least* relevant to the main idea of the paragraph?

   (A) 1
   (B) 2
   (C) 3
   (D) 4
   (E) 5

9. Which of the following assumptions most influenced the writer's argument in the passage?

   (A) Teachers enjoy writing books about their pupils.
   (B) Children shouldn't be taught until they are at least 7 years old.
   (C) Annie Sullivan should not have written to Mrs. Hopkins.
   (D) Teachers and pupils can recount their experiences to provide insight for others.
   (E) Mrs. Hopkins should not have abandoned Annie Sullivan.

Read the passage below; then answer the five questions that follow.

In the late 1960s, I used to see full-page advertisements in magazines featuring a picture of an exotic and winsome 4-year-old captioned, "She speaks fluent Mandarin. Why can't you?" These were advertisements for foreign language schools that specialized in preparing Americans to speak a variety of foreign languages fluently. The advertisement was <u>compelling</u>. Certainly, an adult could learn to do anything a 4-year-old could do—and it shouldn't take very long. Right?

This ad hasn't appeared for a long time. Perhaps it has been banned under the law that prohibits false and misleading advertising. _____ Children are able to learn to speak a language without consulting grammars or dictionaries. They become fluent in their mother tongue, like the young speaker of Mandarin, by the time they are about 4 years old—and some do it considerably earlier.

10. Which of the following persuasive techniques is used in the passage above?

(A) Appealing to emotions
(B) Challenging assumptions
(C) Identifying with readers
(D) Using a telling example
(E) Using vivid language

11. Which of the following best describes the writer's opinion of the 1960s advertisement for an adult language school?

(A) It showed adults how easy it is to learn a second language.
(B) It helped Americans learn to speak Mandarin.
(C) It was deliberately misleading.
(D) It was not effective.
(E) It showed a 4-year-old who had learned to speak Mandarin as a second language.

12. Which sentence, if inserted into the blank line in the second paragraph, would be most consistent with the writer's purpose and intended audience?

(A) The advertisement's writers were hoping their audiences were not critical thinkers.
(B) It's never easy to learn a foreign language.
(C) Many false advertisements about diet pills have recently been banned.
(D) People are too easily tempted into buying things they don't really need.
(E) None of the above

13. Which of the following is the best meaning of the word *compelling* as it is used in the first paragraph of the passage?

    (A) Unconvincing
    (B) Persuasive
    (C) Demeaning
    (D) Elegant
    (E) Comical

14. Which of the following statements expresses an underlying assumption used in the advertisement described in the reading selection?

    (A) Everyone wants to be bilingual.
    (B) Children and adults learn language in the same way.
    (C) Girls learn languages more quickly than boys.
    (D) Adults believe they are more competent than children.
    (E) None of these

> Read the passage below; then answer the five questions that follow.

Features of the baby talk register include speaking in short utterances, a good deal of repetition of utterances, and speaking at a higher than usual pitch with exaggerated intonation. Speaking more slowly and clearly than usual is also sometimes a baby talk register feature. Simplifying the pronunciation of words such as *l'il* for *little, tweetie* for *sweetie,* and *faw* for *fall* is probably less frequently a feature than others, in part at least because we have been taught that doing this interferes with young children's learning to pronounce words correctly. They will try to pronounce what they hear.

The features just mentioned do not exhaust the list that has been proposed for the baby talk register. There is no hard and fast list, _____there is a short list of ways in which the features of the register make it a better means of communication with very young children than the adult register, including clarifying and expressive characteristics that foster communication. _____, the adult's pronouncing *little* as *l'il* does not help babies' language development.

15. According to the information presented in the passage, what should an adult do when attempting to teach a baby how to communicate?

    (A) Avoid simplifying pronunciation.
    (B) Avoid speaking more clearly than usual.
    (C) Avoid using short phrases.
    (D) Avoid using exaggerated expression.
    (E) Avoid pronouncing words slowly.

16. Which words or phrases, if inserted in order into the blanks in the passage, would help the reader understand the sequence of the writer's ideas?

    (A) first, However
    (B) but, On the other hand
    (C) nevertheless, Similarly
    (D) then, Furthermore
    (E) meanwhile, For example

17. Which of the following would be the most appropriate title for this passage?

    (A) How Not to Talk to Babies
    (B) How Young Children Communicate
    (C) Gender Differences in Communication Skills
    (D) Basics of Baby Talk Register
    (E) The Child's Developing Language Skills

18. Which of the following best summarizes the main point of the passage?

    (A) Some kinds of talk are more effective than others in helping a baby learn to communicate.
    (B) No one knows the whole range of effective strategies for communication with babies.
    (C) Some babies like to hear baby talk register, while others don't.
    (D) Babies become language users in the course of their everyday experience.
    (E) Repetition is a good idea to help babies hear, remember, and figure out words.

19. Which of the following is the best meaning of *register* as it is used in the passage?

    (A) Record
    (B) Enroll
    (C) Characteristics
    (D) Bilingualism
    (E) Language subset

Use the index below to answer the two questions that follow.

Anderson, R., 148–9, 179
Anglin, J., 172–173, 174, 177
Animal, 2
    alarm cries, 39
    in contact with people, 2, 17–34
    as experimental, 23–5, 28
    imprinting, 18–19
    as pets, 21–3,
    signal systems in the wild, 2, 7–16
Ants, behavior of, 12–13
Apes, 2, 121
    aggressiveness in, 13–14, 15
    alarm cries, 14
    behavior analogous to humans, 9
    generic memory, 191
    and language ability, 3, 27–34

20. On which pages should one look to find information about ferrets as pets?

(A) 17–34
(B) 23–25
(C) 18–19
(D) 21–23
(E) 13–14

21. On which page(s) would one find information about the similarities between humans and apes?

(A) 2
(B) 9
(C) 17–34
(D) 121
(E) 191

Use the chart below to answer the two questions that follow.

The pie chart below shows the fractions of dogs in a dog competition in seven different groups of dog breeds. We can see from the chart that four times as many dogs competed in the sporting group as in the herding group. We can also see that the two most popular groups of dogs accounted for almost half of the dogs in the competition.

Dogs in the AltoTrainer Dog Competition, by Group

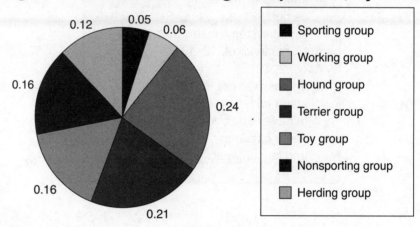

22. Participation by what group was the highest in this competition?

    (A) Toy group
    (B) Working group
    (C) Nonsporting group
    (D) Sporting group
    (E) Terrier group

23. What two groups of dogs participated equally in the competition?

    (A) sporting and nonsporting group
    (B) hound group and working group
    (C) herding group and toy group
    (D) terrier group and hound group
    (E) sporting group and working group

Read the passage below; then answer the following questions.

Chemical signals called pheromones are involved in the social behavior of many animals. Anyone who has had a dog for a pet is aware of the importance of pheromones (smells) in the social life of the dog. E. O. Wilson has demonstrated that the social life of insects is <u>mediated</u> largely by pheromones. He studied a type of ant whose behavior evidenced a feeling of fellowship according to entomologists. Those ants seem to bury their dead. They do not exactly bury, _____ they carry dead ants to a spot somewhat removed from the ant hill. Wilson was able to demonstrate that the sign stimulus for the burying behavior was a pheromone given off by dead ants. He smeared a live ant with the candidate pheromone and, shortly after, two ants picked up the live ant and carried it to the burial spot.

_____, ants use pheromones to leave a trail of scent when returning from a food source to their hill. Other ants in the hill are attracted by the odor and follow the trail back to the food source. Pheromones lose their potency after a short time, so the trail to an exhausted food source soon disappears.

24. Which of the following is the best meaning of the word *mediated* as it is used in the first paragraph of the passage?

(A) Influenced
(B) Antagonized
(C) Diminished
(D) Signaled
(E) Buried

25. Which words or phrases, if inserted *in order* into the blanks in the passage, would help the reader understand the sequence of the writer's ideas?

(A) yet, However
(B) then, Nevertheless
(C) in addition, Next
(D) similarly, In addition
(E) but, Furthermore

26. Which of the following best organizes the main topics addressed in this passage?

    (A) I. Pheromones used by dogs
         II. Pheromones used by ants
    (B) I. How animals find their way with pheromones
         II. How humans use pheromones
    (C) I. Ant pheromones and burying behavior
         II. Ant pheromones and food trail behavior
    (D) I. Pheromones used by dogs and ants
         II. How to deceive animals using pheromones
    (E) I. Examples of mammals using pheromones
         II. Theory behind pheromones

27. According to the information in the passage, what would most likely happen if a biologist left a trail of "food source" pheromones from a plastic cup to an ant colony?

    (A) The ants would travel to the plastic cup.
    (B) The ants would bury the plastic cup.
    (C) Two ants would pick up the plastic cup and take it away from the ant hill.
    (D) Ants that traveled to the plastic cup would die.
    (E) None of these

28. Which of the following would be the most appropriate title for this passage?

    (A) Ant Behavior
    (B) Pheromone Signals
    (C) Facts about Dogs and Ants
    (D) Sign Stimulus
    (E) The Social Life of Insects

Use the chart below to answer the two questions that follow.

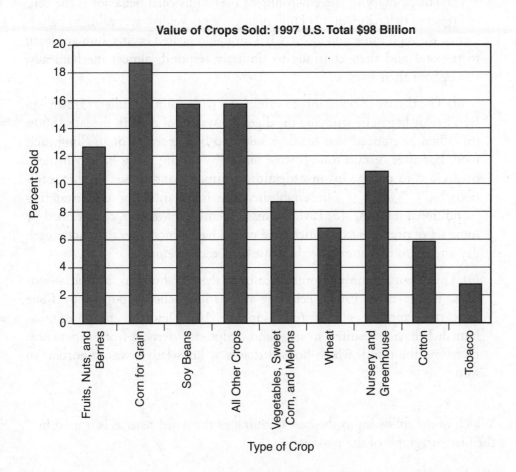

Value of Crops Sold: 1997
U.S. Total $98 Billion

29. What does the chart show?

(A) The value of the crops sold by the United States in 1997
(B) The value of crops sold by the United States in 1997 by percentage
(C) The types of crops needed to feed the United States in 1997
(D) The amount of waste of crops in 1997 by percentage
(E) The popularity of food in the United States in 1997 by percentage

30. Which groups, together, make up approximately half of the crops sold?

(A) Corn for grain; soybeans; all other crops
(B) Corn for grain; fruits, nuts, and berries; tobacco
(C) Fruits, nuts, and berries; nursery and greenhouse; wheat
(D) Wheat; vegetables, sweet corn, and melons; all other crops
(E) Soybeans; all other crops; vegetables, sweet corn, and melons

Read the passage below; and then answer the five questions that follow.

(1) The primacy of the environment over individual behavior is the central <u>tenet</u> of behaviorism. (2) Human behavior develops, according to behaviorists, through cause and effect. (3) Through repeated events, humans learn to respond and then continue to similarly respond, almost mechanically, throughout their lives.

(4) The theory of behaviorism originated with animal studies. (5) Russian Ivan Pavlov began by studying the digestive system of dogs in the late 1800s. (6) When he noticed that his dogs salivated before seeing or smelling their food, but after certain sounds were made (by tuning forks, bells, whistles), he decided to change his investigations to understand these "psychic secretions." (7) _____ he established the foundation for understanding "conditional reflexes." (8) Pavlov himself seems to have been conditioned by some set of previous experiences: He would have lunch at exactly noon each day and go to bed at exactly the same time each evening.

(9) This theory assumed dominance in analysis of humans, as well as animals, in the early 1900s, eclipsing the earlier belief, espoused by Rene Descartes, another scientist/philosopher. (10) Descartes proposed that human behavior resulted in new knowledge not derived from experience; therefore, the mind, which housed that new knowledge, was important to study.

31. Which of the following is the best meaning of the word *tenet* as it is used in the first paragraph of the passage?

    (A) Principle
    (B) Dweller
    (C) Explanation
    (D) Stronghold
    (E) Flavor

32. Which of the following numbered sentences is *least* relevant to the main idea of the second paragraph?

    (A) 4
    (B) 5
    (C) 6
    (D) 7
    (E) 8

33. Which of the following best organizes the main topics addressed in this passage?

    (A) I. Definition of behaviorism
        II. Origin of behaviorism
        III. Comparison to earlier dominant behavior theory

    (B) I. Beginnings of behaviorism
        II. How human cause–effect reactions were discovered
        III. Behaviorism originator Rene Descartes

    (C) I. Animal behaviorism
        II. Definition of behaviorism
        III. Purpose of behaviorism

    (D) I. Conditioned response explained
        II. Pavlov's dogs
        III. 20th century theories

    (E) I. Why behaviorism dominated behavioral theories
        II. Psychic secretions
        III. The importance of the mind

34. Based on the information in the passage, Pavlov's and Descartes' ideas differ because:

    (A) they were developed during different time periods.
    (B) they were competing philosopher/scientists.
    (C) one approaches behavior as mechanical; the other sees it as affected by the rational mind.
    (D) one is based on animal behavior; the other is based on human behavior.
    (E) one studied animals; the other studied the mind.

35. The best title for this passage is

    (A) Origins of Behaviorism
    (B) Cause and Effect
    (C) Leading Theories of Human Behavior
    (D) Theories and Their Originators
    (E) Pavlov's Experiments

Read the passage below; and then answer the five questions that follow.

Samples, representing the entire group being studied, are often used in scientific research. To be a sound sample, the subgroup of the whole must be similar enough to all of the members of the group that conclusions drawn from the sample are likely to be true of the whole group. This "generalizability," or ability to be representative, is extremely important, so researchers must be able to demonstrate that their sample's internal validity can be applied to outside the laboratory, or its external validity. In addition, a study based on a representative sample should include the margin of error, which indicates the mathematically derived amount of random variation underlying the survey's results. That is, the margin of error expresses the amount of variation one would see if the same study, experiment, or poll were conducted multiple times.

Before gathering a sample, it is important to find out as much as possible about the population. Population refers to the larger group from which the sample is taken. Researchers should at least know some of the overall demographics: age, sex, class, etc., about their population. This information will be needed later during the data analysis stage of the research, but it is also relevant to determining sample size. The greater the diversity and differences that exist in the population, the larger the sample size should be. Capturing the variability in the population allows for more variation in the sample, and many statistical tests operate on these principles of variation.

36. Between the first and second paragraphs, the writer's approach shifts from

    (A) demonstration to analysis.
    (B) description to application.
    (C) cause to effect.
    (D) persuasion to narration.
    (E) description to analysis.

37. The writer's argument in the passage is directed mainly at

    (A) students of literature.
    (B) special populations.
    (C) researchers.
    (D) mathematicians.
    (E) census takers.

38. Which of the following assumptions is most influential in the writer's argument in the excerpt?

    (A) Research involves a lot of experience and effort.
    (B) Respecting diversity is critical in a research study.
    (C) Laboratory studies are more valid than field studies.
    (D) Understanding mathematical concepts can be the key to good research.
    (E) Scientific research intends to be unbiased and accurate.

39. A logical conclusion to draw from the information in the passage is that

    (A) the best research is done with several subgroups.
    (B) internal validity is more important than external validity.
    (C) the larger the margin of error, the less confidence one has in the internal validity of the study, experiment, or polls.
    (D) random variation is commonplace in small research studies and should be encouraged whenever possible.
    (E) personal interviews will elicit better research information than phone interviews.

40. If a school has 600 students, consisting of 360 females and 240 males, and researchers looking into nutrition related to gender intend to sample 10% of the population, then which of the following is untrue?

    (A) The sample size should be 60 students.
    (B) The sample should consist of 36 females and 24 males.
    (C) The study's internal validity should be 10% of the study's external validity.
    (D) The researchers should reveal the margin of error, along with their other results.
    (E) The researchers should recommend that future studies be based on a sample that more closely represents the entire group's demographic diversity, rather than just its gender proportions.

Read the passage below, and then answer the four questions that follow.

(1) _____ the human eye sees something, the process involves light passing through the cornea, a tough, transparent tissue on the front of the eyeball, to the aqueous humor, which is a thin, watery fluid. (2) The aqueous humor chamber supplies oxygen and other nutrients to the cornea. (3) From the aqueous humor, light moves through the pupil, an opening in the center of the iris, made of colored tissue.

(4) Muscles in the iris cause contraction or expansion of the pupil, depending on the level of light entering the eye. (5) That's why it is important for adults to ensure children don't look directly into the sun. (6) Pupil size also changes with levels of emotional intensity, such as excitement and interest. (7) _____ a professional gambler, then, may be able to know other players' cards in a poker game by simply looking at the size of the card players' pupils.

41. Which of the sentences numbered in the passage expresses an opinion, rather than a fact?

    (A) 1
    (B) 2
    (C) 3
    (D) 4
    (E) 5

42. What is the best description of the order of events when light goes into the human eye?

    (A) The light passes through the cornea, where it gets oxygen, then on to the pupil, causing contraction of the pupil.

    (B) The light passes through the cornea, where it gets oxygen, then on to the transparent tissue in front of the eyeball, then to the pupil, causing contraction of the pupil.

    (C) The light passes through the cornea, where it gets oxygen, then on to the pupil, causing contraction or expansion of the pupil; the light passes through the cornea, then to the aqueous humor where it gets oxygen, then on to the pupil, causing contraction or expansion of the pupil.

    (D) The light passes through the cornea, then to the aqueous humor where it gets oxygen, then on to the pupil, causing contraction or expansion of the pupil.

    (E) The light passes through the aqueous humor where it gets oxygen, then on to the pupil, causing contraction or expansion of the pupil.

43. Which of the following numbered sentences is *least* relevant to the main idea of the second paragraph?

    (A) 1
    (B) 2
    (C) 3
    (D) 6
    (E) 7

44. Which of the following best organizes the main topics addressed in this passage?

    (A) I. How the Eye Works
        II. Changes in the Pupil

    (B) I. How the Eye Works
        II. What the Eye Needs to Function Properly

    (C) I. Types of Eye Functions
        II. Eye Diseases

    (D) I. Structure of the Eye
        II. Eye Protection

    (E) I. Cornea Function
        II. Pupil Function

Read the passage below, and then answer the six questions that follow.

Different ways of remembering have their own anatomy in the brain. Long-term memory, LTM, is either declarative or procedural. Declarative memory, which is learned facts and events, is processed in the brain's medial temporal region, not in the frontal lobes, as thought earlier.

(1) The first type of declarative memory, "generic memory," is based on general facts. (2) _____, when we attempt to locate our cell phones using our general knowledge of where misplaced things are often found, we are using our "generic memory." (3) _____. (4) "Episodic memory" is knowledge acquired from specific memories of real events. (5) When we look for our cell phones using the memory of where we found them the last time, we are using "episodic memory." (6) Both kinds of declarative memory can be measured through neuroimaging.

45. Which phrase, if inserted into the blank in the second paragraph, would best connect Sentence 1 and Sentence 2?

(A) However,
(B) Finally,
(C) That is,
(D) In addition,
(E) For instance,

46. Which sentence, if inserted into the blank labeled Sentence 3, would be most consistent with the writer's purpose and intended audience?

(A) Generic memory is also sometimes called semantic memory.
(B) The second type of declarative memory is episodic.
(C) Humans are specifically using the frontal lobes of our brains.
(D) Animals use more generic memory than episodic memory.
(E) Locating other misplaced things would follow the same process.

47. A conclusion that can be logically drawn from the passage is that

(A) Neuroimaging would show activity in the brain's frontal lobes when a person is looking for car keys.
(B) Neuroimaging would show activity in the brain's frontal lobes when a person is remembering where he or she last left the car keys.
(C) Neuroimaging would should activity in the brain's medial temporal region when a person is looking for car keys.
(D) Neuroimaging would show activity in the brain's medial temporal region when a person has found lost car keys.
(E) None of these

48. The next part of this excerpt can be expected to

    (A) explain why some doctors do not conduct neuroimaging on their patients.
    (B) provide a definition and explanation of procedural memory.
    (C) give an example of a person using both generic and declarative memory.
    (D) provide an explanation of the steps to becoming a neuroscientist.
    (E) provide a comparison of generic and episodic memory.

49. Which of the following would be the most appropriate title for this passage?

    (A) Varieties of Long-Term Memory
    (B) Neuroimaging Memory
    (C) Procedural Memory
    (D) The Function of Memory
    (E) Developing Strong Long-Term Memory

50. Which of the following best summarizes the main point of the passage?

    (A) Generic memory is more effective than declarative memory.
    (B) Long-term memories are accessed in different parts of the brain.
    (C) Long-term memory is based on either general knowledge or past experience.
    (D) The frontal lobes and the medial temporal region of the brain process all memories.
    (E) Generic memories deteriorate, while declarative memories do not.

Answer Key
MODEL EXAM 1: READING

1. **A**	14. **D**	27. **A**	39. **C**
2. **C**	15. **A**	28. **A**	40. **C**
3. **C**	16. **B**	29. **B**	41. **C**
4. **B**	17. **D**	30. **A**	42. **D**
5. **B**	18. **A**	31. **A**	43. **E**
6. **A**	19. **E**	32. **E**	44. **A**
7. **E**	20. **D**	33. **A**	45. **E**
8. **C**	21. **B**	34. **C**	46. **B**
9. **D**	22. **C**	35. **A**	47. **C**
10. **D**	23. **D**	36. **B**	48. **C**
11. **C**	24. **A**	37. **C**	49. **A**
12. **A**	25. **E**	38. **E**	50. **C**
13. **B**	26. **C**		

ANSWERS FOR MODEL EXAM 1: READING

1. **(A)** See Chapter 3.

2. **(C)** See Chapter 3.

3. **(C)** See Chapter 3.

4. **(B)** See Chapter 3.

5. **(B)** Using the substitution strategy explained in Chapter 3, we can determine that "In fact, in Helen Keller's book . . . " is the best of the first of the paired choices, and "Therefore, the early chapters are relevant to the question . . . ." makes best sense in the last sentence.

6. **(A)** The paragraph describes Keller's deaf state; sentence 5 states that Keller's book is relevant to "what it is like to be without language": therefore, answer (A) is the best answer. It even uses some of the same wording as in sentence 5.

7. **(E)** Opinions represent a person's personal evaluation of something; therefore they have a bias that may not be held by everyone else. It is easy, then, to find statements of opinion, like "The book is fascinating as . . . " because while some may agree with this opinion, it is unlikely that everyone would.

8. **(C)** Sentence 3 provides information about Mrs. Hopkins, a minor "character" in this passage; Annie Sullivan and Helen Keller are the important people. All other sentences that are answer choices describe something about Sullivan or Keller. So answer (C) is the best answer; in fact, it is quite irrelevant to the overall point of the passage.

9. **(D)** Since the information in the passage is based on a book Helen Keller wrote about her relationship to Annie Sullivan, her teacher, the best assumption is that the author holds a fundamental belief in the useful insights which books about teachers and students provide.

10. **(D)** The suggestion that learning Mandarin is so easy a young child can do it is not a rational basis for attending the advertised foreign language school. But it is a telling example of the fact that children learn their first language fluently and effortlessly.

11. **(C)** The second sentence in the second paragraph hypothesizes that the ad was removed because it was illegal; this leads us to know that answer (C) is the best answer.

12. **(A)** If you have underlined key words and phrases in this passage, you have noted that the second paragraph is about false and misleading ideas concerning language learning. Answer (C) about diet pills and answer (D) about making unnecessary purchases do not relate to false ideas and learning languages. Additionally, answer (B) is not a good choice since it is illogical to first indicate that learning foreign languages is difficult and then follow with "Children are able to speak a language without consulting grammars or dictionaries." However, answer (A)'s statement about critical thinking being a problem for advertisers does match the main idea of the false ideas in the ad, so it is the best answer.

13. **(B)** Using the substitution strategy provided in Chapter 3, you can determine that "The advertisement was *persuasive*," answer (B), is the best choice since that sentence is followed by another which articulates the ad's persuasive, not *unconvincing, demeaning, elegant,* or *comical,* message: an adult can learn anything a 4-year-old can learn.

14. **(D)** The advertisement was compelling because it is based on a fundamental belief that adults are more competent than children. This assumption is suggested by the fourth sentence, which describes the indirect message of the foreign language school ad: "An adult could learn to do anything a 4-year-old could do—and it shouldn't take very long."

15. **(A)** Having read this question before reading the passage, it should have been relatively easy to choose the best answer. Underlining and annotating the passage should have helped, also. The only type of baby talk register criticized in the passage is answer (A): "Simplifying the pronunciation of words . . . interferes with young children's learning to pronounce words correctly."

16. **(B)** Testing the first transition word in each pair, we conclude that "but" and "nevertheless" are the only two that truly fit in the indicated sentence. Then, checking the second word choice in answers (B) and (C), we find that "Similarly" is not a logical transition to begin the last sentence in the passage. Thus (B) is the best choice.

17. **(D)** Based on your underlining and annotating of the passage, you probably noted that the most frequent phrase is "baby talk register." In addition, your annotations probably indicate that answers (A), (B), and (C) are not specifically discussed in the passage. And the passage is clearly about adult talk to babies; it is not about the baby's "developing language skills"—answer (E).

18. **(A)** Having read the question before reading the passage, you most likely noticed that baby talk register is preferable for adults to use than "adult register," and that simplifying word pronunciation "does not help babies' language development." Using short phrases, repetition, and a "higher than usual pitch," however, are good means of communicating with babies. Answer (A) condenses all of these ideas into one sentence.

19. **(E)** While "register" may mean "record" or "enroll" in other contexts, in this context it is what is spoken to babies. So it must be answer (E).

20. **(D)** Under the larger category "Animal," we find "as pets" referenced to pages 21–23, answer (D).

21. **(B)** Under the larger category "Apes," "behavior analogous to humans" is explained on page 9.

22. **(C)** The chart gives two visual clues to the correct answer. First, the largest part of the pie chart is noted on the key as "nonsporting group." And 0.24 (out of 1.0) of nonsporting group dogs in the competition is a larger decimal than any other circle in the pie chart.

23. **(D)** Simply finding the two decimals which are the same (0.16) and correlating them to the group names in the key (terrier and hound) allow you to know that answer (D) is the correct choice.

24. **(A)** Using the context of the passage, a strategy explained in Chapter 3, you know that pheromones are the trigger for ants' burying behavior and for creating a food source trail. So pheromones mediate or . . . do something to the social life of insects. They don't *antagonize*, answer (B), *diminish*, answer (C), *signal*, answer (D), or *bury*, answer (E) the social life; they *influence* the social life of insects, such as ants.

25. **(E)** Focusing on the first transition in each pair, you can eliminate answer (B) and (C) and (D) because neither *then, in addition*, nor *similarly* is an appropriate transition in the indicated position. Considering the two remaining possibilities, answer (A) is eliminated because placing "however" before "*ants use pheromones to leave a trail . . .*" does not create an appropriate transition from the previous paragraph. Answer (E) remains, and both transitions make sense when placed in order in the blanks.

26. **(C)** Based on your outlining and annotating, you can see that the first paragraph is centered on ant behavior—the burying. Five of the eight sentences in the paragraph are about ants. So, reviewing the Roman numeral I choices, we can eliminate (A) because the first paragraph is not mainly about dogs; answer (B) because that paragraph is not mainly about following a trail or "finding their way." Since the first paragraph is about dog and ant behavior, it can't be condensed into examples of mammals, which is answer (E). Looking only, then, at Roman numeral II choices for (C) and (D) allows us to eliminate answer (D) because the second paragraph does not explain deception using pheromones. Therefore, answer (C) is the best choice.

27. **(A)** As explained in the second paragraph, ants will follow a "food source" pheromone, so they would leave the ant colony and follow the trail to the plastic cup.

28. **(A)** Eight of the eleven sentences in this passage are about ants, and your underlining and marginal notes probably brought out that focus. Therefore, since only answer (A) focuses on ants, it is the best choice.

29. **(B)** While both answers (A) and (B) are accurate, answer (B) is more precise, so it is the best choice.

30. **(A)** Each of the answers lists three of the types of crops, so the best answer will be the three types that add up to 50% or more. Answer (A) includes the three highest categories by percentage; adding them (18%, 15%, and 15%) results in approximately 50%. This is the largest possible sum from any of the five answer choices, so it is the best answer.

31. **(A)** Substituting each answer choice, "principle" is the best choice to adequately complete the phrase *the central* principle of *behaviorism.*

32. **(E)** Your underlining and marginal notes probably emphasized the idea that Pavlov's studies elicited ideas about "conditional reflexes" which are part of the theory of behaviorism. All the sentences listed as (A) through (D) answer choices are about Pavlov, his study, and behaviorism. So answer (E), though containing a comical, little-known fact about Pavlov, is the sentence with the least relevance to the whole.

33. **(A)** Again, using the strategy explained in Chapter 3, we check the statements given in each Roman numeral I part of the potential answers. We eliminate (B) because it is the second paragraph, not the first, that discusses the beginnings of behaviorism. We eliminate answer (C) because the first paragraph is not specifically about animals and their behavior. We eliminate answer (D) because conditioned response is explained in the second paragraph, not the first. And the statement in Roman numeral I of answer (E) is a condensed version of the third paragraph, not the first. Therefore, without having to consider the rest of the rough outline information, we know that answer (A) is the best choice.

34. **(C)** Having read the questions before reading the passage, you have anticipated spotting Pavlov's and Descartes' names. Descartes is only mentioned in the third paragraph; it says Descartes' beliefs were *earlier* than Pavlov's. However, answer (A) seems like an answer that could be given for a multitude of different theories. Is there a better answer? The further explanation of their different theories is contained in sentence 10. That sentence emphasizes "knowledge" and "mind," so Descartes' ideas revolve around those concepts. Answers (C) and (D) mention "mind," but which one is better? In the first paragraph, behaviorism, Pavlov's theory, is described as happening *almost mechanically.* So answer (C) is more precise than answer (E).

35. **(A)** Did you formulate your own title? Behaviorism is the focus of every sentence in the passage except the last one, so it should definitely be named in the title. Only answer (A) does this.

36. **(B)** The first paragraph contains many definitions—of a *sound sample,* of *external validity,* of *margin of error,* for instance. Therefore, it is not a demonstration, answer (A), an explanation of cause, answer (C), or a persuasive paragraph, answer (D). It describes samples used in research studies, and the second paragraph explains how to select a *sound sample* with *external validity*— knowing overall demographics. Thus, the second paragraph describes how to apply the concepts explained about sampling in the first paragraph. Answer (B), rather than answer (E), then, is the best choice.

37. **(C)** Since the passage is written in formal language, with several technical terms, it is created for an educated reader. It explains "how to" make decisions before collecting a research sample, so it is for researchers.

38. **(E)** The emphasis on a research study's validity, on demographics concerning a population's age, sex, and class, and disclosure of the margin of error all add up to the underlying belief that science *intends to be unbiased and accurate.*

39. **(E)** Only answer (E) is clearly an untrue statement, based on the information in the reading passage.

40. **(C)** Answers (A) and (B) are true because 10% of 600 is 60, and 10% of 360 and 240 is 36 and 24, respectively. Answers (C), (D), and (E) must be examined in relation to the passage. At first reading, answer (C) may have seemed odd. One approach is to skip it to return to later. Examining answer (D), you notice that in the first paragraph, the selection states that studies based on representative samples should include the margin of error, so (D) is also a true choice. Then, the second paragraph centers on the idea of population variety, that "the greater the diversity . . . in the population the larger the sample size should be." Therefore, answer (E) is also true. By process of elimination, then, answer (C) is the only untrue statement—whatever it means.

41. **(C)** Sentences 1, 2, 3, and 4 describe sections of the human eye and the progress of light through those sections. The sentences are written in serious, scientific language and are not opinions. On the other hand, a sentence that begins with "it is important" is likely to be an opinion, since whether something is important is a relative judgment. It cannot be verified and unanimously accepted.

42. **(D)** Based on short annotations or underlining of the passage, you can see that answer (E) is not the best choice because it begins with the aqueous humor, which is not the first stage of the process. Your annotations probably emphasized (1) cornea, (2) aqueous humor + oxygen, and (3) pupil. The answer that contains, in the same order, these key points in the process is (D).

43. **(E)** Sentences 1, 2, 3, and 6 contain scientific information. The first three sentences explain the beginning stages of light as it registers something on the mind. Sentence 7, though, does not present more scientific information; instead, it offers a side note to emphasize the ideas about pupil size change. In itself, then, it is the least relevant; of the choices given it is the sentence that is the least related to the overall purpose of the passage. Sentence 5, introducing the role of parents protecting children, is also somewhat unrelated to the purpose of the passage, but it is not an answer choice.

44. **(A)** Again, you should have underlined or annotated the passage based on a preview of the questions directed to this reading selection. Then, determine that answers (C), (D), and (E) do not present an accurate summation of the first paragraph, which is generally about *the process* when *the human eye sees something*. To select the best choice from answers (A) and (B), annotations or underlining of the second paragraph should easily indicate that it is all about the pupil and the iris. Therefore, answer (A) is the best choice.

45. **(E)** Sentence 2 in the second paragraph discusses locating cell phones, a very specific activity. Thus, the sentences moved from general (an overall definition of declarative memory) to a specific instance of using generic memory when locating a cell phone. Therefore, Sentence 2 should be introduced with "For instance."

46. **(B)** The first paragraph emphasizes declarative memory. The second paragraph begins with the description of the *first type* of declarative memory. And the last sentence tells something about *both kinds of declarative memory*. Therefore, a second type of declarative memory must be the *episodic memory* mentioned just before the blank line. Answer (B) provides a clear lead-in, then, to *episodic memory* as the second kind of declarative memory.

47. **(C)** Since the passage clearly says that the frontal lobes are not where long term memory is stored, answers (A) and (B) can be eliminated. The passage centers on remembering—memory—so the inference should be based on memory, not the brain's activity when experiencing a new situation, like finding lost car keys. So answer (D) can be eliminated. Carefully reading answer (C), you can see that it is a good choice because the passage states that declarative memory, whether generic or episodic, is processed in the medial temporal region. In addition, declarative memory, memories about learned facts and events, is memories accessed by use of general knowledge or specific memories of events. To find misplaced car keys, one could use either general knowledge about where lost items usually appear, or search for a specific memory of putting down the keys. Therefore, looking for misplaced car keys would activate the medial temporal region of the brain.

48. **(C)** To make a logical inference, you should have noted that the first paragraph introduces two kinds of long-term memory—declarative and procedural. The rest of the passage gives details about declarative memory, but nothing about procedural memory. It is highly likely, then, that procedural memory would be discussed following the given reading selection.

49. **(A)** While none of these titles may have been similar to the title you created in your mind, you should attempt to find the one that is the closest. The passage has yet to discuss procedural memory, so answer (C) can not be the most appropriate title. The passage is classifying long-term memory, so it is not discussing the purpose or *function* of memory or how one strengthens long-term memory, so answers (D) and (E) are eliminated. Neuroimaging is introduced in the last sentence in the passage, and an appropriate title would not focus on a small part of the whole, which eliminates answer (B), so answer (A) contains the most appropriate title.

50. **(C)** Since we have determined that "Varieties of long-term memory" is the best title for the passage, we can use that conclusion to help find the best answer for this item. Given this clue, the statement that presents something about "varieties" of memory is answer (C), which defines generic memory as split into two types. We can also determine that answers (A), (B), (D), and (E) are not better choices than (C) because they are all incorrect readings of the passage.

Model Exam 2: Reading
ANSWER SHEET

1 (A) (B) (C) (D) (E)
2 (A) (B) (C) (D) (E)
3 (A) (B) (C) (D) (E)
4 (A) (B) (C) (D) (E)
5 (A) (B) (C) (D) (E)
6 (A) (B) (C) (D) (E)
7 (A) (B) (C) (D) (E)
8 (A) (B) (C) (D) (E)
9 (A) (B) (C) (D) (E)
10 (A) (B) (C) (D) (E)
11 (A) (B) (C) (D) (E)
12 (A) (B) (C) (D) (E)
13 (A) (B) (C) (D) (E)

14 (A) (B) (C) (D) (E)
15 (A) (B) (C) (D) (E)
16 (A) (B) (C) (D) (E)
17 (A) (B) (C) (D) (E)
18 (A) (B) (C) (D) (E)
19 (A) (B) (C) (D) (E)
20 (A) (B) (C) (D) (E)
21 (A) (B) (C) (D) (E)
22 (A) (B) (C) (D) (E)
23 (A) (B) (C) (D) (E)
24 (A) (B) (C) (D) (E)
25 (A) (B) (C) (D) (E)
26 (A) (B) (C) (D) (E)

27 (A) (B) (C) (D) (E)
28 (A) (B) (C) (D) (E)
29 (A) (B) (C) (D) (E)
30 (A) (B) (C) (D) (E)
31 (A) (B) (C) (D) (E)
32 (A) (B) (C) (D) (E)
33 (A) (B) (C) (D) (E)
34 (A) (B) (C) (D) (E)
35 (A) (B) (C) (D) (E)
36 (A) (B) (C) (D) (E)
37 (A) (B) (C) (D) (E)
38 (A) (B) (C) (D) (E)

39 (A) (B) (C) (D) (E)
40 (A) (B) (C) (D) (E)
41 (A) (B) (C) (D) (E)
42 (A) (B) (C) (D) (E)
43 (A) (B) (C) (D) (E)
44 (A) (B) (C) (D) (E)
45 (A) (B) (C) (D) (E)
46 (A) (B) (C) (D) (E)
47 (A) (B) (C) (D) (E)
48 (A) (B) (C) (D) (E)
49 (A) (B) (C) (D) (E)
50 (A) (B) (C) (D) (E)

MODEL EXAM 2: READING

Here is your chance to practice another full test. Use the answer sheet preceding this test; then check your answers with the answer key.

> Read the passage below, and then answer the five questions that follow.

(1) A persistent debate remains among scientists about a critical period for language development. (2) Some research suggests that this critical period does exist. (3) After the age of 12, people are seldom able to achieve total fluency in a second language because their brains use an entirely different neural pathway to process the foreign language than they used when processing their native language.

(4) _____ Linguist Eric Lenneberg claims that if a child learns no language before the age of 12 years, language can never be learned in a fully functional sense. (5) This assertion's validity has been demonstrated only rarely, when highly unusual circumstances have led to a child being isolated from communication for those years. (6) _____ in these few, recent cases, such as "Genie," isolated at $1\frac{1}{2}$ years in 1958 from any human communication until the age of 13 years, and Oxana Malaya, a feral child found in the Ukraine in 1991 at the age of 9 years, the children were never able to master language, despite concentrated assistance from social workers and scientists.

1. Which of the following would be the most appropriate title for this passage?

   (A) Why Language Learning Is Difficult for Adults
   (B) Feral Children in the 20th Century
   (C) Second Language Fluency, a Myth?
   (D) A Critical Period for Language Development?
   (E) Lenneberg's Theory

2. Which of the following persuasive techniques is used in the passage?

   (A) Challenging assumptions
   (B) Identifying with readers
   (C) Using vivid language
   (D) Using real examples
   (E) Appealing to emotions

3. Which words or phrases, if inserted in order into the blanks in the passage, would help the reader understand the sequence of the writer's ideas?

   (A) For example, For instance
   (B) Nevertheless, In fact
   (C) Since, On the other hand
   (D) In contrast, Consequently
   (E) In addition, To illustrate

4. Between the first and second paragraphs of the passage, the writer's approach shifts from

   (A) demonstration to analysis.
   (B) generalization to exemplification.
   (C) analysis to inquiry.
   (D) description to persuasion.
   (E) cause to effect.

5. What pattern of organization does the author use in the second paragraph of the excerpt?

   (A) General to specific
   (B) Order of importance
   (C) Spatial order
   (D) Problem–solution order
   (E) Chronological order

Read the passage below, and then answer the five questions that follow.

Since the human brain size increases significantly and rapidly after birth, there is an extended period of time for language learning, when humans are compared to other animals. Unlike other mammals except chimpanzees, the juvenile brain's plasticity allows for development after birth, coinciding with the period of the most efficient language learning. This is the time period when children receive constant language input in daily, meaningful situations, allowing stronger neurological connections to continually develop.

In addition to <u>cerebral</u> development, a child's speech muscles, actually hundreds of small muscles, develop over time. That is why the ability to form certain complex sounds, such as "r" and "l," can only be done with fluency at an early age. If children are positively reinforced when they make these sounds, their ability to use their speech muscles to form those sounds will develop. If there is no reinforcement, the ability fades. Awareness of these factors has led some linguists to develop a "nativism" theory of language acquisition.

6. One inference that can be drawn from this passage is that

   (A) chimpanzee brains develop over time, unlike the brains of other animals.
   (B) only adults can make sounds like "r" and "l."
   (C) human brains are larger than those of other mammals.
   (D) a child's speech muscles develop exactly like a chimpanzee's speech muscles.
   (E) when a child's speech muscles develop, their brains develop.

7. Which of the following is the best meaning of the word *cerebral* as it is used in the second paragraph of the passage?

(A) Child-like
(B) Slow
(C) Speech
(D) Mammalian
(E) Brain

8. Based on the information contained in the passage, it is reasonable to conclude that

(A) children act a lot like primates.
(B) neurological connections are no longer formed when a child becomes an adult.
(C) "r" and "l" are easy sounds for children to make.
(D) adults who haven't learned to form "r" and "l" sounds as children will not be able to make those sounds fluently.
(E) language learning isn't important after the first few childhood years.

9. Which of the following would be the most appropriate title for this passage?

(A) Efficient Language Learning
(B) Childhood Language Fluency
(C) Developing a Child's Brain
(D) Brain Size
(E) Children and Animal Brain Development

10. The writer's main purpose in this passage is to

(A) persuade.
(B) use telling examples.
(C) appeal to emotion.
(D) cite authorities.
(E) None of these

> Read the passage below, and then answer the five questions that follow.

As infants, human beings are influenced by their innate urges to form close bonds with their primary care takers. Adults are often surprised at the strength of infants' tendencies to connect emotionally with their caregivers. Toddlers, _____, demonstrate joy at success and frustration at failure. These emotion-driven behaviors seem to be inborn. Yet the drive to form social bonds and to establish power is not only derived from the evolutionary mandate to survive and reproduce, but is also based on the role models and values presented to the child by his or her society. Personal desire for power, social bonds, self-esteem, and success, called psychosocial needs, are, _____ , biological as well as psychological.

11. Which words or phrases, if inserted in order into the blanks in the passage, would help the reader understand the sequence of the writer's ideas?

    (A) If, Then
    (B) In fact, In addition,
    (C) Likewise, Therefore,
    (D) When, consequently,
    (E) In fact, In contrast,

12. Which of the following is the best meaning of the word *innate* as it is used in the passage?

    (A) Child-like
    (B) Natural
    (C) Slow
    (D) Mammal
    (E) Strong

13. Which of the following would be the most appropriate title for this passage?

    (A) Emotional Bonds
    (B) Nature and Nurture
    (C) Infants and Toddlers
    (D) Children Need Self-Esteem
    (E) Toddlers and Adults

14. The author's main purpose in the passage is to

    (A) explain the bases of human needs.
    (B) show how children develop with adult care.
    (C) examine the ways in which children's needs are met.
    (D) compare infant and toddler behavior.
    (E) describe how an infant acts toward a care giver.

Read the passage below; and then answer the four questions that follow.

Competitiveness is a complex dynamic, especially in growing children. Those who are highly competitive enjoy being challenged and accomplishing difficult assignments. Additionally, they may be motivated just as strongly to avoid failure.

Children often believe that their failures are due to forces beyond their control. _____, as they grow up, children desire to avoid public humiliation and strive to master skills and meet socially defined standards. Therefore, many children grow up believing they can do anything if they "try hard enough." At the same time, and paradoxically, these children will avoid challenges since they may result in failure and shame.

15. Which sentence, if inserted into the blank line in the second paragraph, would be most consistent with the writer's purpose and intended audience?

   (A) Therefore, the loss of self-esteem that comes with failure is also beyond their control.
   (B) Then they are embarrassed, and that's so terrible because the children can remember that shame for a long time!
   (C) Children also believe in fairies and other magical creatures.
   (D) Their competitiveness is the basis of this counter-productive belief.
   (E) Even when adults tell them differently, they maintain this idea.

16. Information in the passage supports which of the following conclusions?

   (A) Adults should ensure that children do not experience failure.
   (B) If children try hard enough, they can accomplish difficult tasks.
   (C) Children select certain tasks based on their desire to avoid failure, as much as their need to succeed.
   (D) Children will do anything to avoid humiliation.
   (E) Challenges are especially appropriate for children since they lead to psychological growth.

17. Which of the following would be the most appropriate title for this passage?

   (A) Children's Beliefs
   (B) Childhood Challenges
   (C) Children Must Fail
   (D) Challenges
   (E) Competing Desires

18. From the information in the passage, it is possible to project that on a snow day

    (A) competitive children may stay on the baby slopes to avoid falling, while those who are less competitive will try to ski a slope of greater difficulty.
    (B) competitive children may try the hardest slopes first, demonstrating their desire to take on challenges.
    (C) children know if they try hard enough, they'll be able to ski on the difficult slopes.
    (D) competitive children will set up contests to "beat" the children who are less competitive.
    (E) competitive children will wait to see what others are doing before beginning to ski.

> Read the passage below, and then answer the five questions that follow.

(1) When a society is filled with people who feel alienated, unfairly treated, or baffled by rapid cultural change, they listen to charismatic leaders who represent confidence and strength of personality. (2) These leaders generally base their visions of the future on expectations of a better life with less suffering and pain. (3) The kind of uplifting message proposed by charismatic leaders is the opposite of a critical <u>diatribe</u> against the status quo. (4) A type of leader common today, as in most periods of intense social change, is the charismatic leader who inspires followers by the strength of his or her personality. (5) John F. Kennedy, Martin Luther King, Jr., Mahatma Gandhi, and Nelson Mandela were charismatic leaders whose political messages were not entirely <u>pragmatic</u> because they were filled with idealistic, positive messages.

19. Which of the following best describes the writer's pattern of organization in the passage?

    (A) Order of importance
    (B) Problem-solving format
    (C) Spatial order
    (D) Explaining with examples
    (E) Chronological order

20. Which of the following is the best meaning of the word *diatribe* as it is used in sentence 3?

    (A) Philosophy
    (B) Attack
    (C) Demeaning
    (D) Opposition
    (E) Symbol

Model Exam 2: Reading 249

21. The author's main purpose in the passage is to

    (A) explain how charismatic leaders win political office.
    (B) show how charismatic leaders address the psychological needs of their followers.
    (C) examine types of charismatic leaders from history.
    (D) show how alienated people dislike charismatic leaders.
    (E) describe how leaders develop charisma.

22. Which sentence is *least* relative to the main idea of the passage?

    (A) 1
    (B) 2
    (C) 3
    (D) 4
    (E) 5

23. Which of the following is the best meaning of the word *pragmatic* as it is used in the second paragraph of the passage?

    (A) Practical
    (B) Visionary
    (C) Likeable
    (D) Strong
    (E) Intellectual

Read the passage below, and then answer the three questions that follow.

The most common neurological disorder is autism, which affects approximately 1.5 million Americans today. The rate of autism is growing at a startling 10–17% per year, so in the next ten years there will be about 4 million autistic Americans. Although boys are four times more likely to be diagnosed with autism than girls, there are no other statistically outstanding factors. Neither race, ethnicity, family income, nor education level correlates with autism.

Autism manifests itself in abnormal patterns of behavior, social interaction, and communication ability. Children are often diagnosed before the age of three based on the delayed presence of social communication or imaginative play. Although researchers do not know the specific etiology of autism, they suspect that it is the result of seven specific genes present in individuals diagnosed as autistic.

Model Exam 2: Reading

24. Which of the following is the best meaning of the word etiology as it is used in the second paragraph of the passage?

(A) Background
(B) Results
(C) Methodology
(D) Validity
(E) Cause

25. According to information presented in the passage, autism is correlated with

(A) family income.
(B) ethnicity.
(C) education level.
(D) race.
(E) None of these

26. Which of the following inferences can be drawn from the information presented in the passage?

(A) Three-year-olds get autism more frequently than children of other ages.
(B) American children are more often diagnosed with autism than other children.
(C) The study of genetics could help in understanding autism.
(D) Girls enjoy social interaction more than boys.
(E) Seven genes are responsible for adult-onset autism.

Read the passage below, and then answer the three questions that follow.

"Row, Row, Row Your Boat" is a favorite children's round, a musical composition in which two or more voices sing exactly the same melody, beginning at different times. When three voices sing "Row, Row, Row Your Boat," they are simultaneously singing different notes in the same *tonic triad*, like C, E, and G, which is pleasing to the ear.

"Three Blind Mice" is the type of round called a canon. In this type of song the voices enter at different pitches, and, therefore, it is slightly more complicated to sing.

27. Which of the following best describes the writer's pattern of organization in the passage?

(A) Chronological order
(B) Explaining with examples
(C) spatial order
(D) problem-solving format
(E) order of importance

28. Based on the information in the passage, it is reasonable to infer that

    (A) children enjoy singing canons and rounds.
    (B) canons are best sung by people who can sing on key.
    (C) "Three Blind Mice" is the oldest canon in English.
    (D) rounds and canons were created for children.
    (E) adults are better at singing rounds than children.

29. Based on the information in the passage, a *tonic triad* is

    (A) a group of three singers.
    (B) three notes in sequence.
    (C) three harmonious notes.
    (D) three kinds of seltzer water.
    (E) a soprano, alto, and tenor.

Read the passage below, and then answer the three questions that follow.

(1) Radioactive atoms decay at a predictable rate. (2) The atoms disintegrate depending on the number of radioactive isotopes in the sample. (3) After half of the atoms have decayed, the rate of decay and the
Lines isotope's "half life" can be determined. (4) The half-life expresses the
(5) duration of time taken for half of any given number of isotopes to decompose. (5) _____, after 50% of the isotopes decay, another 25% will decay. (6) Then another approximately 13% will decay, and following that another approximately 7%. (7) Therefore, after four half-lives, over 90% of the radioactive material has disintegrated. (8)
(10) _____, it will take another 56 half-lives to disintegrate the rest. (9) This fact has important implications for policies concerning the disposal of radioactive materials in the ground or water.

30. Which words or phrases, if inserted in order into the blanks in the passage, would help the reader understand the sequence of the writer's ideas?

    (A) Thus, Nevertheless
    (B) Yet, On the other hand
    (C) On the other hand, For example
    (D) In addition, In fact
    (E) In fact, For example

31. Which of the following would be the most appropriate title for this passage?

    (A) Radioactive Material
    (B) Counting Isotope
    (C) Rate of Radioactive Decay
    (D) Disposal of Radioactive Materials
    (E) Sampling Radioactive Isotopes

32. Which sentence in the passage expresses an opinion?

    (A) 1
    (B) 3
    (C) 5
    (D) 7
    (E) 9

Read the passage below, and then answer the four questions that follow.

California was admitted into the United States in 1850 when its population dramatically increased due to the Gold Rush. Prior to that, the area was a free republic. After gold was discovered in the foothills east of Sacramento, thousands of people flocked to the region, making long, <u>arduous</u> inland trips from the east or sailing around South America's Cape Horn.

The nearest seaport was San Francisco Bay, located inland from a narrow strait called the Golden Gate. Therefore, San Francisco became the central location for bankers who financed exploration for gold. In addition, stores selling mining supplies, feed for pack animals, and hardware sprang up along what is now State Highway 49 between San Francisco and Sacramento.

33. One inference that can be drawn from this passage is

    (A) bankers and merchants expected the miners to be searching for gold for many years.
    (B) San Francisco is not far from Sacramento.
    (C) It took longer to travel from the east coast to California by land than by water.
    (D) the Golden Gate area was named after gold was discovered in the foothills east of Sacramento.
    (E) bankers and merchants became rich from their trade with the gold miners.

34. Which of the following best organizes the main topics addressed in this passage?

    (A) I. Mining for Gold
         II. Traveling to San Francisco

    (B) I. Land Travel to San Francisco
         II. Sea Travel to San Francisco

    (C) I. Population Boom in California
         II. Population Boom Near San Francisco

    (D) I. California as Free Republic
         II. California as U.S. State

    (E) I. The Gold Rush
         II. Naming San Francisco Bay

35. The author's main purpose in the passage is to

    (A) show how mob mentality can rule a situation.
    (B) explain the historical development of major cities in California.
    (C) show how capitalism became dominant in California in the 1850s.
    (D) examine the motives of Americans who came to populate California in the 1850s.
    (E) describe how some Americans lost everything they owned during the Gold Rush.

36. Which of the following is the best meaning of the word *arduous* as it is used in the first paragraph of the passage?

    (A) Unusual
    (B) Hot and dusty
    (C) Disappointing
    (D) Fulfilling
    (E) Demanding

Using the table of contents from a book about the San Andreas Fault, answer questions 37, 38, and 39.

The San Andreas Fault

Chapter One: Southern and Central Segments
Chapter Two: Northern Segments
Chapter Three: Notable Earthquakes
Chapter Four: Scientific Research
Chapter Five: Pop Culture References
Chapter Six: The Next "Big One"

37. The reader is looking for a description of the San Andreas fault lines which pass into Mexico. The reader would probably find this information most quickly and easily by looking first in which part of the book?

    (A) Chapter One
    (B) Chapter Two
    (C) Chapter Three
    (D) Chapter Four
    (E) Chapter Five

38. The reader is looking for a description of the 1906 San Francisco earthquake. The reader would probably find this information most quickly and easily by looking first in which part of the book?

    (A) Chapter One
    (B) Chapter Three
    (C) Chapter Four
    (D) Chapter Five
    (E) Chapter Six

39. The reader looking for information about predictions for future earthquakes would probably find this information most quickly and easily by looking at first in which part of the book?

    (A) Chapter One
    (B) Chapter Three
    (C) Chapter Four
    (D) Chapter Five
    (E) Chapter Six

Read the passage below, and then answer the three questions that follow.

Lassen Park in northern California is home to Mount Lassen, an active volcano, which was formed about 27,000 years ago. The volcano began as a dacite lava dome, breaking up overlaying rock as it emerged. Lassen reached its present height of 10,000 feet in only a few years, though it has been eroded by Ice Age glaciers. Later, smaller dacite domes emerged around Lassen, and steam eruptions and lava flows are still in evidence today.

40. According to the information in the passage, what happened first in the formation of Mount Lassen?

    (A) Mount Lassen was an active volcano.
    (B) Mount Lassen was a dacite lava dome.
    (C) Mount Lassen grew to a height of 10,000 feet.
    (D) Mount Lassen erupted.
    (E) Smaller dacite domes emerged around Mount Lassen.

41. Information presented in the passage best supports which of the following conclusions?

    (A) Mount Lassen will erupt some day.
    (B) Mount Lassen's height will continue to grow.
    (C) Visitors to Lassen Park can see lava flows and steam eruptions.
    (D) The smaller dacite domes will become as large as Mount Lassen.
    (E) Most active volcanoes grow to their present height in a few years.

42. What pattern of organization does the author use in the excerpt above?

    (A) Spatial order
    (B) Order of importance
    (C) General to specific
    (D) Problem–solution order
    (E) Chronological order

Read the passage below, and then answer the three questions that follow.

(1) The "Land of Gold" in Africa, the original empire of Ghana, was named in geographic literature as early as the eighth century A.D. (2) Not only was it a place wealthy in gold, but it was also a strong military power. (3) It is said that Ghana could put "200,000 warriors in the field, more than 40,000 being armed with bow and arrow." (4) Needless to say, the king of Ghana was extremely powerful, and he controlled the traffic of salt from the north as well as the trade in gold from the south. (5) The empire of Ghana supposedly had 22 kings before the Muslim era (622 A.D.).

(6) A Berber *jihad* in 1076 A.D. captured the capital of Ghana; the conquering Moroccan Berbers split the empire into small kingdoms, which immediately fell to feuding and destroying each other. (7) Approximately 150 years later, the Malinke in that area overthrew the oppressive Sossos and began the extensive Empire of Mali, the greatest of West Africa's precolonial empires.

43. Which of the following numbered sentences is *least* relevant to the main idea of the passage?

    (A) 2
    (B) 3
    (C) 4
    (D) 5
    (E) 7

44. Which of the following best summarizes the main point of the passage?

    (A) The Berbers destroyed a great empire.
    (B) Gold was the source of the empire of Ghana's strength.
    (C) The great empire of Ghana eventually became the empire of Mali.
    (D) The great empire of Mali, over time, became the empire of Ghana.
    (E) Local feuds ruined the empire of Ghana's chance to rebuild itself.

45. According to information in the passage,

    (A) Berbers from Morocco conquered the empire of Ghana.
    (B) salt was less important than gold to the king of Ghana.
    (C) the empire of Ghana received its name in the eighth century A.D.
    (D) Malinke oppressed Sossos in the region of the former empire of Ghana.
    (E) the Muslim era began in 622 C.E.

Read the passage below, and then answer the three questions that follow.

The participation dance called the "Hokey-Pokey" became popular in the United States in the 1950s, but it has a much earlier origin. Scholars have found dances and lyrics about the "hokey-pokey" or the "hokey-cokey" or the "okey-cokey" dating back to the 17th century. There is a similar Shaker song whose lyrics are: "I put my right hand in/ I put my right hand out/ I give my right hand a shake/ And I turn it all about." The relation between the dance's song title and lyrics has been explained as a <u>corruption</u> of the words "hocus pocus," the traditional magicians' incantation, which might be accompanied by shaking hands or feet.

46. Which of the following would be the most appropriate title for this passage?

    (A) How to Hokey-Pokey
    (B) Shaker Songs in Modern Times
    (C) Origin of the Hokey-Pokey
    (D) The Hokey-Pokey Hoedown
    (E) Variety in Hokey-Pokey Dances

47. What does the writer's closing observation that the "song title and lyrics have been explained as a corruption of the words 'hocus pocus,' the traditional magicians' incantation" suggest about the relationship between the lyrics and the way people participate in the dance?

    (A) People dance the Hokey-Pokey as the Shakers did.
    (B) People dance the Hokey-Pokey as if they were under a magician's spell.
    (C) People can participate in the Hokey-Pokey dance if they know the lyrics.
    (D) People can participate in the Hokey-Pokey using their left or their right hands.
    (E) People dance the Hokey-Pokey by shaking their hands or feet.

48. Which of the following is the best meaning of the word <u>corruption</u> as it is used in the passage?

    (A) Specification
    (B) Derogation
    (C) Ramification
    (D) Demonstration
    (E) Alteration

Using the following graph, answer questions 49 and 50.

Summer: June, July, August
Fall: September, October, November
Winter: December, January, February
Spring: March, April, May

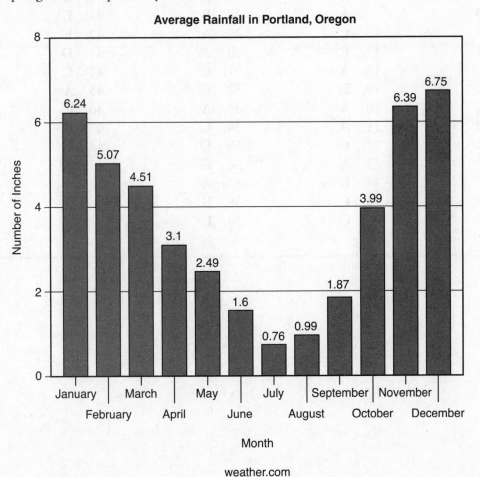

Average Rainfall in Portland, Oregon

weather.com

49. In which season is the average rainfall the greatest in Portland, Oregon?

   (A) Summer
   (B) Fall
   (C) Winter
   (D) Spring
   (E) Fall and Spring are the same

50. In which season is the average rainfall the least in Portland, Oregon?

   (A) Summer
   (B) Fall
   (C) Winter
   (D) Spring
   (E) Summer and Spring are the same

Answer Key
MODEL EXAM 2: READING

1. **D**	14. **A**	27. **B**	40. **B**
2. **D**	15. **A**	28. **B**	41. **E**
3. **E**	16. **C**	29. **A**	42. **E**
4. **B**	17. **E**	30. **A**	43. **D**
5. **A**	18. **A**	31. **C**	44. **C**
6. **A**	19. **D**	32. **E**	45. **A**
7. **E**	20. **B**	33. **A**	46. **C**
8. **D**	21. **B**	34. **C**	47. **B**
9. **B**	22. **C**	35. **D**	48. **C**
10. **E**	23. **A**	36. **E**	49. **C**
11. **C**	24. **E**	37. **A**	50. **A**
12. **B**	25. **C**	38. **B**	
13. **B**	26. **C**	39. **E**	

ANSWERS FOR MODEL EXAM 2: READING

1. **(D)** Only this title embodies, in a more general state, all the ideas within the passage. Did you try to create your own title first before selecting an answer?

2. **(D)** The examples of Genie and Oxana Malaya are used to compel the reader to agree with Lenneberg's claims.

3. **(E)** "In addition" is the only appropriate phrase to introduce the second theorist, and "To illustrate," appropriately precedes the details about the two children used as examples or illustrations.

4. **(B)** General ideas about all people's language fluency are presented in the first paragraph; the second paragraph provides the examples (exemplification) of Genie and Oxana Malaya.

5. **(A)** The second paragraph begins with a general explanation of Lenneberg's theory, followed by specific details related to the two children used as examples of the theory.

6. **(A)** The passage says chimpanzees are the exception to the fact that other mammals' brains are not like the human brain. Therefore, chimpanzee brains develop like human ones, which allow "for development after birth."

7. **(E)** "Cerebral" is used when referring back to the ideas in the previous paragraph, which was about brain development. So the best meaning, among the ones given, is "brain," which can be substituted for "cerebral": *In addition to brain development, the fact that a child's speech muscles . . .*

8. **(D)** The passage states that fluency in forming the complex sounds of *r* and *l* can be done only at an early age, so people who didn't practice those sounds as infants will not be able to say them fluently as adults. None of the other answers is an accurate conclusion drawn from the information in the passage.

9. **(B)** Both paragraphs talk about language learning in childhood.

10. **(E)** The authorities cited are the scientists mentioned in the first paragraph and the linguist Eric Lenneberg whose theory is the focus of the second paragraph.

11. **(C)** By substituting each pair of words/phrases, the correct answer can be seen as generating the sentences, *Toddlers, likewise, demonstrate joy . . .,* and *Personal desire for power, social bonds, self-esteem, and success, called psychosocial needs, are, consequently, biological . . .*

12. **(B)** The urges are described later in the passage as ones which "seem to be inborn." Therefore, innate must mean "natural."

13. **(B)** The topic sentence of the paragraph is the last one, describing a child's psychosocial needs as "biological as well as psychological"; therefore, the needs described in the passage are influenced by nature and nurture.

14. **(A)** The "strength" of children's "tendencies" and "emotion-driven behaviors" are the crux of this paragraph; therefore, the main purpose is to show the reader the bases of human needs.

15. **(A)** Based on the content and word choice, the intended audience is an educated public, and the first answer choice, beginning with "Therefore," matches the neutral, explanatory style of the initial ideas. The ideas are about children's failures, and answer (A) is the only choice that emphasizes the content of the passage.

16. **(C)** This statement accurately conveys the idea that children want to "avoid public humiliation" *and* "strive to master skills," which is explained throughout the passage.

17. **(E)** Several portions of the reading selection point to this being the best title. Avoiding failure and mastering new skills are discussed in this passage as two separate, "paradoxical" (because they are "competing" with each other) urges.

18. **(A)** The item focuses on competitive children in a hypothetical situation. Making a logical inference about the snow day scenario, the children's conflicting desires would prompt them to stay away from the difficult ski slopes—where they may fall when skiing and feel shamed—and remain on the easy slopes where they can more easily experience success.

19. **(D)** The ideas about leadership are not centered on a problem (B), or logically arranged in visual space (C). Nor are they in time order (E). Furthermore, the ideas are not all of equal importance and arranged in ascending or descending order of importance (A). The passage discusses charismatic leaders in the abstract, first, followed by the mention of four specific charismatic leaders. Thus, the passage explains with examples (D).

20. **(B)** Substituting the possible answers results in "attack" as the only selection which makes a meaningful statement: The kind of uplifting message proposed by charismatic leaders is the opposite of a critical "attack" against the status quo.

21. **(B)** Using process of elimination, since political position (A), categories of charismatic leaders (C), or the process of acquiring charisma (E), are not discussed in the passage, and since answer (D) is a misreading of the passage, answer (B) is the correct one. Also, answer (B) does articulate the passage's emphasis on the psychological need for "uplifting messages" of common people living in stressful times.

22. **(C)** The main purpose of the passage, to explain how people's psychological needs are met by charismatic leaders, can be achieved without this sentence, which simply defines "uplifting message" as the opposite of "critical diatribe."

23. **(A)** *Pragmatic* is in the sentence which contains a context clue, the definition of its opposite (signaled by *not . . .* pragmatic because . . .)—"Idealistic, positive messages." Pragmatic message must be the opposite of an ideal message, therefore something that is concrete or practical.

24. **(E)** Substituting the possible answers results in "cause" as a selection which makes the most meaningful or "best" statement. Although researchers do not know the specific *cause* of autism, they suspect that it is the effect of . . . . "Background" may also fit the general meaning of the sentence, but "cause" is a more specific term, thus the better choice.

25. **(C)** The last sentence in the first paragraph provides this answer.

26. **(C)** Answers (A), (B), (D), and (E) are not supported by the passage. Since the passage says that "seven specific genes" are possibly the cause of autism, answer (C) is a logical inference.

27. **(B)** Two types of songs, rounds and canons, are described through the examples of the songs "Row, Row, Row Your Boat" and "Three Blind Mice," respectively.

28. **(B)** Answers (A) and (D) cannot be logical inferences since the passage does not discuss children when discussing canons. Answer (E) cannot be logically deduced since adults are not mentioned in the first paragraph. No mention of time periods is given in the passage, so answer (C) cannot be correct. Since the singers have to begin the song on three different notes, it is logical that people who can sing on key (B) are better choices for singing canons.

29. **(A)** The musical notes C, E, and G are mentioned as examples of a tonic triad; therefore, it is a set of "three harmonious notes."

30. **(A)** Substituting the choices, answer (A) results in the addition of reasonable connections between the ideas: Sentence 5's detail about the second 25% decay follows logically after Sentence 4's information about the first stage of decay. And Sentence 8's fact, that 56 half-lives remain, is somewhat surprising, given that 90% of the isotope has already disintegrated. Therefore, "thus" and "nevertheless" are the best choices.

31. **(C)** The passage does not talk about counting isotopes or the disposing or sampling of radioactive material. It does describe radioactive material (A), but a more specific name for the passage is given in (C) since all the details are about the "predictable rate" of radioactive atomic decay.

32. **(E)** Having read the questions before reading the passage, test-takers should find it easy to spot the only opinion—Sentence 9. Every other choice is statistical or factual.

33. **(A)** Banks and stores would not have been built in the area between San Francisco and Sacramento unless the builders and financers expected the miners to be working there, needing supplies and banks, for many years.

34. **(C)** As explained in Chapter 3, the best answer can be selected by first eliminating the answers in which Roman numeral I is not accurate. These include (B) because the first paragraph is not only about sea travel and (D) because the paragraph mentioned the republic in only one of its sentences. Checking the statements in Roman numeral II, choices (A) and (E) are eliminated because the second paragraph is not mainly about travel, nor is it about naming the bay. Therefore, (C) is the best answer.

35. **(D)** Knowing the main points of the two passages as listed in answer (C) above, the main purpose must have something to do with California's population. Thus, answer (D) is the best choice.

36. **(E)** Substituting the choices, the only two words that would make sense in the sentence are "hot and dusty" and "demanding." Since the trip from the east coast would include regions that are neither hot nor dusty, answer (E) is the best choice.

37. **(A)** Chapter 1 discusses the San Andreas fault in the southern (and central) segments, and Mexico is south of California.

38. **(B)** The 1906 San Francisco earthquake and resulting fires caused immense damage in that area, so it was a "notable earthquake."

39. **(E)** A "future" earthquake could be the next "Big One."

40. **(B)** As the paragraph says, "The volcano began as a dacite lava dome . . . ."

41. **(E)** Since it is an active volcano, lava flows and steam eruptions are likely to be visible. The other statements are less likely or reasonable, based on the information in the passage.

42. **(E)** From 27,000 years ago, the progress of the volcano and mountain formation is described. "Later" as a transition word is a clue that this is in chronological order.

43. **(D)** Sentence 5 names the number of kings in Ghana before 622 A.D. The rest of the passage discusses the wealth and power of the area from 700 A.D. to 1200 A.D. Sentence 2, which brings up the name "Land of Gold", Sentence 3, which cites the number of warriors, Sentence 4, which explains the control of salt and gold traffic, and Sentence 7, which describes the "greatest of West Africa's post-colonial empires" are all important is providing evidence of this wealth and power. Although the number of kings is somewhat related to the wealth and power of the region, Sentence 5 is the "least relevant."

44. **(C)** Did you notice that answers (C) and (D) are opposites? As explained in Chapter 3, one of the two opposing statements is often the correct answer, as it is here.

45. **(A)** All answers except (A) are misreadings of the passage. This is a good example of the importance of actively reading, underlining, and annotating the reading selections.

46. **(C)** The topic sentence, the first sentence in the paragraph, provides a clue to the most appropriate title choice.

47. **(B)** The last sentence says that "hocus pocus" might be said while shaking hands or feet, so since the dance is done by giving the "right hand a shake," etc., the dancers are acting as if they were under a magic spell.

48. **(C)** The reading passage says that "Hokey-Pokey" is a corruption of "hocus pocus." Since the phrases are similar, the meaning of "corruption" here is "alteration," or change.

49. **(C)** Using the information describing the seasons and the graph, it is apparent that the months of December, January, and February are three of the four months of highest average rainfall, so winter would be the season of greatest average rainfall.

50. **(A)** June, July, and August are the three lowest bars on the graph; they are the months of summer. Therefore, summer is the season of lowest average rainfall.

Model Exam 1: Math
ANSWER SHEET

1 Ⓐ Ⓑ Ⓒ Ⓓ Ⓔ 14 Ⓐ Ⓑ Ⓒ Ⓓ Ⓔ 27 Ⓐ Ⓑ Ⓒ Ⓓ Ⓔ 39 Ⓐ Ⓑ Ⓒ Ⓓ Ⓔ
2 Ⓐ Ⓑ Ⓒ Ⓓ Ⓔ 15 Ⓐ Ⓑ Ⓒ Ⓓ Ⓔ 28 Ⓐ Ⓑ Ⓒ Ⓓ Ⓔ 40 Ⓐ Ⓑ Ⓒ Ⓓ Ⓔ
3 Ⓐ Ⓑ Ⓒ Ⓓ Ⓔ 16 Ⓐ Ⓑ Ⓒ Ⓓ Ⓔ 29 Ⓐ Ⓑ Ⓒ Ⓓ Ⓔ 41 Ⓐ Ⓑ Ⓒ Ⓓ Ⓔ
4 Ⓐ Ⓑ Ⓒ Ⓓ Ⓔ 17 Ⓐ Ⓑ Ⓒ Ⓓ Ⓔ 30 Ⓐ Ⓑ Ⓒ Ⓓ Ⓔ 42 Ⓐ Ⓑ Ⓒ Ⓓ Ⓔ
5 Ⓐ Ⓑ Ⓒ Ⓓ Ⓔ 18 Ⓐ Ⓑ Ⓒ Ⓓ Ⓔ 31 Ⓐ Ⓑ Ⓒ Ⓓ Ⓔ 43 Ⓐ Ⓑ Ⓒ Ⓓ Ⓔ
6 Ⓐ Ⓑ Ⓒ Ⓓ Ⓔ 19 Ⓐ Ⓑ Ⓒ Ⓓ Ⓔ 32 Ⓐ Ⓑ Ⓒ Ⓓ Ⓔ 44 Ⓐ Ⓑ Ⓒ Ⓓ Ⓔ
7 Ⓐ Ⓑ Ⓒ Ⓓ Ⓔ 20 Ⓐ Ⓑ Ⓒ Ⓓ Ⓔ 33 Ⓐ Ⓑ Ⓒ Ⓓ Ⓔ 45 Ⓐ Ⓑ Ⓒ Ⓓ Ⓔ
8 Ⓐ Ⓑ Ⓒ Ⓓ Ⓔ 21 Ⓐ Ⓑ Ⓒ Ⓓ Ⓔ 34 Ⓐ Ⓑ Ⓒ Ⓓ Ⓔ 46 Ⓐ Ⓑ Ⓒ Ⓓ Ⓔ
9 Ⓐ Ⓑ Ⓒ Ⓓ Ⓔ 22 Ⓐ Ⓑ Ⓒ Ⓓ Ⓔ 35 Ⓐ Ⓑ Ⓒ Ⓓ Ⓔ 47 Ⓐ Ⓑ Ⓒ Ⓓ Ⓔ
10 Ⓐ Ⓑ Ⓒ Ⓓ Ⓔ 23 Ⓐ Ⓑ Ⓒ Ⓓ Ⓔ 36 Ⓐ Ⓑ Ⓒ Ⓓ Ⓔ 48 Ⓐ Ⓑ Ⓒ Ⓓ Ⓔ
11 Ⓐ Ⓑ Ⓒ Ⓓ Ⓔ 24 Ⓐ Ⓑ Ⓒ Ⓓ Ⓔ 37 Ⓐ Ⓑ Ⓒ Ⓓ Ⓔ 49 Ⓐ Ⓑ Ⓒ Ⓓ Ⓔ
12 Ⓐ Ⓑ Ⓒ Ⓓ Ⓔ 25 Ⓐ Ⓑ Ⓒ Ⓓ Ⓔ 38 Ⓐ Ⓑ Ⓒ Ⓓ Ⓔ 50 Ⓐ Ⓑ Ⓒ Ⓓ Ⓔ
13 Ⓐ Ⓑ Ⓒ Ⓓ Ⓔ 26 Ⓐ Ⓑ Ⓒ Ⓓ Ⓔ

MODEL EXAM 1: MATH

1. Simplify:

$$5(7-4)^2 - (-3) = ?$$

(A) 27
(B) 42
(C) 48
(D) 162
(E) 168

2. Find the value of *x*:

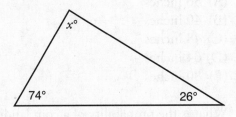

(A) 30
(B) 80
(C) 84
(D) 90
(E) 180

3. Twice a number less 15 is 27. What is the number?

(A) 12
(B) 21
(C) 28
(D) 42
(E) 57

4. Find the value of *x*:

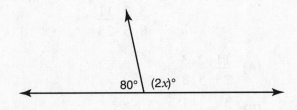

(A) 180
(B) 100
(C) 80
(D) 50
(E) 20

5. Due to its lower gravity, a 180-pound man would weigh only 30 pounds on the moon. If a girl weighed 17 pounds on the moon, what would be her weight on Earth?

(A) $2\frac{2}{3}$
(B) 3
(C) 80
(D) 92
(E) 102

6. Rounded to the nearest whole number, $\sqrt{116} = ?$

(A) 10
(B) 11
(C) 12
(D) 58
(E) 60

7. A sales representative earns a commission of 8% for her first $10,000 in sales and 11% for any additional sales. What would be her commission on $17,000 in sales?

(A) $770
(B) $800
(C) $870
(D) $1,570
(E) $1,870

8. Simplify the following if $x = -2, b = \frac{1}{2}$, and $m = 6$.

$$-2\,(x - m) \div b$$

(A) 32
(B) 16
(C) 8
(D) 4
(E) 2

9. The sophmore class at a local high school enrolled in the following math classes:

Pre-algebra   45 students
Algebra I   60 students
Geometry   85 students
Algebra II   10 students

What percent of the students was enrolled in Algebra I ?

(A) 30
(B) 40
(C) 50
(D) 60
(E) 85

10. What is one-half of one-sixth of twenty-four?

(A) 2
(B) 3
(C) 4
(D) 6
(E) 8

11. Sheila ran the 100-meter dash in the following times on consecutive days:

13.7, 14.4, 13.9, 15.1

To the nearest tenth of a second, what was her average time?

(A) 11.4
(B) 13.2
(C) 14.2
(D) 14.3
(E) 14.4

12. When Juan received his GRE score, the score report indicated the following:

Raw Score	Percentile	Stanine
74	92	9

What can Juan conclude about his score?

(A) He scored as well as or better than 92% of the test-takers.
(B) He scored in the top 9% of test-takers.
(C) His score was 74%.
(D) His stanine score was not in the top category.
(E) 100 people took the test.

13. A square picture has a side length measuring 8 inches and is surrounded by a 2-inch frame. What is the perimeter of the frame?

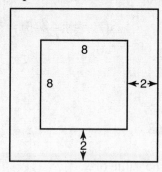

(A) 36 inches
(B) 40 inches
(C) 48 inches
(D) 64 inches
(E) 80 inches

14. What is the probability of a coin landing on tails in four consecutive flips?

(A) $\frac{1}{2}$

(B) $\frac{1}{4}$

(C) $\frac{1}{8}$

(D) $\frac{1}{16}$

(E) $\frac{1}{32}$

15. Place the following fractions in descending order:

$$\frac{3}{8}, \frac{2}{5}, \frac{11}{25}$$

(A) $\frac{11}{25}, \frac{2}{5}, \frac{3}{8}$

(B) $\frac{3}{8}, \frac{2}{5}, \frac{11}{25}$

(C) $\frac{11}{25}, \frac{3}{8}, \frac{2}{5}$

(D) $\frac{2}{5}, \frac{3}{8}, \frac{11}{25}$

(E) $\frac{3}{8}, \frac{11}{25}, \frac{2}{5}$

16. A city with 2,007,243 residents in 1970 had only 1,783,275 residents in 2000. What is the best estimate of the decline in population?

    (A) 200,000
    (B) 180,000
    (C) 80,000
    (D) 20,000
    (E) 15,000

17. The high temperature in Fairbanks during February averages 13°F. By midnight the average temperature drops to −7°F. What is the typical range of temperatures in February?

    (A) −6°
    (B) 6°
    (C) 7°
    (D) 13°
    (E) 20°

18. Solve for *n*:
    $$3n - p = 2r$$

    (A) $\frac{2}{3}r - p$

    (B) $\frac{2}{3}r + p$

    (C) $\frac{2}{3}r + \frac{p}{3}$

    (D) $p + 2r$

    (E) $p - 2r$

19. What is the tens digit in the following problem?

    $$24\overline{)1\boxed{?}7}^{\,6^{r3}}$$

    (A) 2
    (B) 3
    (C) 4
    (D) 5
    (E) 6

20. A jogger ran $8\frac{1}{5}$ miles on Monday and $7\frac{3}{4}$ miles on Tuesday. How much less did the jogger run on Tuesday than on Monday?

    (A) $1\frac{9}{20}$ miles

    (B) $\frac{9}{20}$ mile

    (C) $15\frac{9}{20}$ miles

    (D) $1\frac{2}{5}$ miles

    (E) $\frac{3}{5}$ mile

21. What is the perimeter of a square with a side measuring 7 inches?

    (A) 14 inches
    (B) 24.5 inches
    (C) 25.5 inches
    (D) 28 inches
    (E) 49 inches

22. A school bus can transport 24 students per trip. If 107 students need to be transported, how many trips should be planned?

    (A) 5

    (B) $4\frac{13}{24}$

    (C) $4\frac{11}{24}$

    (D) 4
    (E) 3

23. The Aquino family will begin a road trip next week. On average, they expect to drive 350 miles for each of six consecutive days. If their car travels 32 miles per gallon of gasoline, what will be the cost for gasoline?

What additional information do the Aquino's need to calculate their cost?

(A) Weather conditions for next week.
(B) The total miles to be traveled.
(C) The cost of a gallon of gas.
(D) The number of gallons of gas needed for each day of driving.
(E) The total number of gallons needed for the entire trip.

24. The chart shown below represents a breakdown of students by class at a small high school. If the school's total enrollment is 400 students, how many of the students are 11th graders?

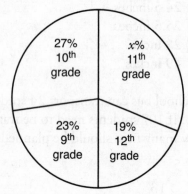

(A) 31
(B) 62
(C) 124
(D) 180
(E) 360

25. Sam received scores of 88, 84, and 91 on his last three tests. What must he score on his fourth test to average 90% for all four of the tests?

(A) 97
(B) 96
(C) 95
(D) 94
(E) 93

26. A rope that measures 81 feet 3 inches is cut into five equal pieces. What is the length of each piece of rope?

(A) 12 feet 3 inches
(B) 15 feet 2 inches
(C) 16 feet $\frac{1}{4}$ inches
(D) 16 feet 3 inches
(E) 18 feet 4 inches

27. A camera that normally sells for $95.00 has a sale price of $76.00. What percent is the camera discounted?

(A) 19
(B) 20
(C) 21
(D) 22
(E) 35

28. Ada works 36 hours per week at an hourly rate of $7.60. Her employer will give her a raise, increasing her weekly pay to $291.60. On an hourly basis, how much was her raise?

(A) $.40
(B) $.50
(C) $.52
(D) $.60
(E) $.65

29. There are three blue marbles, five red marbles, and two clear marbles in a bag. What is the probability of selecting a blue or a red marble on the first draw?

(A) $\frac{1}{5}$

(B) $\frac{3}{10}$

(C) $\frac{1}{2}$

(D) $\frac{7}{10}$

(E) $\frac{4}{5}$

30. What is the best estimate of 2,843 × 7,921?

    (A) 24,000
    (B) 240,000
    (C) 2,400,000
    (D) 24,000,000
    (E) 240,000,000

31. What number is 20% of 1?

    (A) $\frac{1}{8}$

    (B) $\frac{1}{6}$

    (C) $\frac{1}{5}$

    (D) $\frac{1}{4}$

    (E) $\frac{1}{3}$

Use the graph below to answer questions 32 and 33. The graph represents the average daily circulation (in thousands) of a local newspaper:

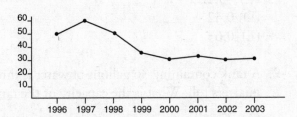

32. During which year did the steepest decline in circulation occur?

    (A) 2003
    (B) 2001
    (C) 1999
    (D) 1998
    (E) 1996

33. What was the greatest decrease in circulation in any given year?

    (A) 10,000
    (B) 14,000
    (C) 16,000
    (D) 18,000
    (E) 22,000

34. In a particular class, one-half of the students left at the ringing of the recess bell. Five minutes later, one-half of the remaining students left the class. If nine students remain in the class, how many students were originally in the class?

    (A) 48
    (B) 36
    (C) 24
    (D) 12
    (E) 6

35. A cubical box, measuring 6 inches on an edge, needs to be gift wrapped with a ribbon and a bow. The ribbon must cross through the middle of each face of the box. An additional 10 inches of ribbon is needed for the bow. How much ribbon is needed to wrap the box and create the bow?

    (A) 24
    (B) 36
    (C) 46
    (D) 48
    (E) 227

36. How many lunch combinations of sandwich, drink, and side order are available at a restaurant if it offers 5 different sandwiches, 3 different drinks, and 2 different side orders?

    (A) 10
    (B) 20
    (C) 30
    (D) 40
    (E) 50

37. If *x* and *y* have a unique relationship, find the missing value?

x	y
-2	-6
0	0
3	9
11	?
15	45

(A) 22
(B) 33
(C) 36
(D) 42
(E) 48

38. Which of the following mathematical statements is correct?

(A) $5\frac{1}{3} > 4\frac{3}{8} > 4\frac{1}{8}$

(B) $5\frac{1}{3} < 4\frac{3}{8} < 4\frac{1}{8}$

(C) $5\frac{1}{3} > 4\frac{1}{8} > 4\frac{3}{8}$

(D) $4\frac{3}{8} > 4\frac{1}{8} > 5\frac{1}{3}$

(E) $4\frac{1}{8} < 5\frac{1}{3} < 4\frac{3}{8}$

39. $0.004 < x < 0.04$

Which of the following values for *x* will satisfy this expression?

(A) 0.0005
(B) 0.031
(C) 0.44
(D) 0.68
(E) 4.0

40. No woman in the Diaz family is taller than 5 feet 6 inches tall. Which of the following conclusions can be made based on this statement?

(A) Any woman shorter than 5 feet 6 inches tall is in the Diaz family.
(B) Some women in the Diaz family are taller than 5 feet 6 inches.
(C) No woman who is exactly 5 feet 6 inches tall could be in the Diaz family.
(D) Only one woman in the Diaz family is taller than 6 feet tall.
(E) A certain woman, who stands 5 feet 8 inches tall, cannot be a member of the Diaz family.

41. What is a good estimate for the value of point *A* on the number line?

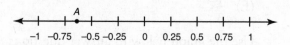

(A) -0.63
(B) -0.42
(C) -0.22
(D) 0.42
(E) 0.63

42. A tank containing 36 gallons of water is three-quarters full. What is the capacity of the tank?

(A) 27 gallons
(B) 32 gallons
(C) 40 gallons
(D) 45 gallons
(E) 48 gallons

43. Which of the following is an appropriate unit to express the weight of a bowling ball?

(A) pounds
(B) quarts
(C) ounces
(D) yards
(E) cubic inches

44. 7 ★ 4 = 27

    Which of the following rules explains this made-up function?

    (A) Multiply the two numbers.
    (B) Divide the two numbers.
    (C) Multiply the two numbers and decrease the product by 1.
    (D) Multiply the two numbers and increase the product by 3.
    (E) Divide the two numbers and subtract 1.

45. The distance between two towns is 390 miles. A trucker must leave one town and arrive at the other no later than 10:00 P.M. If the trucker drives at an average rate of 60 miles per hour, at what time should the trucker depart?

    (A) 2:30 P.M.
    (B) 3:00 P.M.
    (C) 3:30 P.M.
    (D) 4:00 P.M.
    (E) 4:30 P.M.

46. William will rent a car for one day. He must choose between two car rental agencies. Company A offers a daily rate of $30.00 and charges $.10 per mile. Company B offers a daily rate of $24.00 and charges $.20 per mile. At what number of miles will each agency charge the same amount?

    (A) 24
    (B) 32
    (C) 48
    (D) 54
    (E) 60

47. Tom goes to school Monday through Friday. If Tom is sick, he does not go to school. If the day is a holiday, Tom does not go to school. Which of the following must be true?

    (A) If Tom is not in school, he must be sick.
    (B) If Tom is in school, it must be Tuesday.
    (C) If Tom is not in school, it must be a holiday.
    (D) If Tom is in school, it is not a holiday nor is he sick.
    (E) Tom goes to school on some holidays.

48. The amount of water needed to fill a bath tub would be best expressed in which unit of measurement?

    (A) ounces
    (B) pounds
    (C) cups
    (D) gallons
    (E) tons

49. Tammy's purchases at the home improvement center were $8.89, $11.17, and $41.37. To the nearest dollar, what is the best estimate of the cost of her purchases?

    (A) $61.43
    (B) $61.00
    (C) $60.37
    (D) $60.00
    (E) $50.00

50. A train was traveling from San Diego to Los Angeles. The average speed of the train was 75 miles per hour. If the train arrived in Los Angeles at 2:00 P.M., how many miles had it traveled?

    What additional information is necessary to answer the question above?

    (A) The number of stops made during the trip
    (B) The speed of the train
    (C) Average speeds the train traveled on other days
    (D) The departure time from San Diego
    (E) Weather conditions on the day of this particular trip

ANSWERS AND EXPLANATIONS FOR MODEL EXAM 1: MATH

1. **(C)** Order of operations: $5(7 - 4)^2 - (-3)$
   Simplify parentheses: $5 \cdot 3^2 - (-3)$
   Simplify exponent: $5 \cdot 9 - (-3)$
   Multiply: $45 - (-3)$
   Subtract: $45 - (-3) = 45 + 3 = 48$

2. **(B)** The sum of the measures of the angles in a triangle equals 180°. Therefore,

   $$x + 74 + 26 = 180$$
   $$x + 100 = 180$$
   $$x = 80$$

3. **(B)** Let x = the number

   $$2x - 15 = 27$$
   $$2x = 42$$
   $$x = 21$$

4. **(D)** A straight line (also known as a straight angle) equals 180°.

   $$80 + 2x = 180$$
   $$2x = 100$$
   $$x = 50$$

5. **(E)** Use the ratio $\dfrac{\text{weight on the moon}}{\text{weight on Earth}}$

   $$\frac{30}{180} = \frac{17}{x}$$

   Reduce $\dfrac{30}{180} : \dfrac{1}{6} = \dfrac{17}{x}$

   Cross-multiply: $x = 102$

6. **(B)** $\sqrt{100} = 10$ $\sqrt{121} = 11$

   Since 116 is closer to 121, $\sqrt{116}$ is closer to 11.

7. **(D)**

   $10,000 @ 8\% : 10,000(0.08) = \$800$
   $7,000 @ 11\% : 7,000(0.11) = \$770$
   Total: $1,570

8. **(A)** Substitute values:

$$-2\left(-2-6\right)\div\frac{1}{2}$$
$$-2\left(-8\right)\div\frac{1}{2}$$
$$16\div\frac{1}{2}$$
$$16\times 2=32$$

9. **(A)** Percent formula:

$$\frac{\text{Part}}{\text{Whole}}=\frac{x}{100}$$
$$\frac{60}{45+60+85+10}=\frac{x}{100}$$
$$\frac{60}{200}=\frac{x}{100}$$
$$200x=6,000$$
$$x=30$$

10. **(A)** Of means multiply :

$$\frac{1}{2}\cdot\frac{1}{6}\cdot 24=\frac{1}{12}\cdot 24=2$$

11. **(D)**

$$(13.7 + 14.4 + 13.9 + 15.1) \div 4$$
$$57.1 \div 4 = 14.275$$

Round to the nearest tenth of a second: 14.3 seconds

12. **(A)** Since Juan scored in the 92nd percentile, his score was equal to or greater than 92% of the test takers.

13. **(C)**

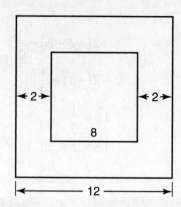

The length of one side of the frame is 12 inches (see diagram). Since the frame is also a square, it has four equal sides. Multiply one side length by 4 to find the perimeter:

$$4 \times 12 = 48$$

Some test-takers add the width of only one border, resulting in the incorrect selection of answer choice B.

14. **(D)** The probability of a flipped coin landing on heads is $\frac{1}{2}$. Find the probability of a flipped coin landing on heads in four consecutive flips by multiplying $\frac{1}{2}$ by itself four times:

$$\frac{1}{2} \times \frac{1}{2} \times \frac{1}{2} \times \frac{1}{2} = \frac{1}{16}$$

15. **(A)** Convert the fractions into decimals:

$$\frac{3}{8} = 0.375$$

$$\frac{2}{5} = 0.4$$

$$\frac{11}{25} = 0.44$$

$$0.44 > 0.4 > 0.375$$

$$\frac{11}{25} > \frac{2}{5} > \frac{3}{8}$$

16. **(A)** Round each number to the nearest hundred thousand:

2,007,243 rounds to 2,000,000

1,783,275 rounds to 1,800,000

2,000,000 − 1,800,000 = 200,000

17. **(E)** To find the range, subtract the lower temperature from the higher temperature:

$$13 - (-7) = 20$$

18. **(C)**

$$3n - p = 2r$$
$$3n - p + p = 2r + p$$
$$3n = 2r + p$$
$$\frac{3n}{3} = \frac{2r}{3} + \frac{p}{3}$$

$$n = \frac{2r}{3} + \frac{p}{3}$$

19. **(C)** Multiply 6 by 24 then add 3:

$$6 \times 24 + 3 = 147$$

The missing digit in the tens place is 4.

20. **(B)** Subtract $7\frac{3}{4}$ from $8\frac{1}{5}$:

$$
\begin{array}{ccccc}
8\frac{1}{5} = 8\frac{4}{20} & & \overset{7}{\cancel{8}} + \frac{20}{20} + \frac{4}{20} & & 7\frac{24}{20} \\
& \rightarrow & & \rightarrow & \\
-7\frac{3}{4} = 7\frac{15}{20} & & -\quad\quad 7\frac{15}{20} & & -7\frac{15}{20} \\
& & & & \overline{\quad\frac{9}{20}}
\end{array}
$$

21. **(D)** To find the perimeter of a square, multiply one side length by 4:

$$4 \times 7 = 28$$

22. **(A)** Divide the number of students, 107, by the maximum capacity of the bus, 24 :

$$24\overline{)107} \quad 4\frac{11}{24}$$

The bus cannot make $\frac{11}{24}$ of a trip, so round the answer to 5, the nearest whole number.

23. **(C)** To find the fuel cost for the entire trip, calculate the number of gallons needed:

$$350 \text{ (miles per day)} \times 6 \text{ (days)} = 2{,}100 \text{ miles}$$

Divide the total miles to be traveled by 32, the miles the car can travel on a single gallon of gas:

$$2{,}100 \div 32 = 65\frac{3}{8} \text{ gallons of gas needed for the trip}$$

Without knowing the cost of a gallon of gas, the total fuel cost cannot be calculated.

24. **(C)** To find the number of 11th graders, find the percentage of the students who are 11th graders:

$$27\% + 23\% + 19\% + x\% = 100\%$$
$$x = 31\%$$

Convert 31% to 0.31 and multiply by 400, the number of students in the entire student body:

$$(0.31)(400) = 124$$

25. **(A)** Let $x =$ Sam's fourth test score.

$$\frac{88 + 84 + 91 + x}{4} = 90$$
$$\frac{263 + x}{4} = 90$$
$$263 + x = 360$$
$$x = 97$$

26. **(D)** Convert 81 feet 3 inches into inches (remember 1 foot = 12 inches):

$$(81 \times 12) + 3 = 975 \text{ inches}$$

Divide the length by 5:

$$975 \div 5 = 195$$

Reconvert 195 inches into feet:

$$\begin{array}{r} 16 \text{ remainder } 3 \\ \hline 12)195 \end{array}$$

Each rope is 16 feet 3 inches long.

27. **(B)**
Use the formula

$$\frac{\text{discount}}{\text{original price}} = \frac{x}{100}$$

Find the discount by subtracting the sale price from the regular price:

$$\$95.00 - \$76.00 = \$19.00$$

$$\frac{19}{95} = \frac{x}{100}$$

$$1,900 = 95x$$

$$20 = x$$

28. **(B)** Find Ada's current weekly pay:

$$36 \times \$7.60 = \$273.60$$

Subtract her current weekly pay from her future weekly pay:

$$\$291.60 - \$273.60 = \$18.00$$

Divide the difference by 36, the number of hours Ada works each week:

$$\$18.00 \div 36 = \$.50$$

29. **(E)** Use the ratio

$$\frac{\text{favored outcomes}}{\text{all outcomes}}$$

There are 3 blue marbles and 5 red marbles for a total of 8 favored outcomes. There are 10 marbles altogether which represent all outcomes. Therefore the probability that a red or blue marble will be chosen is $\frac{8}{10}$, which reduces to $\frac{4}{5}$.

30. **(D)** Round to the nearest thousand:
2,843 rounds to 3,000
7,921 rounds to 8,000
$3,000 \times 8,000 = 24,000,000$

31. **(C)** Let $x =$ the unknown number:

$$x = (0.20)(1)$$
$$x = 0.20$$

Convert 0.20 to a fraction:

$$0.20 = \frac{20}{100} = \frac{1}{5}$$

32. **(D)** The largest decline in circulation occurred in 1998 (see graph).

33. **(C)** The largest decline in circulation, which occurred in 1998, was approximately 16,000.

34. **(B)** Let $x =$ the number of students originally in the class.

$$\left(x - \frac{1}{2}x\right) - \left(\frac{1}{2}\right)\left(\frac{1}{2}x\right) = 9$$

$$x - \frac{1}{2}x - \frac{1}{4}x = 9$$

$$\frac{1}{4}x = 9$$

$$x = 36$$

This problem can also be done using a "plug-and-check" strategy:

$$36 - \left(\frac{1}{2}\right)(36) = 18$$

$$18 - \left(\frac{1}{2}\right)(18) = 9$$

35. **(C)** A cube has six square faces. Each square requires 6 inches of ribbon. Additionally, 10 inches of ribbon are needed for the bow:

$$(6 \times 6) + 10 = 46$$

36. **(C)** Multiply the number of sandwiches by the number of drinks. Multiply that product by the number of side orders:

$$5 \times 3 \times 2 = 30$$

37. **(B)** By inspection, we see that each y-value is triple the corresponding x-value. Since x equals 11, y must equal 33.

38. **(A)** Reading from left to right in selection A, we find each value is smaller than the preceding value.

39. **(B)** Adding zero place holders may be helpful:

$$0.04 = 0.040$$

Therefore:

$$0.004 < 0.031 < 0.040$$

40. **(E)** No woman in the Diaz family is taller than 5 feet 6 inches tall. Choice E, stating that a certain woman who stands 5 feet 8 inches tall cannot be in the Diaz family, must be correct.

41. **(A)** Point A appears to lie midway between -0.50 and -0.75. A reasonable estimate would be -0.63.

42. **(E)** Let $x =$ the capacity of the tank.

$$36 = \frac{3}{4}x$$

$$\left(\frac{4}{3}\right)(36) = \left(\frac{3}{4}x\right)\left(\frac{4}{3}\right)$$

$$x = 48$$

43. **(A)** Of the answer choices, only pounds and ounces are measures of weight. Ounces are appropriate units of measure for smaller, lighter items such as a bag of cough drops.

44. **(C)**

$$(7 \times 4) - 1 = 28 - 1 = 27$$

45. **(C)** Find the time needed to drive 390 miles at 60 miles per hour. Since rate × time = distance, it follows that time = distance ÷ rate:

$$r \times t = d$$

$$\frac{r \times t}{r} = \frac{d}{r}$$

$$t = \frac{d}{r}$$

$390 \div 60 = 6.5$ hours or 6 hours 30 minutes.
Subtract 6 hours 30 minutes from 10:00 P.M.

10 hours 0 minutes	=	9 hours 60 minutes
− 6 hours 30 minutes	=	− 6 hours 30 minutes
		3 hours 30 minutes

The trucker must leave by 3:30 P.M.

46. **(E)** Let $x =$ the number of miles in which costs are equal.
Company A: $30 + 0.1x$
Company B: $24 + 0.2x$

Find the number of miles in which both companies charge the same amount by setting the two expressions equal to one another:

$$30 + 0.1x = 24 + 0.2x$$

$$6 = 0.1x$$

$$60 = x$$

47. **(D)** Tom is not in school on Saturdays, Sundays, holidays, or when he is sick. If Tom is in school, it must be true that it is not a holiday nor is he sick.

48. **(D)** Only fluid measurements can be used to measure liquids (i.e. gallons, ounces, and cups). Compare the size of a bath tub to a gas tank in an automobile. Gallons are the most suitable units of measure when evaluating the capacity of a bath tub.

49. **(B)** Round each purchase to the nearest dollar and find the sum:
$8.89 rounds to $9.00.
$11.17 rounds to $11.00.
$41.37 rounds to $41.00.
$9.00 + $11.00 + $41.00 = $61.00

50. **(D)** Use the formula rate × time = distance. The rate, 75 miles per hour, is known but the time traveled is not. If the departure time was known, the traveling time could be calculated by subtracting it from the 2:00 P.M. arrival time.

Model Exam 2: Math

ANSWER SHEET

1 Ⓐ Ⓑ Ⓒ Ⓓ Ⓔ   14 Ⓐ Ⓑ Ⓒ Ⓓ Ⓔ   27 Ⓐ Ⓑ Ⓒ Ⓓ Ⓔ   39 Ⓐ Ⓑ Ⓒ Ⓓ Ⓔ

2 Ⓐ Ⓑ Ⓒ Ⓓ Ⓔ   15 Ⓐ Ⓑ Ⓒ Ⓓ Ⓔ   28 Ⓐ Ⓑ Ⓒ Ⓓ Ⓔ   40 Ⓐ Ⓑ Ⓒ Ⓓ Ⓔ

3 Ⓐ Ⓑ Ⓒ Ⓓ Ⓔ   16 Ⓐ Ⓑ Ⓒ Ⓓ Ⓔ   29 Ⓐ Ⓑ Ⓒ Ⓓ Ⓔ   41 Ⓐ Ⓑ Ⓒ Ⓓ Ⓔ

4 Ⓐ Ⓑ Ⓒ Ⓓ Ⓔ   17 Ⓐ Ⓑ Ⓒ Ⓓ Ⓔ   30 Ⓐ Ⓑ Ⓒ Ⓓ Ⓔ   42 Ⓐ Ⓑ Ⓒ Ⓓ Ⓔ

5 Ⓐ Ⓑ Ⓒ Ⓓ Ⓔ   18 Ⓐ Ⓑ Ⓒ Ⓓ Ⓔ   31 Ⓐ Ⓑ Ⓒ Ⓓ Ⓔ   43 Ⓐ Ⓑ Ⓒ Ⓓ Ⓔ

6 Ⓐ Ⓑ Ⓒ Ⓓ Ⓔ   19 Ⓐ Ⓑ Ⓒ Ⓓ Ⓔ   32 Ⓐ Ⓑ Ⓒ Ⓓ Ⓔ   44 Ⓐ Ⓑ Ⓒ Ⓓ Ⓔ

7 Ⓐ Ⓑ Ⓒ Ⓓ Ⓔ   20 Ⓐ Ⓑ Ⓒ Ⓓ Ⓔ   33 Ⓐ Ⓑ Ⓒ Ⓓ Ⓔ   45 Ⓐ Ⓑ Ⓒ Ⓓ Ⓔ

8 Ⓐ Ⓑ Ⓒ Ⓓ Ⓔ   21 Ⓐ Ⓑ Ⓒ Ⓓ Ⓔ   34 Ⓐ Ⓑ Ⓒ Ⓓ Ⓔ   46 Ⓐ Ⓑ Ⓒ Ⓓ Ⓔ

9 Ⓐ Ⓑ Ⓒ Ⓓ Ⓔ   22 Ⓐ Ⓑ Ⓒ Ⓓ Ⓔ   35 Ⓐ Ⓑ Ⓒ Ⓓ Ⓔ   47 Ⓐ Ⓑ Ⓒ Ⓓ Ⓔ

10 Ⓐ Ⓑ Ⓒ Ⓓ Ⓔ   23 Ⓐ Ⓑ Ⓒ Ⓓ Ⓔ   36 Ⓐ Ⓑ Ⓒ Ⓓ Ⓔ   48 Ⓐ Ⓑ Ⓒ Ⓓ Ⓔ

11 Ⓐ Ⓑ Ⓒ Ⓓ Ⓔ   24 Ⓐ Ⓑ Ⓒ Ⓓ Ⓔ   37 Ⓐ Ⓑ Ⓒ Ⓓ Ⓔ   49 Ⓐ Ⓑ Ⓒ Ⓓ Ⓔ

12 Ⓐ Ⓑ Ⓒ Ⓓ Ⓔ   25 Ⓐ Ⓑ Ⓒ Ⓓ Ⓔ   38 Ⓐ Ⓑ Ⓒ Ⓓ Ⓔ   50 Ⓐ Ⓑ Ⓒ Ⓓ Ⓔ

13 Ⓐ Ⓑ Ⓒ Ⓓ Ⓔ   26 Ⓐ Ⓑ Ⓒ Ⓓ Ⓔ

MODEL EXAM 2: MATH

1. Simplify:

    $$7 - |-2| = ?$$

    (A) –14
    (B) 2
    (C) 5
    (D) 9
    (E) 14

2. On a highway map, the scale was 1 inch = 35 miles. If a distance on the map is 1.7 inches, how far is the actual distance, rounded to the nearest mile?

    (A) 58
    (B) 59
    (C) 60
    (D) 61
    (E) 62

3. 17 is what percent of 25?

    (A) 17
    (B) 34
    (C) 51
    (D) 61
    (E) 68

4. The probability of an event occurring is $\frac{3}{7}$. What is the probability of the event *not* occurring?

    (A) $\frac{4}{7}$

    (B) $\frac{7}{4}$

    (C) $\frac{7}{3}$

    (D) $\frac{3}{10}$

    (E) $\frac{2}{5}$

5. In a certain survey, 440 of 500 respondents watched the Super Bowl. If 140,000,000 television sets were tuned in at that time, how many sets were actually tuned into the game?

    (A) 120,000,000
    (B) 122,500,000
    (C) 123,000,000
    (D) 123,200,000
    (E) 123,500,000

6. What is a good estimate of the circumference of the circle?

    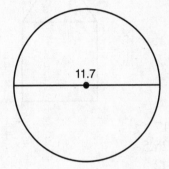

    (A) 48
    (B) 36
    (C) 24
    (D) 12
    (E) 6

7. In the number 7,613,215.0749, what digit is in the ten thousandths place?

    (A) 1
    (B) 2
    (C) 3
    (D) 5
    (E) 9

8. The ratio of the angles in a triangle is 1:2:3. What is the measure of the largest angle?

    (A) 30°
    (B) 60°
    (C) 90°
    (D) 120°
    (E) 150°

9. A flag pole that is 18 feet tall casts a 24-foot shadow. How long is the shadow cast by a woman whose height is 5 feet?

   (A) 6 feet
   (B) 6 feet 2 inches
   (C) 6 feet 4 inches
   (D) 6 feet 6 inches
   (E) 6 feet 8 inches

10. In the diagram, an equilateral triangle with length 8.5 is placed on top of a square. What is the perimeter of the figure?

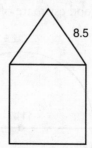

   (A) 17
   (B) 25.5
   (C) 42.5
   (D) 51
   (E) 59.5

11. An isosceles triangle has one side of length 4 and another of length 6. What is the greatest measure of its perimeter?

   (A) 12
   (B) 14
   (C) 16
   (D) 18
   (E) 24

12. Li, Sally, and Juanita each bowled one game. Their average score was 168 and Juanita bowled 185, the highest score.

   Which of the following *cannot* be deduced from the information provided above?

   (A) The total pins knocked down by the three players
   (B) The highest of the three scores
   (C) The sum of the two lower scores
   (D) The average of the three scores
   (E) The lowest score

13. Toyo threw a softball 12 feet farther than she threw yesterday. If the sum of her two throws was 216 feet, what was the length of her longer throw?

   Which of the following equations will correctly solve this problem?

   (A) $x + 12 = 216$
   (B) $2x = 216$
   (C) $2x + 12 = 216$
   (D) $\dfrac{216}{2} = x - 12$
   (E) $\dfrac{216}{2} = x + 12$

14. The seventh-grade students at a middle school need pencils. The five seventh-grade teachers pooled their pencils together. The number of pencils is as follows:

   Teacher A: 68 pencils
   Teacher B: 71 pencils
   Teacher C: 59 pencils
   Teacher D: 78 pencils
   Teacher E: 48 pencils

   If there are 108 students in all five of the classes, how many pencils will each student receive?

   (A) 3
   (B) 6
   (C) 9
   (D) 12
   (E) 15

15. A blouse that normally sells for $25 is being offered at a 20% discount. What is the sale price of the blouse?

   (A) $23.00
   (B) $20.00
   (C) $18.00
   (D) $16.00
   (E) $15.00

16. If Brittany can type two pages in 11 minutes, how long will it take her to type 15 pages?

    (A) $82\frac{1}{2}$ minutes
    (B) 82 minutes
    (C) 66 minutes
    (D) $65\frac{1}{2}$ minutes
    (E) 65 minutes

17. Light travels at the rate of approximately 186,000 miles per second. What is the best estimate of the time needed for light to travel 1,000,000 miles?

    (A) 4 seconds
    (B) 5 seconds
    (C) 4 minutes
    (D) 5 minutes
    (E) 50 minutes

18. A tennis racket normally priced at $79.99 is offered at a 10% discount. What is the sale price (exclude sales tax)?

    (A) $71.99
    (B) $72.99
    (C) $73.99
    (D) $74.99
    (E) $75.99

19. A turkey should be cooked for 20 minutes for each pound it weighs. If an $8\frac{1}{2}$ pound turkey needs to be cooked by 5:30 P.M., what time should it be placed in the oven?

    (A) 2:00 P.M.
    (B) 2:10 P.M.
    (C) 2:20 P.M.
    (D) 2:30 P.M.
    (E) 2:40 P.M.

20. Solve for *m*:

    $$3m + 112n = 18q$$

    (A) $6q - 4n$
    (B) $4n - 6q$
    (C) $24qn$
    (D) $10qn$
    (E) $-10qn$

21. Sally needs to measure the perimeter of her living room.

    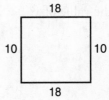

    Which of the following calculations should she use?

    (A) 18×10
    (B) $2 \times 18 \times 10$
    (C) $(2 \times 18) + (2 \times 10)$
    (D) $18 + 10$
    (E) $(18 \times 10) \div 2$

22. Which of the following fractions, when entered into the triangle, makes the statement true?

    $$\frac{3}{8} < \Delta < \frac{13}{24}$$

    (A) $\frac{7}{8}$
    (B) $\frac{5}{8}$
    (C) $\frac{5}{12}$
    (D) $\frac{1}{3}$
    (E) $\frac{1}{4}$

23. $9x = 4y$

Which values of x and y satisfy this equation?

(A) $x = 6, y = 10$
(B) $x = 9, y = 4$
(C) $x = 4, y = 9$
(D) $x = 49, y = 94$
(E) $x = \dfrac{9}{4}, y = \dfrac{4}{9}$

24. The average of 2.7, 6.3, 4.8, and x is 5.7. What is the value of x?

(A) 93
(B) 9
(C) 0.93
(D) 0.92
(E) −9.3

25. A garage floor has an area of 480 square feet. If 65% of the floor is used for car space, how many square feet are used for other purposes?

(A) 168
(B) 226
(C) 386
(D) 312
(E) 400

26. The Key Club and the Girl's Chorus competed in a contest. The Key Club donated

$207\dfrac{1}{3}$ pounds of clothing to the Salvation

Army, while the Girl's Chorus contributed

$187\dfrac{3}{6}$ pounds. How much greater was the

Key Club's donation?

(A) $18\dfrac{1}{6}$ pounds

(B) $18\dfrac{1}{2}$ pounds

(C) $18\dfrac{5}{6}$ pounds

(D) $19\dfrac{1}{2}$ pounds

(E) $19\dfrac{5}{6}$ pounds

27. Bill is taller than Alison. Alison is taller than Reggie. Kathy is not as tall as Bill but is taller than Reggie.

Which of the following *cannot* be concluded from the above information?

(A) Bill is the tallest.
(B) Alison is taller than Reggie.
(C) Bill is taller than Reggie.
(D) Reggie is not as tall as Kathy.
(E) Alison is taller than Kathy.

Use the chart below to answer questions 28 and 29.

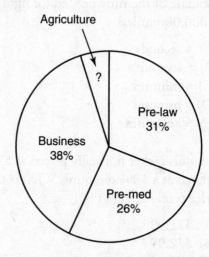

Percentage of declared majors

Total of students declaring majors is 18,000

28. What percentage of the students is agriculture majors?

(A) 5%
(B) 12%
(C) 31%
(D) 37%
(E) 38%

29. How many students are declared Pre-Law majors?

(A) 4,540
(B) 5,440
(C) 5,580
(D) 8,550
(E) 18,000

30. An elevator has a maximum capacity of 15 people. If 68 people need to arrive at the 5th floor, how many trips must the elevator make?

    (A) 3

    (B) $3\frac{8}{15}$

    (C) 4

    (D) $4\frac{8}{15}$

    (E) 5

31. A coin has landed on heads in each of three successive tosses. What is the probability of the coin landing on heads after the next toss?

    (A) $\frac{1}{16}$

    (B) $\frac{1}{8}$

    (C) $\frac{1}{4}$

    (D) $\frac{1}{2}$

    (E) 1

32. What is the product of three squared and four?

    (A) 4
    (B) 12
    (C) 16
    (D) 24
    (E) 36

33. Wilma works 40 hours per week at the rate of $9.50 per hour. If she receives a 10% raise in her hourly pay, how much greater will her weekly paycheck be?

    (A) $38.00
    (B) $36.00
    (C) $35.50
    (D) $35.00
    (E) $24.00

34. Gary has eight more marbles than his brother. Together they have 38 marbles. How many marbles does Gary have?

    (A) 23
    (B) 19
    (C) 15
    (D) 12
    (E) 8

35. Which of the following statements is false?

    (A) $\frac{1}{5} < \frac{1}{2}$

    (B) $0.03 < 0.3$

    (C) $-8 > -2$

    (D) $\frac{1}{3} > \frac{1}{6}$

    (E) $\frac{-5}{8} > -1$

36. Sheree has 7 blouses, 3 skirts, and 4 pairs of shoes. How many different combinations of blouses, skirts, and shoes does she have?

    (A) 96
    (B) 84
    (C) 48
    (D) 40
    (E) 14

37. Charlie wants to mentally calculate the product of 15 and 12. Which of the following expressions will help him?

    (A) $(10 + 15) \div (10 + 12)$
    (B) $(10 \times 15) + (2 \times 15)$
    (C) $(10 + 10) + (5 + 2)$
    (D) $(10 \div 2) + (10 \div 5)$
    (E) $(15 - 2) \times (10 - 10)$

38. The square root of 89 is closest to which integer?

    (A) 6
    (B) 7
    (C) 8
    (D) 9
    (E) 10

39. Which expression is equivalent to $r \times t = d$?

    (A) $t = \dfrac{r}{d}$

    (B) $d = \dfrac{r}{t}$

    (C) $r = \dfrac{t}{d}$

    (D) $d \times r = t$

    (E) $r = \dfrac{d}{t}$

40. If $2n = 24$, what is the value of $3n - 6$?

    (A) 10
    (B) 20
    (C) 30
    (D) 40
    (E) 50

41. The sum of two integers is 28. The difference between the same two integers is 4. What are the two integers?

    (A) 20 and 8
    (B) 10 and 18
    (C) 26 and 2
    (D) 16 and 12
    (E) 24 and 4

42. Which of the following number lines represents the expression $x > -6$?

    (A)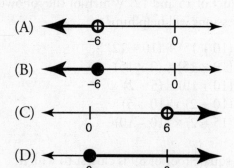

    (B)

    (C)

    (D)

    (E)

43. Jamie biked and ran a total of 6 miles. The time he spent jogging was double the time he spent biking. What was his average speed for the entire 6 miles?

    What additional information is needed to answer this question?

    (A) The total distance traveled
    (B) The number of miles traveled on foot
    (C) The number of miles traveled by bike
    (D) The time spent biking
    (E) The time Jamie arrived at home

44. $xyz = 12$

    Solve for x if $y = -2$ and $z = \dfrac{1}{2}$.

    (A) 12
    (B) 6
    (C) −2
    (D) −6
    (E) −12

Use the following table to answer questions 45 and 46. The table highlights the average attendance at the Girls' Field Hockey games:

Date:	9/9	9/17	9/21	9/28	10/2
Attendance:	140	162	140	188	155

45. Which attendance figure represents the mode of the data?

    (A) 48
    (B) 140
    (C) 155
    (D) 157
    (E) 188

46. Which attendance figure represents the median of the data?

    (A) 48
    (B) 140
    (C) 155
    (D) 157
    (E) 188

47. What is the perimeter of the figure?

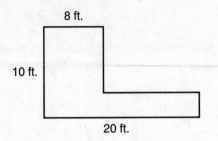

(A) 180
(B) 120
(C) 60
(D) 38
(E) 30

48. At 6:00 A.M., the temperature in City A was −8°F. By noon, the temperature had risen to 11°F. How much had the temperature risen in that period?

(A) −3°
(B) 0°
(C) 3°
(D) 12°
(E) 19°

49. At the start of the college's Math 65 class, the enrollment was 60 students. After the first test, one-third of the students dropped the class. After the second test, one-fourth of the remaining students dropped the class. After the second test, how many students were still enrolled in Math 65?

(A) 40
(B) 30
(C) 28
(D) 22
(E) 18

50. If 1 ounce of jelly beans cost $.60, what would be the cost of $\frac{5}{8}$ pound of jelly beans (1 pound = 16 ounces)?

(A) $6.00
(B) $5.40
(C) $4.80
(D) $4.20
(E) $3.00

ANSWERS AND EXPLANATIONS FOR MODEL EXAM 2: MATH

1. **(C)** The absolute value of any positive or negative number is positive. Since $|-2| = 2$, $7 - |-2| = 7 - 2 = 5$.

2. **(C)** Use the ratio: $\dfrac{\text{inches}}{\text{miles}}$

$$\frac{1}{35} = \frac{1.7}{x}$$
$$x = (3.5)(1.7) = 59.5$$

Round to the nearest mile: 60

3. **(E)**

Method A
$$\frac{\text{part}}{\text{whole}} = \frac{x}{100}$$
$$\frac{17}{25} = \frac{x}{100}$$
$$25x = 1,700$$
$$x = 68\%$$

Method B
$$17 \div 25 = 0.68$$

Move the decimal two places to the right to convert to a percent:

$$0.68 = 68\%$$

4. **(A)** The probability of an event occurring *or* not occurring is 1 (i.e., 100% probability). If we let x equal the probability of an event not occurring, we get the equation:

$$x + \frac{3}{7} = 1$$
$$x = \frac{4}{7}$$

5. **(D)** Use the ratio $\dfrac{\text{surveyed respondents watching the Super Bowl}}{\text{all surveyed respondents}}$

$$\frac{440}{500} = \frac{x}{140,000,000}$$
$$500x = 61,600,000,000$$
$$x = 123,200,000$$

6. **(B)** Use the formula circumference = π × diameter (π is approximately equal to 3.14). Round to the nearest whole number:

   3.14 rounds to 3

   11.7 rounds to 12

   3 × 12 = 36

7. **(E)** Eliminate answers A though D. They are not decimals:

   0 is in the tenths place.

   7 is in the hundredths place.

   4 is in the thousandths place.

   9 is in the ten thousandths place.

8. **(C)** The sum of the measures of the angles of a triangle is 180°. If the ratio of the angles is 1:2:3, then:

   $$x = \text{measure of the smallest angle}$$
   $$2x = \text{measure of the middle-sized angle}$$
   $$3x = \text{measure of the largest angle}$$

   $$x + 2x + 3x = 180$$
   $$6x = 180$$
   $$x = 30$$
   $$3x = 90$$

   The largest angle measures 90°.

9. **(E)** Use the ratio

   $$\frac{\text{height}}{\text{length of shadow}}$$

   $$\frac{18}{24} = \frac{5}{x}$$
   $$18x = 120$$
   $$x = 6\frac{2}{3} \text{ feet}$$

   Since 1 foot = 12 inches, $\frac{2}{3}$ of one foot equals 8 inches ($\frac{2}{3} \times 12 = 8$).

   The woman's shadow measures 6 feet 8 inches.

10. **(C)** The base of the triangle is also the length of one side of the square.

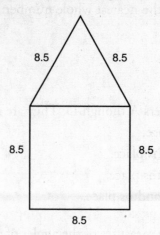

Perimeter is the distance around a figure. Therefore the base of the triangle should not be included in the perimeter.

$$8.5 \times 5 = 42.5$$

11. **(C)** An isosceles triangle has two equal sides. The triangle could have different pairs of equal sides:

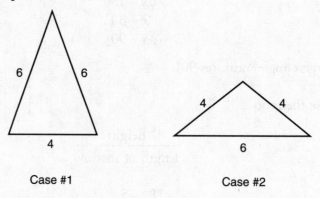

Since the problem asks for the greatest measure of the perimeter, select diagram 1:

$$6 + 6 + 4 = 16$$

12. **(E)** Multiply the average score, 168, by the number of players, 3:

$$168 \times 3 = 504$$

Since 504 is the number of pins knocked down, eliminate A.

Eliminate B since it is known that Juanita scored 185, the highest score.

Subtracting Juanita's score from the total pins knocked down eliminates C.

Eliminate D as this information was provided in the problem.

Based on the given information, we do not know whether Li or Sally scored the lowest of the three scores. Therefore, E cannot be deduced from the information provided.

13. **(C)** Let

$$x = \text{the length of Toyo's first throw}$$
$$x + 12 = \text{the length of Toyo's second throw}$$

The sum of the two throws is 216:

$$x + (x + 12) = 216$$
$$2x + 12 = 216$$

14. **(A)** Add all the pencils:

$$68 + 71 + 59 + 78 + 48 = 324$$

Divide the number of pencils by the number of students:

$$324 \div 108 = 3$$

15. **(B)** Calculate the discount:

$$(\$25.00)(0.20) = \$5.00$$

Subtract the discount from the regular price to find the sale price:

$$\$25.00 - \$5.00 = \$20.00$$

16. **(A)** Use the ratio

$$\frac{\text{pages typed}}{\text{minutes}}$$

$$\frac{2}{11} = \frac{15}{x}$$
$$2x = 165$$
$$x = 82\frac{1}{2}$$

17. **(B)** Round to the nearest one hundred thousand:
186,000 rounds to 200,000
1,000,000 ÷ 200,000 = 5

18. **(A)** Find the discount and subtract it from the regular price:

$$\$79.99 - (0.1)(\$79.99) = \$79.99 - \$7.999 = \$79.99 - \$8.00 = \$71.99$$

19. **(E)** Multiply $8\frac{1}{2}$ minutes by 20 to get the number of minutes needed to cook the turkey:

$$8\frac{1}{2} \times 20 = 170$$

Convert 170 minutes into hours by dividing by 60:

$$170 \div 60 = 2 \text{ hours } 50 \text{ minutes}$$

Subtract 2 hours 50 minutes from 5:30:

5 hours 30 minutes	=	4 hours 90 minutes
−2 hours 50 minutes		− 2 hours 50 minutes
		2 hours 40 minutes

The turkey should be placed in the oven at 2:40 P.M.

20. **(A)**

$$3m + 12n = 18q$$
$$3m + 12n - 12n = 18q - 12n$$
$$3m = 18q - 12n$$
$$\frac{3m}{3} = \frac{18q}{3} - \frac{12n}{3}$$
$$m = 6q - 4n$$

21. **(C)** The perimeter of a rectangle is found by using the formula (2 × length) + (2 × width) or $P = 2\ell + 2w$:

$$(2 \times 18) + (2 \times 10)$$

22. **(C)** Find the common denominator of $\frac{3}{8}$ and $\frac{13}{24}$.

$$\frac{3}{8} \times \frac{3}{3} = \frac{9}{24} \qquad \frac{13}{24} \times \frac{1}{1} = \frac{13}{24}$$

The value in the triangle must be greater than $\frac{9}{24}$ and less than $\frac{13}{24}$. Choice C, $\frac{5}{12}$, when expressed as the equivalent fraction $\frac{10}{24}$, is correct.

23. **(C)**

$$(9)(4) = (4)(9)$$
$$36 = 36$$

24. **(B)**

$$\frac{2.7+6.3+4.8+x}{4}=5.7$$

$$4\left(\frac{13.8+x}{4}\right)=4(5.7)$$

$$13.8+x=22.8$$

$$x=9$$

25. **(A)** Since 65% of the garage space is used for cars, 35% represents the balance of the floor space.

$$480\,(0.35)=168$$

26. **(D)**

$$207\frac{1}{3}\times\frac{2}{2}=207\frac{2}{6}=206+\frac{6}{6}+\frac{2}{6}=206\frac{8}{6}$$
$$-187\frac{5}{6}\times\frac{1}{1}\quad -187\frac{5}{6}\quad -187+\frac{5}{6}\quad -187\frac{5}{6}$$

$$19\frac{3}{6}=19\frac{1}{2}$$

27. **(E)**

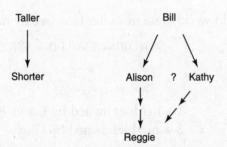

No information is provided comparing the heights of Alison and Kathy.

28. **(A)** Add up the known percentages of the other majors and subtract from 100%:

$$100-(31+38+26)=5$$

29. **(C)** Multiply the percent of Pre-Law majors, 31%, by the total number of students, 18,000:

$$(0.31)(18,000)=5,580.$$

30. **(E)** Divide 68 by 15:

$$68 \div 15 = 4\frac{8}{15}$$

Since an elevator cannot make $\frac{8}{15}$ of a trip, round up to 5, the next consecutive whole number.

31. **(D)** The outcomes of previous tosses do not affect the outcomes of future tosses. The probability of a coin landing on heads on the fourth toss is $\frac{1}{2}$

32. **(E)**

$$3^2 \cdot 4 = 36$$

33. **(A)** Find Wilma's current weekly pay:

$$\$9.50 \times 40 = \$380.00$$

Find her new hourly rate:

$$\$9.50 + (\$9.50)(0.10) = \$10.45$$

Find her new weekly rate:

$$\$10.45 \times 40 = \$418.00$$

Subtract her old weekly rate from her new weekly rate:

$$\$418.00 - \$380.00 = \$38.00$$

34. **(A)** Let

$$x = \text{marbles owned by Gary's brother}$$
$$x + 8 = \text{marbles owned by Gary}$$

$$x + (x + 8) = 38$$
$$2x + 8 = 38$$
$$2x = 30$$
$$x = 15$$

Since Gary has 8 more marbles than his brother, he owns 23 marbles.

35. **(C)** On a number line, −8 is to the left of −2. Therefore −8 < −2.

36. **(B)** Calculate the number of different combinations of blouses, skirts, and shoes by finding the product of all three:

$$7 \times 3 \times 4 = 84$$

37. **(B)**

$$15 \times 12 = 180$$
$$(10 \times 15) + (2 \times 15) = 150 + 30 = 180$$

38. **(D)**

$$\sqrt{81} < \sqrt{89} < \sqrt{100}$$
$$9 < \sqrt{89} < 10$$

Since 89 is closer to 81 than it is to 100, $\sqrt{89}$ is closer to 9.

39. **(E)**

$$r \times t = d$$
$$\frac{r \times t}{d} = \frac{d}{t}$$
$$r = \frac{d}{t}$$

40. **(C)** Solve for n, then substitute that value into the expression:

$$2n = 24$$
$$n = 12$$
$$3(12) - 6 = 30$$

41. **(D)**

$$16 + 12 = 28$$
$$16 - 12 = 4$$

42. **(E)** Graph shows values greater than −6 on a number line.

43. **(D)** Since rate × time = distance, then rate = distance ÷ time:

$$r \times t = d$$
$$\frac{r \times t}{t} = \frac{d}{t}$$
$$r = \frac{d}{t}$$

The distance, 6 miles, is known. If the time spent biking were known, it could be doubled to find the jogging time. Adding the two times together would provide the total time, which is the missing information.

44. **(E)** Substitute the known values and solve for x:

$$x(-2)\left(\frac{1}{2}\right) = 12$$
$$x = 12$$
$$x = -12$$

45. **(B)** The mode is the value that occurs most frequently.

46. **(C)** To find the median, array the data in ascending order:

$$140, 140, 155, 162, 188$$

The median, 155, is the value that appears in the middle.

47. **(C)** Let x, y, and z represent the unknown lengths in the figure. Note that $x + z = 10$. Furthermore, $8 + y = 20$, so $y = 12$.

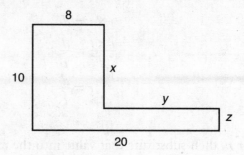

Add all the lengths to find the perimeter:

$$10 + 8 + 10 + 12 + 20 = 60$$
$$\quad\quad\quad\quad \downarrow \quad\quad \downarrow$$
$$\quad\quad\quad (x + z) \ (y)$$

48. **(E)** Subtract the lower temperature from the higher temperature:

$$11 - (-8) = 11 + 8 = 19$$

49. **(B)** Find the class size after the first test by subtracting $\frac{1}{3}$ of 60 from 60:

$$60 - \left(\frac{1}{3} \times 60\right) = 60 - 20 = 40$$

Find the number of students remaining in the class after the second test by subtracting $\frac{1}{4}$ of 40 from 40:

$$40 - \left(\frac{1}{4} \times 40\right) = 40 - 10 = 30$$

50. **(A)** Find the number of ounces in $\frac{5}{8}$ pound and multiply by \$.60:

$$\frac{5}{8} \times 16 = 10 \text{ ounces}$$
$$10 \times 0.60 = \$6.00$$

Model Exam 3: Math

ANSWER SHEET

1 Ⓐ Ⓑ Ⓒ Ⓓ Ⓔ	14 Ⓐ Ⓑ Ⓒ Ⓓ Ⓔ	27 Ⓐ Ⓑ Ⓒ Ⓓ Ⓔ	39 Ⓐ Ⓑ Ⓒ Ⓓ Ⓔ
2 Ⓐ Ⓑ Ⓒ Ⓓ Ⓔ	15 Ⓐ Ⓑ Ⓒ Ⓓ Ⓔ	28 Ⓐ Ⓑ Ⓒ Ⓓ Ⓔ	40 Ⓐ Ⓑ Ⓒ Ⓓ Ⓔ
3 Ⓐ Ⓑ Ⓒ Ⓓ Ⓔ	16 Ⓐ Ⓑ Ⓒ Ⓓ Ⓔ	29 Ⓐ Ⓑ Ⓒ Ⓓ Ⓔ	41 Ⓐ Ⓑ Ⓒ Ⓓ Ⓔ
4 Ⓐ Ⓑ Ⓒ Ⓓ Ⓔ	17 Ⓐ Ⓑ Ⓒ Ⓓ Ⓔ	30 Ⓐ Ⓑ Ⓒ Ⓓ Ⓔ	42 Ⓐ Ⓑ Ⓒ Ⓓ Ⓔ
5 Ⓐ Ⓑ Ⓒ Ⓓ Ⓔ	18 Ⓐ Ⓑ Ⓒ Ⓓ Ⓔ	31 Ⓐ Ⓑ Ⓒ Ⓓ Ⓔ	43 Ⓐ Ⓑ Ⓒ Ⓓ Ⓔ
6 Ⓐ Ⓑ Ⓒ Ⓓ Ⓔ	19 Ⓐ Ⓑ Ⓒ Ⓓ Ⓔ	32 Ⓐ Ⓑ Ⓒ Ⓓ Ⓔ	44 Ⓐ Ⓑ Ⓒ Ⓓ Ⓔ
7 Ⓐ Ⓑ Ⓒ Ⓓ Ⓔ	20 Ⓐ Ⓑ Ⓒ Ⓓ Ⓔ	33 Ⓐ Ⓑ Ⓒ Ⓓ Ⓔ	45 Ⓐ Ⓑ Ⓒ Ⓓ Ⓔ
8 Ⓐ Ⓑ Ⓒ Ⓓ Ⓔ	21 Ⓐ Ⓑ Ⓒ Ⓓ Ⓔ	34 Ⓐ Ⓑ Ⓒ Ⓓ Ⓔ	46 Ⓐ Ⓑ Ⓒ Ⓓ Ⓔ
9 Ⓐ Ⓑ Ⓒ Ⓓ Ⓔ	22 Ⓐ Ⓑ Ⓒ Ⓓ Ⓔ	35 Ⓐ Ⓑ Ⓒ Ⓓ Ⓔ	47 Ⓐ Ⓑ Ⓒ Ⓓ Ⓔ
10 Ⓐ Ⓑ Ⓒ Ⓓ Ⓔ	23 Ⓐ Ⓑ Ⓒ Ⓓ Ⓔ	36 Ⓐ Ⓑ Ⓒ Ⓓ Ⓔ	48 Ⓐ Ⓑ Ⓒ Ⓓ Ⓔ
11 Ⓐ Ⓑ Ⓒ Ⓓ Ⓔ	24 Ⓐ Ⓑ Ⓒ Ⓓ Ⓔ	37 Ⓐ Ⓑ Ⓒ Ⓓ Ⓔ	49 Ⓐ Ⓑ Ⓒ Ⓓ Ⓔ
12 Ⓐ Ⓑ Ⓒ Ⓓ Ⓔ	25 Ⓐ Ⓑ Ⓒ Ⓓ Ⓔ	38 Ⓐ Ⓑ Ⓒ Ⓓ Ⓔ	50 Ⓐ Ⓑ Ⓒ Ⓓ Ⓔ
13 Ⓐ Ⓑ Ⓒ Ⓓ Ⓔ	26 Ⓐ Ⓑ Ⓒ Ⓓ Ⓔ		

MODEL EXAM 3: MATH

1. What is 24% of 600?

   (A) 34
   (B) 51
   (C) 61
   (D) 68
   (E) 144

2. The expression:

   $$-12 - (15 - 30)$$

   simplifies to which of the following?

   (A) −33
   (B) −30
   (C) −3
   (D) 3
   (E) 33

3. When Fran received her SAT math score, she noticed the following data:

Score	Stanine	Percentile
640	7	77

   Fran now knows:

   (A) 640 students took the SAT.
   (B) Fran did as well as or better than 640 students.
   (C) 77% of the test-takers did better than she.
   (D) Fran did as well as or better than 77% of the test-takers.
   (E) Her stanine score is the same as her SAT score.

4. A pair of running shoes that normally sells for $69.00 is being discounted by one-third. How much will a buyer save with this discount?

   (A) $46.00
   (B) $33.00
   (C) $26.00
   (D) $24.00
   (E) $23.00

5. Solve for *n*:

   $$2n + 5 + 3n = -20$$

   (A) −10
   (B) −5
   (C) 0
   (D) 5
   (E) 10

6. Which of the following numbers is greater than 7,461,200 but less than 7,851,500?

   (A) 7,308,400
   (B) 7,461,185
   (C) 7,461,190
   (D) 7,623,158
   (E) 7,855,230

7. If four out of every seven junior college students go on to a four-year college, how many of the 8,400 students enrolled at a certain junior college will go on to a four-year school?

   (A) 4,800
   (B) 4,300
   (C) 3,600
   (D) 3,000
   (E) 2,880

8. Of the 40 students in a class, 22 weigh more than 100 pounds. What percent of the class weighs more than 100 pounds?

   (A) 22%
   (B) 25%
   (C) 45%
   (D) 55%
   (E) 65%

9. In the floor plan, 1 inch = 6 feet. If the actual width of the bedroom is 15 feet, what would be the width on the floor plan?

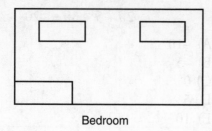

Bedroom

(A) 1.5 inches
(B) 2 inches
(C) 2.5 inches
(D) 3 inches
(E) 3.5 inches

10. Phyllis can make 3 pies with 2 pounds of flour. If she needs to make 11 pies, how many pounds of flour does she need?

(A) $6\frac{2}{3}$

(B) 7

(C) $7\frac{1}{3}$

(D) $7\frac{2}{3}$

(E) 8

11. Which of the following is the best way to estimate 49,627 ÷ 5,113?

(A) 5,000,000 ÷ 5
(B) 5,000 ÷ 500
(C) 50,000 ÷ 5,000
(D) 49,000 ÷ 6,000
(E) 48,000 ÷ 5,000

12. What is one-half of one-eighth of 96,000?

(A) 60
(B) 96
(C) 160
(D) 600
(E) 6,000

13. An astronomical unit (a.u.) is defined as the distance between the Earth and the Sun. The distance between the Earth and the Sun is approximately 93,000,000 miles. What information is needed to calculate the number of astronomical units that separates Neptune and the Sun?

(A) The number of miles that separate Earth and Jupiter.
(B) The number of miles that separate the Sun and Neptune.
(C) The number of miles in an astronomical unit.
(D) The distance, in astronomical units, between Mars and Neptune.
(E) The definition of the word *astronomical*.

14. Solve for *x*:

$$\frac{3}{7}x - 11 = 16$$

(A) $\frac{4}{7}$

(B) $\frac{7}{3}$

(C) 27
(D) 36
(E) 63

15. A coat normally sells for $90.00. To reduce inventory, a vendor reduced the price by 10%. The following week, she reduced the sales price by $\frac{1}{3}$. What is the coat's new sales price?

(A) $18.00
(B) $36.00
(C) $45.00
(D) $54.00
(E) $81.00

16. A square and an equilateral triangle have the same perimeter. If one side of the triangle measures 6 inches, how long is one side of the square?

    (A) 3 inches
    (B) 3.5 inches
    (C) 4 inches
    (D) 4.5 inches
    (E) 9 inches

17. In the figure below, *ABCD* and *BFGE* are adjacent squares. If *AD* measures 40 feet and *FG* measures 60 feet, what is the perimeter of the figure?

    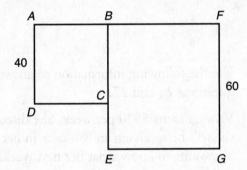

    (A) 230
    (B) 280
    (C) 320
    (D) 360
    (E) 5,200

18. A rectangle has a perimeter of 96 inches. If the width is 12, what is the measure of the length?

    (A) 48
    (B) 36
    (C) 24
    (D) 12
    (E) 6

19. Naomi has received a score of 85 on each of two tests. She wants to know what score she needs on the next test to have at least a 90% average for the three tests. To calculate the minimum score of the next test, Naomi should:

    (A) Add 85, 85, and 90 and divide the sum by 3.
    (B) Subtract 85 from 90.
    (C) Add 85 and 90 and divide by 2.
    (D) Multiply 90 by 2 and subtract 85.
    (E) Multiply 90 by 3 and subtract the sum of 85 and 85.

20. The typical school year for American high school students is 180 days. In Japan, the school year is 225 days. What percent longer is the Japanese school year?

    (A) 45%
    (B) 35%
    (C) 30%
    (D) 25%
    (E) 20%

21.

x	y
2	4
3.5	7
4	8
5.5	11

    Which equation describes the relationship between x and y?

    (A) $x = 2y$
    (B) $y = 2x$

    (C) $y = \dfrac{1}{2}x$

    (D) $\dfrac{x}{y} = 2$

    (E) $\dfrac{y}{x} = 2$

22. $\frac{7}{10} > \square > \frac{2}{5}$

Which value should be placed in the box to satisfy the inequality?

(A) $\frac{3}{5}$

(B) $\frac{3}{10}$

(C) $\frac{2}{5}$

(D) $\frac{1}{10}$

(E) $\frac{2}{25}$

23. Toni swam the 100-yard freestyle on each of four consecutive days. Her times, in seconds, were 58.8, 61.4 , 59.2, and 60.2. To the nearest tenth of a second, what was her average time?

(A) 59.7
(B) 59.8
(C) 59.9
(D) 60
(E) 60.2

24. Simplify the following expression:

$$8^2 - 2(3 - 6)$$

(A) 10
(B) 16
(C) 58
(D) 64
(E) 70

25. What is the best estimate for point A on the number line?

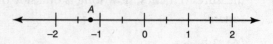

(A) $-1\frac{1}{4}$

(B) $\frac{-3}{4}$

(C) $\frac{-1}{4}$

(D) $\frac{1}{4}$

(E) $1\frac{1}{4}$

Use the following information to answer questions 26 and 27.

Vanessa earns $520 per week. She discovers she will be receiving an 8% raise in her pay. She wants to know what her new weekly pay will be.

26. Which of the following equations will help Vanessa calculate her new weekly pay?

(A) 0.08×520
(B) 0.8×520
(C) 1.8×520
(D) 0.18×52.0
(E) $520 + (520 \times 0.08)$

27. What will Vanessa's new weekly pay be?

(A) $561.60
(B) $553.70
(C) $528.00
(D) $520.00
(E) $494.00

28. Find the value of *x*:

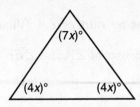

(A) 12
(B) 24
(C) 48
(D) 90
(E) 180

29. If five 9-inch pieces are cut from a rope that is $4\frac{1}{2}$ feet long, how much rope will remain?

(A) 5 inches
(B) 6 inches
(C) 7 inches
(D) 8 inches
(E) 9 inches

30. If an individual serving of salad contains 2 celery stalks, how many celery stalks are needed for three dozen individual salads?

(A) 75
(B) 72
(C) 45
(D) 36
(E) 12

31. Tara earns $9 per hour at her job. Beginning next week, her hourly rate will be increased by 9%. What will be the increase in her hourly rate?

Which of the following expressions will help Tara calculate the increase in her hourly rate?

(A) $\$9.00 \times \frac{1}{9}$

(B) $\$9.00 \times 0.9$

(C) $\$9.00 \times \frac{9}{100}$

(D) $\left(\$9.00 \times \frac{9}{100}\right) + \$9.00$

(E) $\$9.00 \div 9$

32. Omar ran $6\frac{2}{3}$ miles yesterday. Today he ran twice the distance he ran yesterday. How many miles did Omar run yesterday and today?

(A) $20\frac{1}{3}$

(B) 20

(C) $19\frac{2}{3}$

(D) $19\frac{1}{3}$

(E) $16\frac{2}{3}$

33. Tori caught 2 fish. The heavier fish weighed 8 pounds 4 ounces. The lighter fish weighed 6 pounds 11 ounces. What is the difference in their weights?

(A) 19 ounces
(B) 1 pound 9 ounces
(C) 2 pounds 4 ounces
(D) 5 pounds 6 ounces

34. The Dow Jones Industrial Average closed at 11,241.42, an increase of 59.68 over yesterday's closing figure. What was the closing figure yesterday of the Dow Jones Industrial Average?

(A) 11,788.47
(B) 11,181.74
(C) 11,192.63
(D) 11,207.48
(E) 12,217.43

35. During the month of March, a basketball player scored 64 of her 80 foul shots. What percentage of her foul shots was successful?

(A) 50
(B) 64
(C) 72
(D) 80
(E) 90

36. Tenai paid $18.47 for each of 50 shares of stock. Later that month, she noticed the stocks were currently worth $16.89 per share. Tenai wants to know how much money she lost. Which of the following operations will correctly calculate Tenai's financial loss?

    (A) Subtract $16.89 from $18.47.
    (B) Subtract $16.89 from $18.47 and divide by 50.
    (C) Subtract $18.47 from $16.89 and multiply by 50.
    (D) Subtract $16.89 from $18.47 and multiply by 50.
    (E) Add 50 to $16.89 and $18.47.

37. Experts suggest that during rainy driving conditions, drivers should allow an extra 15% in the braking distance for a particular speed. If a driver traveling on a sunny day at 45 miles per hour needs 86 feet to stop, how many feet will he need on a rainy day?

    (A) 98.9
    (B) 88.4
    (C) 88.3
    (D) 87.9
    (E) 12.9

38. Harry has 4 red socks, 2 white socks, and 7 black socks. What is the probability he will reach in and pull out a red sock?

    (A) $\frac{13}{4}$

    (B) $\frac{4}{13}$

    (C) $\frac{5}{13}$

    (D) $\frac{4}{7}$

    (E) $\frac{7}{13}$

39. The measure of $\angle A$ is 81°. The measure of $\angle B$ is $\frac{1}{3}$ the measure of $\angle A$. What is the sum of the measures of $\angle A$ and $\angle B$?

    (A) 27°
    (B) 54°
    (C) 81°
    (D) 108°
    (E) 180°

40. Which of the following statements is FALSE?

    (A) $\frac{3}{4} = \frac{12}{16}$

    (B) $\frac{1}{2} > \frac{1}{4}$

    (C) $\frac{3}{5} = 0.6$

    (D) $-4.3 > -8.6$
    (E) $-4.3 < -8.6$

41. $\sqrt{53}$ is between which two whole numbers?

    (A) 8 and 9
    (B) 7 and 8
    (C) 6 and 7
    (D) 5 and 6
    (E) 4 and 5

42. How much is one-half of one-half?

    (A) One whole
    (B) One-half
    (C) One-fourth
    (D) One-eighth
    (E) Zero

43. Kristina can type two pages in 14 minutes. At this rate, how long will it take her to type 17 pages?

    (A) 19 minutes
    (B) 28 minutes
    (C) 1 hour 37 minutes
    (D) 1 hour 59 minutes
    (E) 2 hours 11 minutes

44. Tim can deliver 392 newspapers in 4 hours and 53 minutes. Which expression will best help him estimate the average number of newspapers distributed in one hour?

    (A) 392×4.53
    (B) $400 \div 5$
    (C) $392 \div 4.53$
    (D) 400×5
    (E) $392 - 453$

45. Between movie showings, the theater's staff needs 18 minutes to clean the theater. In the following movie schedule, find the unknown time.

Movie	Start Time	Duration
The Man of the Moment	2:15	108 minutes
Leave 'Em Laughin'	?	94 minutes

    (A) 3:23
    (B) 3:45
    (C) 4:16
    (D) 4:21
    (E) 4:30

46. How many hours is 9,000 seconds?

    (A) 150
    (B) 15
    (C) 6
    (D) 3
    (E) 2.5

47. On Tuesday, the sun rose at 5:48 A.M. and set at 6:18 P.M. How much time elapsed between sunrise and sunset?

    (A) 10 hours 42 minutes
    (B) 11 hours 18 minutes
    (C) 12 hours 18 minutes
    D) 12 hours 30 minutes
    (E) 13 hours 8 minutes

48. Gil noticed when he put 12 gallons of gas into his automobile the fuel gauge indicated $\frac{3}{4}$ full. What is the total number of gallons the tank will hold?

    (A) 9
    (B) 12
    (C) 16
    (D) 18
    (E) 20

49. Express $\frac{3}{8}$ as a percent.

    (A) 38%
    (B) 37.5%
    (C) 37%
    (D) 30%
    (E) 3%

50. On the three sections of a college placement test, Isabel correctly answered the number of questions shown below.

Section	Number of Questions	Questions Answered Correctly
Reading	35	29
Math	25	14
Grammar	20	17

    What percentage of the questions did Isabel answer correctly?

    (A) 25
    (B) 45
    (C) 55
    (D) 60
    (E) 75

ANSWERS AND EXPLANATIONS FOR MODEL EXAM 3: MATH

1. **(E)**

$$600(0.24) = 144$$

2. **(D)**
   Order of operations:

   Simplify the quantity in the parentheses:

   $$-12 - (-15)$$

   Subtract:

   $$-12 - (-15) = -12 + 15 = 3$$

3. **(D)** The percentile refers to those test-takers whose scores were equal to or less than Fran's score.

4. **(E)**

$$\left(\frac{1}{3}\right)(\$69.00) = \$23.00$$

5. **(B)**

$$2n + 5 + 3n = -20$$
$$5n + 5 = -20$$
$$5n = -25$$
$$n = -5$$

6. **(D)**

$$7{,}461{,}200 < 7{,}623{,}158 < 7{,}851{,}500$$

7. **(A)** Use the ratio

$$\frac{\text{junior college students going on to 4-year colleges}}{\text{all junior college students}}$$

$$\frac{4}{7} = \frac{x}{8{,}400}$$
$$7x = 33{,}600$$
$$x = 4{,}800$$

8. **(D)** Use the formula

$$\frac{\text{part}}{\text{whole}} = \frac{x}{100}$$

$$\frac{22}{40} = \frac{x}{100}$$

$$40x = 2,200$$

$$x = 55$$

9. **(C)** Use the ratio

$$\frac{\text{inches}}{\text{feet}}$$

$$\frac{1}{6} = \frac{x}{15}$$

$$6x = 15$$

$$x = 2.5$$

10. **(C)** Use the ratio

$$\frac{\text{pies}}{\text{pounds of flour}}$$

$$\frac{3}{2} = \frac{11}{x}$$

$$3x = 22$$

$$x = 7\frac{1}{3}$$

11. **(C)** Round each number to the nearest thousand:

49,627 rounds to 50,000

5,113 rounds to 5,000

$$50,000 \div 5,000 \text{ is the best way to estimate } 49,627 \div 5,113.$$

12. **(E)** *Of* means multiply:

$$\frac{1}{2} \times \frac{1}{8} \times 96,000 = \frac{1}{16} \times 96,000 = 6,000$$

13. **(B)** If the distance in miles between the Sun and Neptune were known, it could be divided by 93,000,000 to calculate the number of astronomical units that separate them.

14. **(E)**

$$\frac{3}{7}x - 11 = 16$$

$$\frac{3}{7}x = 27$$

$$\frac{7}{3}\left(\frac{3}{7}x\right) = (27)\frac{7}{3}$$

$$x = 63$$

15. **(D)**

Price of the coat after 10% discount: $90 - (90)(0.10) = \$81$

Price of the coat after discounted by $\frac{1}{3}$: $81 - \left(\frac{1}{3}\right)(81) = \$54$

16. **(D)** An equilateral triangle has three equal sides. If each side is 6 inches, the perimeter of the triangle is 18 inches. A square has four equal sides. Since its perimeter must also be 18 inches, divide 18 by 4:

$$18 \div 4 = 4.5$$

17. **(C)**

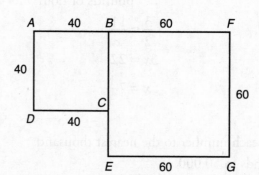

The perimeter is the distance around a figure. Since *BC* is in the interior of the figure, it is not included in the perimeter. Therefore, add the lengths of the following:

$$AB = 40$$
$$AD = 40$$
$$DC = 40$$
$$FG = 60$$
$$EG = 60$$
$$BF = 60$$

Subtract the length of *BC*, 40, from the length of *BE*, which is 60. The result, 20, is the length of *CE*:

$$40 + 40 + 40 + 60 + 60 + 60 + 20 = 320$$

18. **(B)**

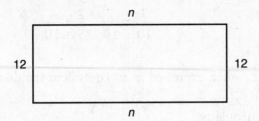

Let n = the length of the rectangle:

$$n + n + 12 + 12 = 96$$
$$2n + 24 = 96$$
$$2n = 72$$
$$n = 36$$

19. **(E)** To earn an average of 90 on three tests, Naomi must score a total of 270 points ($3 \times 90 = 270$). To calculate the score Naomi needs on her third test, subtract the sum of her first two tests from 270:

$$270 - (85 + 85) = 100$$

Naomi needs a score of 100% on her third test to have a 90% average on the three tests.

20. **(D)** To find the percentage increase, use the formula

$$\frac{\text{increase}}{\text{original}} = \frac{x}{100}$$

Subtract 180 from 225 to find the increase:

$$225 - 180 = 45$$
$$\frac{45}{180} = \frac{x}{100}$$
$$4,500 = 180x$$
$$25 = x$$

21. **(B)** The chart indicates that each x value must be doubled to equal the corresponding y value, so $y = 2x$.

22. **(A)** Express both fractions with a common denominator:

$$\frac{7}{10} = \frac{7}{10} \quad \frac{2}{5} = \frac{4}{10}$$

Choice A, $\frac{3}{5}$, when expressed as an equivalent fraction, is the only value that satisfies the inequality:

$$\frac{3}{5} = \frac{6}{10}$$

$$\frac{7}{10} > \frac{6}{10} > \frac{4}{10}$$

$$\frac{7}{10} > \frac{3}{5} > \frac{2}{5}$$

23. **(C)**

$$\frac{58.8 + 61.4 + 59.2 + 60.2}{4} = 59.9$$

24. **(E)**
Order of operations:

$$8^2 - 2(3 - 6) = 8^2 - 2(-3) = 64 - 2(-3) = 64 + 6 = 70$$

25. **(A)** The point appears to be midway between -1 and $-1\frac{1}{2}$, so $-1\frac{1}{4}$ is the best estimate.

26. **(E)** Find the value of an 8% raise:

$$(0.08)(520)$$

Add the value of the raise to the existing weekly pay to find the new weekly pay:

$$520 + (520)(0.08)$$

27. **(A)** $520 + (520)(0.08) = \$561.60$

28. **(A)** The sum of the measures of the angles in a triangle equals 180°:

$$7x + 4x + 4x = 180$$
$$15x = 180$$
$$x = 12$$

29. **(E)** Convert the length of the rope into inches (1 foot = 12 inches)

$$4\frac{1}{2} \times 12 = 54$$

Find the length of five, nine-inch pieces of rope and subtract that number from the length of the rope:

$$5 \times 9 = 45$$
$$54 - 45 = 9$$

30. **(B)** Use the ratio

$$\frac{\text{celery stalks}}{\text{individual salad}}$$

Remember that one dozen equals 12 units.

$$\frac{2}{1} = \frac{x}{36}$$
$$x = 72$$

31. **(C)** Percents can be expressed as decimals or fractions. As a fraction, 9% is expressed as $\frac{9}{100}$. Multiply $9.00 by $\frac{9}{100}$ to find the increase in the hourly rate.

32. **(B)**

$$6\frac{2}{3} + (2)\left(6\frac{2}{3}\right) = 6\frac{2}{3} + 13\frac{1}{3} = 20$$

33. **(B)** Subtract 6 pounds 11 ounces from 8 pounds 4 ounces (1 pound = 16 ounces):

8 pounds 4 ounces	=	7 pounds + 16 ounces + 4 ounces	=	7 pounds 20 ounces
− 6 pounds 11 ounces		− 6 pounds 11 ounces		− 6 pounds 11 ounces
				1 pound 9 ounces

34. **(B)** Subtract today's increase in the Dow Jones Industrial Average from today's close to get yesterday's closing figure:

$$
\begin{array}{r}
11,241.42 \\
-\quad 59.68 \\
\hline
11,181.74
\end{array}
$$

35. **(D)** Use the formula

$$\frac{\text{part}}{\text{whole}} = \frac{x}{100}$$

to find the percentage of successful foul shots:

$$\frac{64}{80} = \frac{x}{100}$$
$$80x = 6,400$$
$$x = 80$$

36. **(D)**

$$50(\$18.47 - 16.89) = \$79.00$$

The value of Tenai's stock portfolio has decreased by $79.00.

37. **(A)** Find 15% of 86 and add it to 86:

$$(0.15)(86) + 86 = 98.9$$

38. **(B)** Use the formula

$$\frac{\text{favorable outcomes}}{\text{all outcomes}}$$
$$\frac{\text{red socks}}{\text{all socks}} = \frac{4}{7+2+4} = \frac{4}{13}$$

39. **(D)** Find $\frac{1}{3}$ of 81 and add it to 81:

$$\left(\frac{1}{3}\right)(81) + 81 = 27 + 81 = 108$$

40. **(E)** −4.3 is to the right of −8.6 on a number line. Thus it cannot be true that −4.3 < −8.6.

41. **(B)**

$$\sqrt{49} < \sqrt{53} < \sqrt{64}$$
$$7 < \sqrt{53} < 8$$

42. **(C)** *Of* means multiply:

$$\frac{1}{2} \times \frac{1}{2} = \frac{1}{4}$$

43. **(D)** Use the ratio

$$\frac{\text{pages}}{\text{minutes}}$$

$$\frac{2}{14} = \frac{17}{x}$$

$$2x = 238$$

$$x = 119 \text{ minutes}$$

Convert 119 minutes to hours by dividing by 60:

$$119 \text{ minutes} \div 60 = 1 \text{ hour } 59 \text{ minutes}$$

44. **(B)** Use rounding:

392 newspapers rounds to 400

4 hours 53 minutes rounds to 5 hours

Divide to find the number of papers delivered per hour:

$$400 \div 5$$

45. **(D)** Find the ending time of the first movie:

$$2:15 + 108 \text{ minutes} = 2:15 + 1 \text{ hour } 48 \text{ minutes} = 4:03$$

The first movie ends at 4:03. Add 18 minutes for theater cleaning:

$$4:03 + 18 = 4:21$$

The second movie begins at 4:21.

46. **(E)** Find the number of seconds in one hour:

$$60 \text{ minutes} \times 60 \text{ seconds} = 3{,}600 \text{ seconds in one hour}$$

Divide 9,000 by 3,600 to calculate the number of hours:

$$9{,}000 \div 3{,}600 = 2.5$$

47. **(D)** Subtract 5:48 A.M. (5 hours 48 minutes) from 6:15 P.M.:

$$
\begin{array}{rcl}
6 \text{ hours } 18 \text{ minutes} & = & 5 \text{ hours} + 60 \text{ minutes} + 18 \text{ minutes} \\
\underline{- \ 5 \text{ hours } 48 \text{ minutes}} & & \underline{- \ 5 \text{ hours } 48 \text{ minutes}}
\end{array}
$$

$$
\begin{array}{rl}
= & 5 \text{ hours } 78 \text{ minutes} \\
& \underline{- \ 5 \text{ hours } 48 \text{ minutes}} \\
& 30 \text{ minutes}
\end{array}
$$

Add 12 hours to the answer because sunset is 6:18 P.M.:

$$12 \text{ hours} + 30 \text{ minutes} = 12 \text{ hours } 30 \text{ minutes}$$

48. **(C)** Let

$$x = \text{capacity of gas tank in gallons}$$
$$\frac{3}{4}x = 12$$
$$\frac{4}{3}\left(\frac{3}{4}x\right) = (12)\frac{4}{3}$$
$$x = 16 \text{ gallons}$$

49. **(B)** To find the percent, use the formula :

$$\frac{\text{part}}{\text{whole}} = \frac{x}{100}$$
$$\frac{3}{8} = \frac{x}{100}$$
$$300 = 8x$$
$$37.5 = x$$

50. **(E)** Use the formula

$$\frac{\text{part}}{\text{whole}} = \frac{x}{100}$$

to find the percent of questions answered correctly:

Questions answered correctly: 29 + 14 + 17 = 60

All questions: 35 + 25 + 20 = 80

$$\frac{60}{80} = \frac{x}{100}$$
$$6,000 = 80x$$
$$75 = x$$

MODEL EXAM 1: WRITING

Reminder: You will be required to write two essays, Type I "expressive" (personal experience) and Type II "informational," analyzing a given situation or statement. After you have written essays based on the following prompts, you can evaluate them using the process explained in Chapter 7.

Essay Type I

Some people believe that being a good friend is a full-time occupation. Ralph Waldo Emerson said that friendship often requires more time than the average person has to give. Write about a friendship that at some point in time required a lot of time to maintain. What was the outcome of that significant amount of attention given to the friend?

_____

_____

_____

_____

_____

_____

_____

_____

_____

_____

_____

_____

_____

_____

_____

_____

_____

_____

Essay Type II

According to personnel manager and educator Mary Barnett Gilson, education is a failure if it "does not stir in students a sharp awareness of their obligations to society and furnish at least a few guideposts pointing toward the implementation of these obligations." To what extent do you agree or disagree with this observation? Provide specific reasoning and examples in defense of your position.

_____

_____

_____

_____

_____

_____

_____

_____

_____

_____

_____

_____

_____

_____

_____

_____

_____

_____

_____

_____

_____

_____

_____

_____

_____

_____

MODEL EXAM 2: WRITING

Essay Type I

The basic social standards of tolerance, honesty, and responsibility are many of the important pieces of information children learn in the classroom. In this way, they learn how to function in society at large. Write about an experience in a classroom when you learned about one of these standards. Did it have a lasting effect on you? Why or why not?

_____

_____

_____

_____

_____

_____

_____

_____

_____

_____

_____

_____

_____

_____

_____

_____

_____

_____

_____

Essay Type II

In countries around the world, many public and private elementary and secondary schools require their students to wear uniforms. What are the advantages and disadvantages of this requirement?

_____

_____

_____

_____

_____

_____

_____

_____

_____

_____

_____

_____

_____

_____

_____

_____

_____

_____

_____

_____

_____

_____

_____

_____